Underground Ranger

UNDERGROUND RANGER

Adventures in Carlsbad Caverns National Park and Other Remarkable Places

Doug Thompson

University of New Mexico Press | Albuquerque

LIBRARY OF CONGRESS CATALOGING-IN-PUBLICATION DATA
Names: Thompson, Doug, 1943– author.
Title: Underground ranger : adventures in Carlsbad Caverns National Park
and other remarkable places / Doug Thompson.
Other titles: Adventures in Carlsbad Caverns National Park
Description: [First edition] | Albuquerque : University of New Mexico Press, [2016] |
Includes bibliographical references.
Identifiers: LCCN 2016004176 (print) | LCCN 2016010361 (ebook) |
ISBN 9780826357502 (pbk. : alk. paper) | ISBN 9780826357519 (electronic)
Subjects: LCSH: Thompson, Doug, 1943– author. | Carlsbad Caverns National Park (N.M.) |
Park rangers—New Mexico—Carlsbad Caverns National Park—Biography. | Caving—New Mexico—
Carlsbad Caverns National Park. | Spelunkers—United States—Biography. | Carlsbad Caverns (N.M.)
Classification: LCC F802.C28 T57 2016 (print) | LCC F802.C28 (ebook) |
DDC 978.9/42—dc23
LC record available at http://lccn.loc.gov/2016004176

COVER PHOTOGRAPH: Iffy on rope at Gunsight Cave, Lincoln National Forest, courtesy of the author.
All photographs are courtesy of the author except where otherwise indicated.
DESIGNED BY Lila Sanchez and Lisa C. Tremaine
COMPOSED IN Cone & Carter Galliard and Bertold Akzidenz Grotesque

John Milton's description of Satan's Fall is reprinted with permission from *Paradise Lost*, ed. David Scott Kastan (Indianapolis, IN: Hackett Publishing Company, 2005); the words spoken by Tsitctinako in the tale of Ute'tsiti's daughters are from "Emerging into the Upper World" in *American Indian Myths and Legends*, eds. Richard Erdoes and Alfonso Ortiz (New York: Pantheon Books, 1984); Jim White's descriptions of his adventures are from his 1938 memoir *Jim White's Own Story: The Discovery and History of Carlsbad Caverns* (Carlsbad, NM: Carlsbad Caverns–Guadalupe Mountains Association, 1998); Robert Nymeyer's description of Jim White is from his book *Carlsbad, Caves and a Camera* (St. Louis, MO: Cave Books, 1993); the lines from Franz Joseph Haydn's oratorio *The Creation* and Wolfgang Amadeus Mozart's *Requiem* are Doug Thompson's paraphrases; the Thompson River Native's assessment of Old Man Coyote is given in *A Coyote Reader*, ed. William Bright (Berkeley: University of California Press, 1993); the words of John Muir are taken from his 1894 book *The Mountains of California* (Hamburg, Germany: Tradition Classics, 2012); Annie Dillard quotes a sixteenth-century alchemist in *Pilgrim at Tinker Creek* (New York: Harper's Magazine Press, 1974); Geronimo's story of the underworld is recorded in his 1906 autobiography, *Geronimo: His Own Story*, trans. S. M. Barrett (New York: Penguin Group, 1996); Emily Dickinson's verse is from *The Poems of Emily Dickinson*, ed. Thomas H. Johnson (Cambridge, MA: The Belknap Press of Harvard University Press, copyright 1951, 1955, 1979, 1983 by the President and Fellows of Harvard College); the words of Henry David Thoreau are from *Walden* in *Walden and Civil Disobedience*, ed. Sherman Paul (Boston, MA: Houghton Mifflin, 1960); the two lines of poetry by Walt Whitman are from *Walt Whitman: Complete Poetry and Collected Prose* (New York: Literary Classics of the United States, n.d.); the Tennyson quotation is from his poem "In Memoriam" in *Alfred, Lord Tennyson: Complete Works* (Hastings, UK: Delphi Classics, 2013); the verse from "The Gospel According to Thomas" is quoted in *A Joseph Campbell Companion: Reflections on the Art of Living*, ed. Diane K. Osbon (New York: HarperCollins, 1991); Everett Ruess's letters and his poem "Wilderness Song" are quoted in W. L. Rusho's *The Mystery of Everett Ruess*, first revised edition (Layton, UT: Gibbs Smith, 1982).

For my parents and my friends Lance, Dave, and Iffy

Sometimes I go about in pity for myself,
and all the while a great wind is bearing me across the sky.

—OJIBWA SAYING

CONTENTS

CONTENTS

ACKNOWLEDGMENTS

I want to thank everyone who helped me with this project, especially Lance Mattson, Dave Thomas, and Iffy Khan. Without their friendship, I would have no story to tell. A number of friends, former coworkers, acquaintances, and family members read early versions of the manuscript and offered many helpful suggestions, including Lance, Dave, Iffy, Dennis Dunnum, Frank Thompson, my sisters Rose Marie Duley and Beverly Kindred, my brother-in-law Ed Kindred, and three members of the staff at Carlsbad Caverns National Park: Stan Allison, David Kayser, and Virginia Moyers. Stan and Virginia also checked facts and corrected a number of errors, for which I am grateful. My brother Larry and my sister-in-law Orleeta Thompson also read an early version of the manuscript, while other friends and acquaintances read one or more chapters, including Kelly Bridges, Joanne Kozuchowski, Allison Thomas, Marjorie Thomas, Brad Long, Andy Zellner, and Pam L. Cox of the staff at Carlsbad Caverns. Kelly Bridges devoted many hours to developing my website, parkrangerdoug.com, while Jay Foreman was extremely helpful in preparing the map of the Guadalupe Mountains, and Brad Long and Andy Zellner made our trip into Ellison's Cave possible. I also want to thank Marie Marek, chief of interpretation and education at Carlsbad Caverns, and Jason Woldt for their assistance in having the manuscript reviewed. Paul Cox of the staff at Carlsbad Caverns arranged my trip into Spider Cave to take photographs, and Ellen Trautner took time from her busy schedule to accompany me. My thanks also to former park rangers Andrea Lankford, author of *Ranger Confidential: Living, Working, and Dying in the National Parks*, and Jim Burnett, author of *Hey, Ranger! True Tales of*

ACKNOWLEDGMENTS

Humor and Misadventure from America's National Parks, for their advice about the publishing process. Editor Allen Jones of Manuscript Medics was a tremendous help, and I'm grateful for his patience and insight. If the primary purpose of an editor is to make an author rethink his or her manuscript, Allen succeeded many times over. I also want to thank Executive Editor Clark Whitehorn and the staff at the University of New Mexico Press, as well as my copyeditor, Katherine Harper. Her diligence and professionalism gave the book its final form. I also thank the two anonymous reviewers who offered many helpful suggestions for improving the manuscript. Finally, my thanks to friends and coworkers who kindly allowed me to use their real names, including Stan Allison, Kelly Bridges, Harry Burgess, Laura Denny, Craig DiGiulio, Leah Glenn, Iffy Khan, Joanne Kozuchowski, Brad Long, Lance Mattson, Paul Mauermann, Beth Milner, Allison Thomas, Dave Thomas, Marjorie Thomas, Clarence Wadkins, and Andy Zellner. To avoid confusion, it was necessary to change the names of two coworkers: "Dennis" is really Dave Roemer, and "Jake" is David Hall.

AUTHOR'S NOTE

Most of the caves in and around the Guadalupe Mountains of West Texas and southeastern New Mexico are on public lands administered by the National Park Service, the US Forest Service, and the Bureau of Land Management. Entry requires a written permit from the administering agency, available at its office in Carlsbad, New Mexico. Locked gates protect many of the caves, and visitors must stay on designated trails and follow established guidelines for their own safety as well as for the caves' preservation. All caves are subject to periodic closures and other restrictions. Vertical caves require an ability to climb and descend ropes using technical equipment. *The caving activities described in this book are inherently dangerous, especially climbing. Please be cautious underground, and don't attempt vertical caving unless you've had technical training.*

To contact Doug Thompson, or to view a wide selection of color photographs showing the people and places described in *Underground Ranger*, visit parkrangerdoug.com.

Part One

LEARNING

CHAPTER ONE

A Good Career

THE FIRST TIME I saw the Guadalupe Mountains, I thought they were clouds floating above the distant horizon. I was driving east across the plains of West Texas at the beginning of the summer rainy season, when the air of the Chihuahuan Desert is not only unbearably hot but also oppressively humid and muggy. The thick seasonal haze that afternoon carried a tinge of grayish-brown smog from El Paso, which made the eastern horizon invisible. Or so I thought. Ahead of me stretched dry grass, yuccas, and scrubby creosote bushes for as far as I could see, unbroken by anything worth noticing until they disappeared into the haze below what seemed to be a bank of clouds. Despite the haze—or perhaps because of it—the fleecy apparitions reflected the afternoon sunlight in a way that made them appear grand and luminous, like a pale-orange mirage glimmering above the barren landscape.

It was late June 1995, and I was on my way to Carlsbad Caverns National Park for a job interview that I hoped would get my career back on track. For the previous three years, I had worked as the site manager at Gila Cliff Dwellings National Monument, a tiny enclave in the Gila National Forest in southwestern New Mexico that preserves cave dwellings built hundreds of years ago by people of the Mogollon culture. (The name is Spanish,

3

pronounced Moe-go-*yone*.) Yet I wasn't satisfied with my position. The remoteness of the site and personality clashes between staff members had made it both frustrating and stressful.

Only a few months earlier, I had met Carlsbad Caverns' chief of interpretation at a National Park Service conference in Denver and told him I was looking for a change of duty station. My required term of service at the cliff dwellings was ending, and I hoped to find another position as a frontline interpretive ranger at a larger park. He assured me that if I didn't mind working underground, two positions on his staff would become available within a few months. It seemed likely I would qualify for one of them. So there I was, fixating on cloud formations as I drove across West Texas.

Yet the closer I got, the less certain I became that they were clouds. Surely they couldn't be cliffs: they were far too high and imposing for that. And yet . . .

A wave of astonishment swept over me. They were indeed a wall of rugged cliffs, veering away toward the north and rising thousands of feet above the desert floor. It was their imposing foundation of dun-colored talus that had made it seem as though they were floating in the air; it blended convincingly into the smoggy haze. But not the cream-colored cliffs: they shone through like the glorious harbingers of a massive storm front. With each passing mile, I became increasingly captivated by their size and magnificence, and I concluded that they had to be the western flank of what the map showed to be the Guadalupe Mountains. I had no idea how significantly they were going to affect my life.

⌒ Carlsbad Caverns appealed to me for several reasons. As one of the largest and most popular national parks in the desert Southwest—my favorite part of the country—it would be a welcome relief after the isolation of Gila Cliff Dwellings. Moreover, instead of being a manager and supervisor, I would be doing the things I enjoyed most: presenting guided tours and other interpretive programs and interacting with park visitors. Two of the tours were supposed to be very strenuous, but that didn't bother me; I was in good physical condition for a fifty-two-year-old and had always enjoyed hiking, jogging, and bicycling. My experience as an interpreter and interpretive supervisor made me fully qualified for the job, and I felt confident I would do well in the interview.

Yet several unwelcome concerns lurked in the back of my mind, refusing to go away. The first was that I had visited Carlsbad Caverns as a teenager, and it hadn't been a good experience. As my father bought our family's tickets for the guided tour down the Natural Entrance Trail— this was before the later self-guided tours—I felt apprehensive, as though something bad were about to happen. I tried to brush it off, but as we walked down the trail from the visitor center to the cave, my anxiety grew and I began to feel queasy.

When we reached the Natural Entrance, my queasiness turned to panic. Looming before us, under a massive rock overhang that bristled with cactus and other sinister-looking desert plants, was a monstrous opening in the earth, a yawning chasm that seemed ready to devour anyone who approached too closely. Cave swallows, unaware of my apprehension, swooped in and out of the opening, yet I hardly noticed them. The only thing I could see was the trail descending into that evil abyss in a series of steep switchbacks, until it finally disappeared in darkness far below. The group of visitors waiting for the next tour to begin seemed unaware that once they had descended into the cave, the rock overhang was going to collapse behind them and bury them alive. Never again would they enjoy the light and air of the earth's surface. They were about to enter their own grave.

There was no way I could go down that trail, and I desperately tried to think of an excuse that might save me from certain death. My mother apparently felt the same way: she began stammering that she didn't want any part of that big hole in the ground. It was just too scary, and she didn't like being in the dark. Quickly sensing my own salvation, I told my father I would sacrifice myself and wait at the visitor center with my mother, because she obviously needed someone to comfort her. My father appeared to accept this reasoning, and I felt my tensed muscles begin to relax. I had camouflaged my own desperation and salvaged my manhood. While this incident had occurred many years earlier, I still hadn't been into a cave, and I now wondered if I would be able to work underground.

Another concern was that the strenuous tours involved crawling through tight passages, and I was mildly claustrophobic. Several years earlier, I had been reluctant to crawl into the confined space under my house to check a water pipe and had to call a plumber. Would I react the same way to a tight cave passage? Moreover, the chief of interpretation had mentioned that I'd have the option of learning to climb rope, which would be essential if I wanted to become a "caver" and explore some of the many caves in the Guadalupe Mountains. Yet I had a fear of heights. Given my love of adventure and exploration, there was no way I could work in a cave park without learning to cave and climb rope, so I had to ask myself: Would I be up to the challenge?

Looking back, I could see that my National Park Service career hadn't prepared me for working at Carlsbad Caverns. I hadn't gone underground or crawled into tight spaces, and I hadn't climbed rope or otherwise been exposed to heights. For the most part, I had supervised other employees and worked behind a desk.

⌐ I had been a national park ranger since the early 1970s, when I became a trainee at the Albright Training Academy—named after Horace Albright, the second director of the National Park Service—at Grand Canyon National Park in Arizona. Although I had grown up in suburban San Diego and been hired while living there with my parents, I had always loved the outdoors and had even done some hiking and camping. I had also spent three years in the military, but in a position unrelated to the outdoors. I was an air traffic control officer in a ground-based radar unit, supervising men and women who directed aircraft in flight during inclement weather. I spent most of my days in small, dark rooms lit only by flashing radar screens.

I also had worked for one year as a high school history teacher, a position I found less rewarding than I had expected. Between grading test papers, struggling with malfunctioning audiovisual equipment, and trying to maintain order among students who didn't seem interested in learning, I longed for a job that would challenge me intellectually while also satisfying my love for the outdoors. After resigning my teaching job, unsure of what I wanted to do next, I kicked around for months without doing much of anything. Then I came upon a National Park Service brochure in the career-placement files at my alma mater, San Diego State College. I had always admired the National Park Service and enjoyed working with the public—I had been a student assistant at the library checkout desk while in college—so I took the required government exam and applied for a position. Almost a year later, I received a phone call telling me I had been selected and would begin training the following month.

My time at Grand Canyon was unlike anything I had ever experienced. It included plenty of classroom sessions about the National Park Service and its mission, but it also introduced me to outdoor activities I had never dreamed of doing, such as packing mules and taking part in a simulated wilderness rescue. I had visited several national parks before my arrival at Grand Canyon, but the class field trips that were a part of my training introduced me to additional parks in Arizona. Visiting them provided my first inside look at how the National Park Service managed its areas and confirmed my love for the Sonoran Desert and the Southwest.

My training also introduced me to predators in the wild. One evening our class of about thirty trainees and several instructors was camping in the juniper-piñon forest along the southern rim of the Grand Canyon. The following morning, we were going to hike into the canyon and camp for another night. As our fires slowly died and we began settling into our sleeping bags, we could hear a pack of wolves howling in the distance in that plaintive way that's also common among coyotes. That was odd: I had had the impression there were no longer any wolves in the area. It was a magnificent sound but a little unnerving because the pack seemed to be moving in our direction. Gradually but unmistakably, the howling grew louder until someone remarked that perhaps we should be concerned. When the sound became so loud that it had to be within thirty yards, I sat up in my sleeping bag and fumbled in the dark for my flashlight. Surely a pack of wolves wouldn't come into our camp. Frantically sweeping my light back and forth through the trees, I finally saw them: two of our fellow trainees walking out of the woods with a portable tape recorder playing the sound of howling wolves, laughing at our gullibility.

By the end of our training period, I had fallen in love with the Grand Canyon, as everyone does, and I was reluctant to leave. One night while my roommates were asleep, I lay awake in bed listening to the faraway rumble of thunder along the canyon's northern rim. Like the sound of the "wolves" and almost imperceptibly at first, the rumbling began to move closer, echoing from the cliffs and mesas beyond the Colorado River. Soon it was over the middle of the canyon, where it became deeper and more ominous, and then closer still, above the cliffs and plateaus of the South Rim. On it came, growing ever stronger and more threatening, until the branches of the piñon pines outside our apartment began to lurch in the wind and scratch against the windowpanes. Then the world exploded in brilliant flashes of lightning, deafening peals of reverberating thunder, and the staccato pounding of heavy rain and sleet against the roof. I gradually drifted off to sleep, marveling at how fortunate I was to be in such a place.

Following my graduation from the academy, I went to Jefferson National Expansion Memorial in St. Louis for an additional six months of training in an urban area. Visitors to national parks increasingly tended to come from large cities, so the National Park Service was emphasizing urban problems and concerns in its ranger-orientation courses. My training would acquaint me with the outlook of people who lived in an inner city. It was an enjoyable assignment, and I found St. Louis intriguing, if only because I had never seen so many brick buildings. Because I had always loved children, it was fun and rewarding to present environmental-education programs to schoolchildren in their classrooms.

My first permanent assignment was at Kings Mountain National Military Park, a Revolutionary War battlefield in the rolling hills of the South Carolina Piedmont, where American patriots had defeated a small army of British and Loyalist troops in 1780. I was responsible for the park's law-enforcement and resource-management programs, and I also helped the park historian supervise a few seasonal rangers. Law enforcement was a challenge because my training at Grand Canyon hadn't covered it. Today, park rangers who specialize in law enforcement are fully trained and certified before they begin their duties, but in those days some rangers, especially in the smaller parks, found themselves in law-enforcement positions without being adequately prepared. That was my situation. During my first weeks on the job, two of the seasonal rangers patiently taught me how to make traffic stops in the park's only squad car, and a local police department let me use its firing range to become qualified with a pistol. Beyond that I had no formal law-enforcement training for more than six months after I arrived at Kings Mountain.

Traffic stops introduced me to people who lived in the surrounding area, which was entirely rural. Most of them were friendly in the traditional southern manner. (I liked the local highway custom of waving at other drivers in the oncoming lane of traffic.) I also met plenty of amusing characters. Once when I was patrolling the park's main drive with one of the seasonal rangers, we stopped an elderly woman whose rusty old car was weaving erratically back and forth. When we asked if she was all right, she said yes. Then she proved it by getting out of the car with great effort and walking in a relatively straight line to the shoulder of the road—where she defiantly spit tobacco juice onto the grass.

My favorite law-enforcement duty was patrolling the park's rugged backcountry on foot, not just because I loved the outdoors but also because it was fun to explore and learn the terrain. Hiking through a dense hardwood forest was a new experience. I began to encounter unfamiliar trees and animals. Raccoons and turkeys—which I heard but never saw—were my favorites. I also enjoyed hiking through deep leaves for the first time and kicking them up as I traveled cross-country. One afternoon I even discovered an abandoned moonshine still hidden in one of the remote canyons, complete with copper coils and a supply of large plastic bottles. The park superintendent suspected it had belonged to a local farmer with a dubious reputation, but we couldn't prove it.

The time I devoted to exploring paid off late one night when I awoke to frantic knocking at my front door. Because I lived near the visitor center in the park's housing area, visitors who needed assistance afterhours invariably found their way to my front porch. In this case, it was a distraught man whose wife and children hadn't returned from a hike they had begun that afternoon. Running a hand through his disheveled hair, he pleaded for someone to find his family. Fifteen minutes later, the superintendent was phoning local volunteer fire departments and rescue squads for assistance, and I was hiking into the woods along the trail where the man's family had last been seen. For the rest of the night, I doubled back and forth along the trail, calling the woman's name and getting no response. It was a lonely and somewhat eerie experience, especially when the trail descended into a rocky, thickly wooded canyon and I began walking through hundreds of fireflies, their pale-blue glow lamps undulating slowly back and forth just above the damp ground.

By sunrise almost a hundred volunteers had arrived at the visitor center, where I briefed them on the park's search-and-rescue plan and the terrain we were going to cover. After dividing them into teams, I led one group of about a dozen volunteers to the area we were going to search. By midmorning we hadn't found any sign of the woman and her children, and I was becoming worried, because the overnight temperature had dropped well below freezing. Then we received a welcome radio transmission: they had been found by another search team and were being taken back to the visitor center, cold and disoriented but otherwise in good condition. The first search-and-rescue operation of my career had ended quickly and successfully.

After three years at Kings Mountain, I transferred to Colonial National Historical Park in Virginia, where I served for eighteen years as a district interpreter in one of the park's two districts, initially at Yorktown Battlefield and later at Jamestown. Now I was working in the field of interpretation, which I greatly preferred to law enforcement, and I took to my job enthusiastically. I managed an operation of about twenty permanent and seasonal interpreters who presented guided tours and other programs, and I was in my element.

Yorktown, as every schoolchild knows, was the site of George Washington's momentous victory over General Charles Cornwallis's British army in 1781, which effectively ended the American Revolution. The battle was a siege, with Washington's army of American and French troops surrounding the fortified town and bombarding it with artillery fire. I often conducted guided tours along the British Inner Defense Line near the visitor center, pointing out the reconstructed Allied siege works in the distance and describing the course of the battle.

One of our most popular interpretive programs was a nonfiring artillery demonstration, which we presented near the visitor center using an original French cannon that had been fired at Yorktown. It was called an "eighteen-pounder" because it fired cannonballs weighing eighteen pounds. After explaining the importance of artillery during a siege, we asked for volunteers from the audience to serve as crew members in the demonstration. Then, using a reproduction ramrod and other reproduction equipment, we walked them through the sequence of steps needed to fire an eighteenth-century cannon. The visitors loved it.

One day an interpreter came into my office to tell me a woman needed help at the artillery-demonstration area. When I arrived there, she was almost hysterical. She had placed her miniature poodle in the eighteen-pounder's muzzle, intending to take its photo, but the little dog had become frightened and scooted backward into the barrel. Now it wouldn't come out. After getting a flashlight from my office, I peered into the barrel and saw two little eyes gleaming back at me from the bottom. I had no idea what to do. At that moment, one of the protection rangers arrived. She happened to be a dog lover with several pets of her own. Looking down the barrel, she began speaking to the poodle in baby talk, patiently coaxing it forward. A few moments later, the trembling little dog appeared in the muzzle and the ranger grabbed it by the collar, much to the owner's relief. The second rescue operation of my career had also ended successfully.

Jamestown, the park's second district, was located on the James River at the opposite end of the Colonial Parkway, twenty two miles from Yorktown. Although the operation I managed there was similar to the one at Yorktown, it focused on the beginning of the colonial period rather than the end. Jamestown was the first successful English-speaking settlement in the New World, founded in 1607 by a small group of colonists representing the Virginia Company of London, a joint-stock company chartered by King James I. The venture initially consisted of a few thatch-roofed, mud-plastered buildings surrounded by a rude wooden palisade and mosquito-infested swamps. The earliest colonists suffered terribly from a variety of hardships. During the so-called Starving Time in the winter of 1609–1610, most of them died from malnutrition and disease.

During my years at Jamestown, archaeologists believed the site of the first buildings and palisade had been washed away by the James River, which meant that the existing brick church and several foundations from the later "New Towne" were all that remained of the colony. (Excavations have since unearthed evidence of the earliest buildings and palisade.) Our guided tours centered on the church, where colonists from throughout Tidewater Virginia held the first representative assembly in the New World in 1639.

Our interpretation at Jamestown included living-history programs, and we took great pains to make them accurate. Because the use and pronunciation of English words have changed significantly since 1607, we contracted a local college professor to teach our living-history interpreters how to speak proper Elizabethan English. The resulting presentations were linguistically accurate, but they sounded strange to modern ears.

For instance, when the interpreter who portrayed an indentured servant stated in Elizabethan English that he had come across "poisonous snakes" in the nearby swamps, it sounded like "poisonous snacks," and when he mentioned "the beaches of Jamestown," it sounded like "the bay-ches of Jimes-toon." It was quite engaging.

I enjoyed working at Colonial so much that I remained there for eighteen years, but eventually a job opportunity came along that I couldn't resist. Gila Cliff Dwellings National Monument in southwestern New Mexico was looking for a site manager. I had always wanted to work in the Southwest, and a cultural area with cliff dwellings seemed perfect. I had the necessary qualifications, so I applied for the position and was lucky enough to land it. Three months later, I moved to New Mexico.

Although the cliff dwellings were a unit of the national park system, they were located in such a remote area of the Gila National Forest that the National Park Service and US Forest Service had agreed to administer them jointly, with the National Park Service providing the funding and the Forest Service providing the monument's staff. To work there, I had to transfer to the Forest Service. My assignment was for three years, after which I could rejoin the National Park Service and apply for a position at another park in the Southwest. If necessary, the regional office would assist in placing me.

It was gratifying to work at Gila Cliff Dwellings, although adjusting to a prehistoric site took some effort. The people and events commemorated at my previous parks had been fully documented by letters, diaries, memoirs, and other written sources, but the cliff dwellings lacked any documentation because the Mogollon people who built them had no form of writing. Visitors usually wanted to know why a small band of people had decided to settle there, why they eventually chose to leave, and where they had gone; yet those are things we probably will never know. It was an interesting interpretive challenge.

The dwellings were perched in shallow caves within a narrow side canyon of the Gila River's West Fork. I lived in the nearby site manager's house and had never been stationed in such a remote place. The surrounding Gila Wilderness was so mountainous and rugged that it took visitors almost two hours to drive the forty-four miles from Silver City, the nearest town. It was a country of deep canyons and high cliffs, stately ponderosas, prickly pears, violent thunderstorms, and wildflowers that carpeted the meadows with vibrant color every spring and fall. In historic times, the area was part of the Chiricahua Apache homeland, and most Chiricahua sources today agree that Geronimo was born nearby, despite his claim that he was born in Arizona.

I fell in love with the Gila and spent much of my off-duty time hiking the trails and enjoying the magnificent scenery. Occasionally I would stop along a trail to watch bald eagles circling overhead, and once I paused briefly while a hummingbird zoomed back and forth within inches of my shoulders, investigating the brightly colored straps on my daypack. I also favored hiking up the Middle Fork of the Gila River to the local hot springs, where visitors and nearby residents liked to soak in the shallow pools. At night I often fell asleep listening to the distant howling or yapping of coyotes.

I also witnessed my first flash floods, which frequently occurred without warning along the Gila's three forks and in side canyons. Even when no rain had fallen locally, a cloudburst many miles away could send a life-threatening wall of water surging downstream. We routinely had to warn hikers about this danger during the rainy season. One afternoon I received word at the visitor center that a family was stranded on the trail to the cliff dwellings. They had walked only a short distance into the canyon when it started to rain, and when they turned around they encountered a flash flood that had just washed away the trail behind them. Several Forest Service firefighters and I had to climb the steep side of the canyon to bypass the washout and help the family across the treacherously churning water. I'll always remember how one of the firefighters carried their baby, wrapped warmly in a blanket, up the rocky slope.

Despite my affinity for the country, there was one aspect of my job I didn't enjoy: it was highly stressful to manage such an isolated site. Few people wanted to live two hours away from the nearest grocery store, so it was hard to find qualified staff. We had wonderful volunteers, but they had schedules of their own, and there was nothing to keep them at the monument after their terms of service ended. Also, the isolation seemed to intensify personality clashes between staff members, and I was constantly trying to quell arguments—usually without success. Things eventually became so strained that I began to question whether I wanted to continue working as a supervisor. I had never enjoyed supervision as much as the interpretive aspects of my job, and the idea of becoming a frontline interpreter without any supervisory or managerial responsibilities seemed very appealing. After giving it a great deal of thought, I finally decided to seek a frontline position when I completed my three years at Gila Cliff Dwellings.

I had been a national park ranger for twenty-two years. It had been a good career, yet it hadn't prepared me for the challenges of Carlsbad Caverns. As I drove across the plains of West Texas, pondering my concerns about working in a cave, crawling through tight spaces, and learning to climb rope, I had to wonder if I was doing the right thing by traveling several hundred miles for a job interview. Still, I wanted the position. How many other large parks in the desert Southwest had a vacancy that was exactly the kind of interpretive job I was looking for? Besides, I had overcome other fears in the past, so why couldn't I do the same for these? My plan for the coming interview wasn't to hide my fears, but to act—no, to *be*—completely confident and make a good impression.

A New Beginning

MY OPTIMISM CONTRASTED sharply with the West Texas landscape, which seemed to have given up all hope of rain. It was as desiccated as the scrawny coyotes that padded between its scant water holes, and for anyone who didn't know how to contend with its harsh conditions it could be as venomous as a rattlesnake. If I had been making the same trip 150 years earlier in a creaking wagon or on horseback, I would have been living on meager rations of salted pork, parched corn, hard bread, and warm, brackish water, and I would have been acutely aware that the Mescalero Apaches were probably on my trail. Yet despite the aridity and desolation, I loved the desert's openness and couldn't get enough of it. I had always preferred deserts to landscapes blessed with everything they needed. Deserts were lean and tough. They knew how to take care of themselves, especially when things got dicey. Like coyotes, they were survivors, and I admired their pluck.

One of the volunteers at Gila Cliff Dwellings, a widowed grandmother from Pennsylvania, had characterized the desert fairly accurately when she turned to me one morning in the visitor center and said, "You know, Doug, I never realized how different the Southwest would be. Distances here are so much longer than they are back East, and what with flash floods and all, I pay much closer attention to the weather."

Cresting a low rise, I encountered the first in a series of additional landmarks that would shape my future profoundly: an immense salt basin that spread before me like a dazzling white sea washing against the base of the cliffs. It was even more desolate than the grass-covered plains, quintessentially desert and something I definitely liked. On the far side of the basin, the highway curved broadly toward the cliffs, sweeping behind a range of low hills to approach them from the south. I now began climbing a steep grade toward a massive block of limestone that towered over the highway like the impregnable keep of a medieval castle, rising almost a thousand feet above its chaotic talus slope. It was the southernmost tip of the Guadalupe Mountains, and its name was El Capitán. I could see it as the prow of a great ship.

Below this marvel, the highway veered sharply to the northeast and crossed the wide canyon that was Guadalupe Pass. Now the cliffs were behind me, replaced by the grass-covered slopes of the Guadalupes rising majestically on my left. A large sign told me I was passing through Guadalupe Mountains National Park, and a short drive through more low hills took me over the state line into the endless sweep of desert that was southeastern New Mexico. Now I was seeing mesquite, jimsonweed, and barbed-wire fences. Cattle country.

As the highway veered further northward to parallel the Guadalupe Mountains, I was struck by how different their eastern face looked from the massive cliffs I had seen earlier. It was an escarpment, a high and abrupt ridge of limestone stretching over forty miles from El Capitán toward the northeast, almost to the small town of Carlsbad. It had a treacherous slope to it, but I could see a few places where a good climber could make it to the top without using ropes. I had no idea that I would spend countless hours exploring the escarpment's canyons and caves over the coming years, or that my explorations would teach me the greatest lessons of my six years at Carlsbad Caverns.

Almost directly ahead and still ten or twelve miles away, I could see a cluster of white buildings on top of the escarpment. The map showed Carlsbad Caverns National Park in that area, so one of the buildings had to be the park's visitor center. A second small cluster of buildings at the bottom of the escarpment and farther to the east would be Whites City, located just outside the park's entrance.

I found Whites City to be one of those small communities that often cater to visitors at the entrances to popular national parks. (Think Gatlinburg, Tennessee, only much smaller.) Along with three motels and a restaurant, it featured nightly entertainment at Granny's Opera House, a Million-Dollar Museum, and an old-time boardwalk—incongruously made of concrete—stretching along the fronts of several western-style buildings. The gift shop offered every imaginable souvenir of the Southwest, from feathery dream catchers to ceramic chili peppers and T-shirts proclaiming, "I Did It in a Cave." Thumbing through one of the travel books on a sales rack, I read that Whites City had stood at the entrance to Carlsbad Caverns since 1928, four years after the area became a national monument and two years before it would be designated a national park. The singular name "Carlsbad Cavern" refers to the park's largest and best-known cave—there are at least 120 others—while the plural "Carlsbad Caverns" refers to the park itself.

⌁ Leaving Whites City after a brief rest, I drove past the Carlsbad Caverns entrance sign and started up Walnut Canyon. The road now meandered below rugged limestone cliffs pocked with small caves, following the rocky dry wash. Desert willows and mesquite choked parts of the canyon, while the roadside bristled with thorny ocotillo plants, the tips of their spidery branches blazing with magnificent red blossoms. I even noticed bees and other insects swarming around the yellow flowers on the prickly pears.

Several miles into the canyon, the road ascended steeply to the top of the cliffs and emerged onto the broad desert expanse above the escarpment, revealing a breathtaking panorama of the arid plains below washing against the blue peaks of the Guadalupe Mountains. The visitor center near the edge of the escarpment was a simple stucco building with a stubby tower, which I assumed marked the elevator shaft that descended to the Big Room, the largest known chamber in Carlsbad Cavern. That meant the cave must be directly below. I thought it was an odd location for a cave, but that was only because I didn't yet know anything about caves or limestone.

The visitor center lobby was appropriately cavernous and echoed with the noise of visitors crowded into a long ticket line. I told one of the rangers at the information desk that I had an appointment with the operations supervisor, and she directed me to the park's Division of Interpretation and Visitor Services, housed in a small temporary building behind the visitor center. There I found a middle-aged man named Pete sitting in his cramped office, working diligently on the next week's work schedule. He had close-cropped hair and a friendly smile—despite my having interrupted his concentration—and I liked him right away. He gave the impression of being a capable manager, someone who could handle a very complex job without becoming flustered or stymied. Even his short, wiry physique added to a look of poise and self-confidence, despite a bit of middle-age spread. After greeting me and offering me a chair, he got right to the point.

"Doug, I need to begin by asking you a few questions. First, how do you feel about working in a cave? Is that something you can handle?" The question startled me. Pete evidently was a mind reader who knew exactly what I had been thinking, and I reminded myself to sound confident and make a good impression.

"It won't bother me at all, Pete."

"I ask because we've had a couple of incidents in the past where interpreters have accepted positions and then realized they didn't like working underground, where it's dark and relatively cold. You'll be spending a big portion of your time in the park's caves, patrolling the trails and giving tours, so if that doesn't sound appealing, you probably shouldn't work here." He certainly knew how to be blunt.

"No, I'll be able to handle it."

"Some of the trails are strenuous, too," he continued. "The trail from the Natural Entrance down to the Big Room is a mile long and descends about 750 vertical feet, which is seventy-five stories if you figure ten feet per story. It's a long hike, and you'll usually be walking uphill. Have you seen the Natural Entrance yet?"

"Uh, no. I just got here."

"We call it the Natural Entrance to distinguish it from the elevator shafts that go straight down to the Big Room. The elevators are no sweat, obviously, but the Natural Entrance Trail can be intimidating for some people. And the trail up to Slaughter Canyon Cave is long and steep, too."

"Well, I've always enjoyed hiking, jogging, and bicycling," I replied, "so I think I can handle just about anything that comes my way. I'm up for the challenge."

"That's good, because the job definitely requires stamina. And one other thing: How do you feel about crawling through tight passages on the strenuous caving tours?"

"It shouldn't be a problem, Pete."

"Matlock's Pinch on the Hall of the White Giant tour is about as tight as they come, and some of the passages in Spider Cave are almost as bad. You'll really have to exert yourself in places where it's difficult to maneuver, and you'll be getting dirty." Pete had anticipated almost all my concerns, and I felt as though he could see right through me.

I kept my voice level as I answered, "Sounds good to me, Pete."

"Great. Now, do you have any questions before we get into the interview?"

I had noticed several coils of rope, a caving helmet, and other gear stored around the room or hanging on a wall. I gestured toward the helmet. "Do you use your caving equipment very often?"

"All the time. I've been a caver for years, even before I started working here. I really love it. Most weekends I'm up in the Guadalupe Mountains, caving with friends. Quite a few people on the park staff are into caving, so if you're interested you'll have plenty of opportunities to learn all about it. And if you want to go along on some of our trips, you'll be welcome."

"That would be great, Pete."

"Have you ever been on rope?"

"No, never."

"It isn't required for the job, but if you want to do any caving or take part in our rope-climbing demonstrations, you'll have to learn how to climb. If that's agreeable, we'll put you on rope during your training period."

"Yes, I'd like that."

Pete then asked about my background, especially my experience as an interpreter. I described the various types of guided tours and other programs I had given over the years as well as the interpretive-training programs I had developed as a supervisor. We talked for about thirty minutes, and I warmed to Pete's friendly demeanor. He seemed pleased with what I had to say and assured me at the end of our meeting that I was qualified for either of the available positions. However, the park's chief of interpretation would make the final decision, so Pete had to meet with him before they could let me know where things stood. Still, he felt certain I would soon be working at Carlsbad Caverns. Despite my unexpressed concerns, I felt pleased with the interview as I watched Pete sign a guest pass that would allow me to enter the cave.

"Here you go, Doug," he said, handing it to me. "The Natural Entrance Trail closed for the day at three o'clock, but you can still use this to go down on the elevators and walk around the Big Room Trail. It's open until five, and since it's self-guided, you'll be seeing things from the visitors' point of view." I accepted the pass, hoping it wouldn't be my downfall. I certainly didn't want to come back and tell Pete I had been dead wrong about my ability to venture underground.

"Thanks, Pete. I'm curious to see if the Big Room lives up to its reputation."

"It does, and then some. Enjoy the cave, and you should be hearing from the chief of interpretation within a week or so." Pete offered me his hand. I hoped it would be a momentous handshake.

⌒ After walking back to the visitor center, I found my way to the elevators and joined a dozen or so other visitors in a hushed, dimly lit waiting room. This was the moment that would determine whether I could work at Carlsbad Caverns. I wasn't feeling anxious or queasy, as I had decades earlier, but I nonetheless slipped my hands into my pockets and crossed my fingers.

A young park ranger closed the doors behind us and began a brief orientation by instructing us to stay on the trail and not touch the cave formations, because body oils can impede their growth and cause them to deteriorate. His short hair and clean-cut appearance reminded me of my own early years as a park ranger at Kings Mountain. He seemed completely self-confident and obviously didn't have any qualms about working underground. I had to envy him. After completing his introduction, he ushered us into one of four elevators for our one-minute descent to the cave. I felt a brief tingling sensation as it started down, but otherwise I was fine—probably because I had been on so many elevators before. I took this to be a good omen. When the elevator came to a stop and the door pulled open, we stepped into a brightly lit room with stucco walls and a glass revolving door leading into the underground lunchroom.

I had done it. I had descended into the cave without mishap and was now seventy-five stories below the visitor center. Passing through the revolving door, I gazed in wonder at the dark limestone ceiling about twenty feet overhead and paused for a moment to savor my modest achievement. Over the past decades, although I couldn't explain when or how, I had outgrown my fear of caves, and I would no longer be intimidated by the thought of going underground. I could work at Carlsbad Caverns. And having overcome one fear, it seemed likely I could overcome the others as well. My optimism soared.

Ignoring the noise and bright lights of the lunchroom, I followed a sign to the Big Room Trail and entered a narrow, dimly lit passage decorated with an array of small cave formations that stood like sentinels, some of which appeared to be covered with popcorn made of limestone. The passage opened almost immediately into a much larger chamber, while the ceiling rose dramatically to create an imposing vault. A second trail branched to the right, disappearing into a narrow gallery filled with massive boulders. I concluded that it must be the Natural Entrance Trail, which Pete had mentioned. The visitors I saw emerging from the gallery had just hiked down from the surface through a series of massive chambers known as the Main Corridor. I was eager to make that descent myself, but not today. This would be just a cursory visit.

I began to notice more limestone popcorn covering the lower two-thirds of the wall. I had read about cave popcorn but hadn't realized its name was so appropriate. Except for its grayish color, it looked just like the stuff I popped in my microwave. The trail eventually curved around an abrupt turn of the wall to reveal three towering stalagmites, the largest rising to the height of a six-story building. This definitely caught my attention. Limestone draperies cascaded down its sides like drizzles of sugar icing on a many-tiered wedding cake—a cake that towered almost to the ceiling. A sign next to the trail told me I had entered the Hall of Giants and that the massive stalagmites had been created by water dripping from the ceiling over countless centuries. Astounded by the enormity and magnificence of the formations, I began to regret that I hadn't overcome my fear and ventured into caves sooner. This was just too good to miss.

Beyond the Hall of Giants, I came upon a forest of limestone soda straws hanging topsy-turvy from the ceiling. Nearby were some squiggly little formations that looked like pigs' tails or baby snakes growing out of the wall. They went up, down, and around in every direction, leaving me to wonder how they had formed. The ceiling now vaulted upward again, rising so high that it almost disappeared in the semidarkness overhead. Spotlights concealed on the floor illuminated a huge opening in the rock at the ceiling's apex. I couldn't stop gazing up at it as I continued along the trail.

"That's called the Spirit World."

I had almost bumped into the park ranger who spoke these words. His name tag identified him as Ronnie, and his friendly nature became apparent as he asked where I was from.

"I'm the site manager at Gila Cliff Dwellings over in the southwest corner of the state. I just had a job interview with Pete up in the temporary building. I've applied for one of the vacant interpreter positions."

"Hey, good luck," he said, smiling broadly. "I know you'll love it here—it's a great park."

"Yeah, I'm finding that out. How high is it up there?"

"The top of Spirit World is 250 feet above the cave floor. That's the height of a twenty-five-story building. Hard to believe, isn't it?"

"I'll say."

I stood in awe, craning my neck as I stared upward, while Ronnie told me the amazing story of Spirit World. Several years earlier, the park's cave-resources staff had used a cluster of helium balloons to raise a long, thin cord into the opening and drape it around a stalagmite visible from the cave floor. After tying one end of the cord to the end of a climbing rope, they used the cord's other end to pull the rope up and around the stalagmite and back to the floor. Then, with the rope anchored securely, two climbers—Ronal Kerbo of the National Park Service and Jim Goodbar of the Bureau of Land Management—had ascended to explore more than seven hundred feet of passages in the ceiling. They named the area Spirit World because it contained a number of white stalagmites that looked like ghosts hiding in the darkness.

As Ronnie told his story, several other visitors stopped to listen. Like them, I could only marvel at the underground world I was discovering, and I realized my walk around the Big Room Trail might be the start of an entirely new and exciting chapter in my life. By putting my fear of caves behind me, I had taken the first step toward improving my job situation and becoming an interpretive ranger at Carlsbad Caverns—and maybe even a caver.

The trail eventually brought me to a massive pit that looked as broad as a football field. I gripped the metal railing with trepidation as I peered into its pervasive darkness. Because of my phobia about heights, the great depth it implied gave me a sinking feeling in the pit of my stomach, and I reflexively sucked in my breath. Eventually, I would learn that the Bottomless Pit does have a bottom, fourteen stories below the trail. At the time, however, I could only wonder what it would be like to descend into that terrible void on one of the ropes I had seen in Pete's office. Riding down in a crowded elevator was one thing, but descending on a rope, all by myself, and trusting my life to the kind of equipment Pete used, was quite another. Yet I was determined to do just that.

⌒ After an hour of fast-paced walking, I arrived back at the elevators, fully convinced that the Big Room lived up to its reputation. Within minutes I was heading across the parking lot toward my car, squinting in the bright sunlight and excited by the prospect of working at such an amazing park. Driving south from Whites City, I felt completely happy and optimistic, and by the time I reached Guadalupe Mountains National Park, I was already setting goals for my new assignment.

The first was to learn as much as I could about Carlsbad Cavern and the other caves of the Guadalupe Mountains, through research and by exploring them in person. Because I knew nothing about caves—I was still confused about the difference between stalactites and stalagmites— this would be a significant challenge, involving many hours of study in the park library as well as ongoing discussions with other interpreters and members of the park's cave-resources staff.

My second goal was to become an experienced caver. I had the required strength and stamina, but now I had to prove I could overcome my fear of tight spaces and heights. This was essential because I would need caving and climbing skills to go on weekend caving trips with Pete and his friends. I didn't yet realize how much work and commitment this would involve, but within weeks I would be struggling to master technical equipment as well as climbing techniques, and enduring many exhausting hours of practice on rope. Eventually I would test my new skills in some of the mountains' deepest vertical caves.

My final goal was to explore and learn about the Chihuahuan Desert. I knew from past experience that visitors to national parks constantly ask questions about things unrelated to a park's primary theme. At Yorktown Battlefield, they had wanted to know about the deer they saw grazing along roadsides and the wildflowers growing on earthworks. At Gila Cliff Dwellings, they had asked about the hot springs and the fish they saw swimming in the river. At Carlsbad Caverns, they would undoubtedly ask about the desert, so I had to be prepared.

I would find, to my surprise, that Carlsbad Caverns is as much a desert park as a cave park. My time there would be divided almost equally between exploring the Chihuahuan Desert and exploring the underworld of caves. It would be an unforgettable adventure, taking me from rocky canyons bristling with spiky lechuguilla plants into twisting cave passages decorated with gypsum flowers and sparking aragonite crystals. Along the way, I would discover that the desert and its caves are linked not only by the creative actions of water and other natural processes, but by nature's inexhaustible desire to create a world of astonishing beauty, both below and above the earth's surface.

Making Friends

ABOUT A WEEK after my interview, the chief of interpretation phoned to tell me I had the job. He would add me to the Carlsbad Caverns payroll in mid-September, which gave me about two months to get ready for my move. I was ecstatic, and as I shared the good news with my coworkers, my mind began racing with thoughts of the guided tours and other programs I would be giving. By the end of the day, I had planned the basic outline for my evening bat flight program at the cave's Natural Entrance.

I had a lot to accomplish before leaving Gila Cliff Dwellings. Besides finishing several projects at work, I had to study the books and other materials Pete sent to me, coordinate with my new park's administrative office, and say good-bye to my coworkers. A going-away party at the visitor center brought home the realization that I was finally leaving. It wasn't long before I was driving back across the plains of West Texas, marveling again at the beauty of the Guadalupe Mountains. This time I saw the open expanse of the Chihuahuan Desert as my new home.

I liked my job at Carlsbad Caverns right away and easily settled into a new routine. The employee-housing area, where I had a two-bedroom duplex apartment, stood several hundred yards behind the visitor center on the far side of a shallow canyon known as Bat Cave Draw—so named because it sheltered the Natural Entrance, where swarms of bats emerged every evening during spring and summer. The housing area was known affectionately among staff members as "On the Hill" because of its location above the canyon. In later years, I would be glad to live there rather than in the town of Carlsbad, as most staff members did, because it allowed me to take part in caving trips and other off-duty activities I might otherwise have missed.

I walked to work every morning along the paved trail that descended into the canyon from the housing area, crossed the small parking lot near the cave entrance, then ascended gradually to the visitor center. I looked forward to being greeted by the soaptree yuccas—the state flower of New Mexico—and the soapberry trees at the bottom of the draw, with their feathery leaves and bright-yellow berries. Often I came upon small desert creatures along the trail, including cactus wrens, tarantulas, and eight-inch-long centipedes. On some days, there might even be a rattle-snake. My favorite sightings were collared lizards, which I could easily identify by the thick black bands around their necks. Occasionally one of them would lead me up the trail toward the visitor center, scurrying along the asphalt on its hind legs with its pale-green skin gleaming in the morning sunlight and its head bobbing frantically back and forth. Invariably, it would dart into the brush and vanish like a heat wave in the morning haze.

At the side door of the visitor center, I often paused to gaze across the parking lot toward the southeastern horizon. The desert below the escarpment seemed timeless, and it always gave me a sense of absolute peace. Sometimes I even walked around to the front of the visitor center, where I could see the broad sweep of the Guadalupe Escarpment receding into the distance. The deep canyons that punctuated its slope meant nothing to me at the time, but I would eventually be able to recite their names from memory: McKittrick Canyon, Big Canyon, Black Canyon, Double Canyon, Slaughter Canyon, Nuevo Canyon, Rattlesnake Canyon, and Walnut Canyon. Mountain lions roamed the area, and it occurred to me that the eight canyons could represent the number of scratch marks left by a lion when she sharpens her claws against the trunk of a fallen juniper or sinks them into the shoulders of a fleeing mule deer. Given the harshness of the country, it seemed like an apt metaphor.

Over the coming weeks, I would also learn that the escarpment had been part of an ancient reef that flourished along the edge of a great sea covering portions of West Texas and southeastern New Mexico. This was during the Permian Era, about 265 million years ago. The reef had been pushed above the surrounding terrain by mountain-building forces long after the sea disappeared; it was studded with fossils and other reminders of the small sea creatures that had once comprised the reef. In time I would be spotting the impressions left by their tiny bodies as I hiked through the canyons or explored passages in the escarpment's many caves, including Carlsbad Cavern.

I felt supremely happy to be living in the Chihuahuan Desert and gratified that I had finally achieved everything I really wanted in my career. I was doing exactly what I most enjoyed doing, and I was being paid to do it. Like Robert Frost's narrator in "Two Tramps in Mud Time," I had realized my object in living by uniting my avocation and my vocation.

At the beginning of each morning, Pete conducted a short staff meeting with the interpreters who were on duty that day—usually between fifteen and twenty of them—in the lunchroom of the temporary building. He was always relaxed and easygoing, giving the impression that anyone could approach him with a problem. I had always tried to be that way with my own subordinates, and I sensed that Pete and I would get along. Before and after the meetings, I began to meet my new coworkers. One of the other permanent interpreters warned me that relationships within the staff could be politically charged, but I tried to keep an open mind. I told him quite honestly that I liked everyone I had met so far and felt certain I could get along.

The operation Pete supervised was far bigger and more complex than anything I had experienced and so required an exceptionally large staff. There were nineteen permanent interpreters who developed and conducted the guided tours and other programs, and an additional five to fifteen seasonal interpreters and park volunteers—depending on the time of year—whose duties included patrolling the cave's trails and serving as "trail rangers" for the guided tours. (A trail ranger walked behind each tour group to prevent straggling and provide backup during emergencies.) The daily and biweekly schedules that Pete was constantly preparing seemed like nightmares of complexity, and I couldn't understand how he was able to manage them. Just trying to remember which interpreters had been trained to give which tours would have taxed my abilities, but Pete seemed to take it all in stride.

I liked the variety of personalities among my fellow interpreters. While some were relatively young, others were middle-aged, and they came from widely divergent backgrounds and almost every region of the country. Mark Twain once wrote that after meeting so many unusual characters while working as a riverboat pilot on the Mississippi River, he never again met a person who was truly unique; he had already "met him on the river." Would I be able to say that I had already "met him in a cave"?

One of my favorite seasonal interpreters was Chandra, a feisty and self-reliant grandmother whose perpetually tanned face and weathered blonde hair made her seem as much a part of southeastern New Mexico as the prickly pears and dust devils. She and her husband owned a cattle ranch about fifteen miles south of the park, and she had been a member of the interpretive staff for several years. Staunchly optimistic and unshakably reliable, she was someone Pete could always count on.

Another favorite was Kenny, a young man whose parents had once been migrant farm workers. He attended college in El Paso during the school year, was active in his local army-reserve unit, and would later serve as a helicopter pilot during the Iraq War. I liked Kenny because he was a gentleman, very soft-spoken and always polite, and because he seemed level-headed in his approach to problems. I was impressed that he spoke fluent Spanish as well as English and was certified to give rope-climbing demonstrations in the underground lunchroom.

Then there was Becky, a friendly young woman who was learning to fly an airplane during her off-duty hours while also learning to climb rope at work. I could easily distinguish her from other staff members, even in the semidarkness of the Big Room, by the way her curly red hair protruded in an explosion of vibrant color under the broad brim of her ranger hat. Her voice was so soft and flowed so beautifully that it was easy to think she might not be very assertive, but anyone who crossed Becky discovered that she knew how to take care of herself.

One of the most popular seasonal interpreters was Monty, an older local man with a thickset frame and bright, expressive eyes. By reputation he was hyper-friendly, loved to tell jokes, and found it difficult to stop talking. Pete once lamented that Monty had never been able to complete an entire patrol around the Big Room Trail because he stopped so often to talk and joke with visitors, pointing out the shapes of animals and objects in the formations: "Look there! Doesn't that look like a gorilla? And do you see that big manta ray swimming just above the trail over there? Isn't that something?" Monty's confident air and close-cropped, neatly combed hair made it easy to guess that he had once been a state-highway patrol officer, and he reveled in the experiences he had accumulated throughout his lifetime, reminding me of a gnarled old juniper growing out in the backcountry. The only thing out of character about him was his extraordinary fear of snakes and women doctors. Whenever he dropped his guard, some of the other staff members would tease him mercilessly.

Because the permanent interpreters had to develop guided tours, they needed more study time than the seasonals and so had their own office, a large room in the visitor center known as "the Roost"—a place where bats live, of course—with two interpreters sharing each desk. My desk partner was a young man named Dennis, who impressed me not only with his knowledge of caves but also with his deeply resonant voice, which made him seem older than he was. He was obviously intelligent and had a studious, intellectual air about him, reinforced by his unruly black hair and neatly trimmed goatee. Dennis was interested in the park's resource-management program and hoped eventually to join the resource-management staff.

I was pleased to learn that Dennis and I would be partnered on weekends to give guided tours through Slaughter Canyon Cave, which was located at the end of a dirt road in the park's remote backcountry. Because the cave had only a primitive trail and no electric lights, visitors brought their own flashlights. One of us would give the morning tour while the other served as trail ranger; then we'd switch places for the afternoon tour. Dennis had given the tour many times, so I hoped to benefit from his experience.

Most of the permanent interpreters had come to Carlsbad Caverns from other NPS areas, including cave parks like Mammoth Cave National Park and Wind Cave National Park. Some had worked in historical areas or other types of natural areas—Gettysburg National Military Park or Grand Tetons National Park, for example—and had been as unfamiliar with caves when they arrived at Carlsbad Caverns as I was. A few of the other permanents had already learned how to climb rope and had become avid cavers, which I found encouraging, as I would be following their example.

Of the permanent interpreters, Lance impressed me the most because he seemed to know more about caves than anyone else, including Dennis. He could explain how and why aragonite crystals had formed along the trail near the underground lunchroom, describe the two species of bats that roosted near the deepest-known point in Carlsbad Cavern at the Lake of the Clouds, and tell visitors anything they wanted to know about Jim White, the Texas cowboy who was one of the earliest explorers of Carlsbad Cavern. I couldn't imagine anyone knowing more about caves than Lance did, and I felt intimidated because he knew so much, while I knew so little.

I saw him for the first time one morning while studying at my desk. He passed so quickly that I had only a vague impression of a tall, lanky figure with long hair striding confidently through the Roost. When we finally talked, he appeared to be studying everything I said or did without knowing what to make of me, and I suspected he wanted to decide later. Although I knew he was well liked, my first impression was that he seemed aloof.

Lance had more caving and rope-climbing experience than any other interpretive staff member, including Pete, and on his days off he usually went caving in the Guadalupe Mountains with Pete and some of his other friends. About a week after I arrived at Carlsbad Caverns, he and several of his caving buddies left for a difficult trip to the remote mountains of central Mexico, where they descended by rope into a limestone pit called Sotano de las Golondrinas, or "Basement of the Swallows." When he told me later that it was one of the deepest underground free-fall drops in the world and that he and his friends had descended to a depth of 1,094 feet—109 stories—individually and while hanging freely on one rope, I was completely amazed. Would I have enough gumption and stamina to do something like that?

Lance seemed even younger than his twenty-four years and had been a permanent interpreter only since June, when he had graduated from the University of Wyoming. For the previous four years, he had worked as a seasonal interpreter at Carlsbad Caverns during the summer months under a college internship program. He was very proud that his father had been a national park ranger for more than two decades and currently held a law-enforcement position at Guadalupe Mountains National Park. "Scotty" was well-known among western national-park employees because he had served at so many large parks, including Yellowstone, Grand Tetons, Sequoia, Big Bend, and even Mt. McKinley—now Denali—in Alaska. Because of Scotty's background, Lance had already learned the ins and outs of the National Park Service and the ranger profession, and he was obviously eager to follow in his dad's footsteps.

I could always recognize Lance from a distance because he stood well over six feet tall and moved with a slow, methodical gait that reminded me of rodeo cowboys from the northern Great Plains, where he had spent most of his youth. Often when I left for work in the mornings, I would see his lanky frame ambling up the trail toward the visitor center on the far side of Bat Cave Draw, his long stride looking as though it could easily measure the rolling plains of eastern Wyoming.

The way Lance moved said everything about his outlook. Whenever he took part in rope-climbing demonstrations in the underground lunchroom or visitor center lobby, or even occasionally at the Natural Entrance, he moved with greater ease and self-assurance than any of the other climbers, however experienced they might be. Something about his movements said he knew exactly what he was doing and could handle himself in any situation. Everyone respected him for that, and those of us with less experience in caving and rope climbing followed his lead implicitly. When I eventually saw Lance on a dance floor, doing a Texas two-step for all he was worth, I noticed the same characteristic: it was all in the way he moved.

Lance was passionate about most outdoor activities, and his garage in the housing area brimmed with evidence that he hadn't been wasting his youth. Neatly tied coils of rope for both caving and rock climbing hung securely on the walls, along with a pair of snow skis and several recurve hunting bows. A much-used mountain bike and a well-worn leather saddle rested nearby. In the center of all this stood his 1984 Honda Magna motorcycle. No one could deny that Lance was a perpetual source of raw energy and the hyperactive all-American boy writ large.

At first I was drawn to Lance because I wanted to learn more about caving and rope climbing, but gradually I saw other reasons for wanting to gain his friendship. I liked that he was my exact opposite in most ways and that he challenged some of my strongly held assumptions about other people, and even about life itself. He was by far the most engaging and unusual person I had ever met. Beyond teaching me everything I know about caving and rope climbing, he would inspire me to do my best when things became difficult, and he ultimately influenced my outlook more than any other person at Carlsbad Caverns.

CHAPTER FOUR

Entering the Underworld

AS A PERMANENT interpreter, my job would be to develop and present six guided tours, including the two strenuous caving tours Pete had mentioned in our interview, along with several programs for the visitor center lobby or theater and an evening bat flight program. So my first task was to begin working in earnest toward one of the three goals I had already set for myself: learning as much as I could about Carlsbad Cavern and the other caves of the Guadalupe Mountains.

Pete said he would schedule me for several hours of project time each day so I could study in the Roost or the park's library. To acquaint me with the operation, he would also schedule me to work at the visitor center information desk, patrol the Big Room and Natural Entrance trails, learn how to turn the cave's lighting system on and off, and trail some of the other rangers' tours. At the end of two weeks, he would expect me to have my first narrative outline ready for the King's Palace tour, which took visitors along a paved trail through the most scenic chambers in the cave: the King's Palace, Queen's Chamber, Papoose Room, and Green Lake Room. I was going to be busy.

I had great fun patrolling the cave and talking with visitors. Because the Big Room and Natural Entrance trails were self-guided, Pete expected us to walk against the flow of visitor traffic so we could greet everyone and answer their questions. One of the most common inquiries was difficult to answer: "Has all of the cave been discovered yet?" Not a bad question, actually, when reworded to express more accurately what the visitors were asking: "Given everything we know about Carlsbad Cavern, is it possible or even likely that some areas of the cave haven't been discovered?" Every visitor seemed greatly impressed by the cave's size, and many asked if the Big Room is the largest cave chamber in the world. They often seemed disappointed to learn that when measured in approximate square footage, the record-holder is Sarawak Chamber on the island of Borneo, which is many times larger than the Big Room. Visitors also wanted to know if Carlsbad Cavern is one of the Seven Wonders of the World. I had to explain that, while the park had been designated a World Heritage Site by the United Nations, it wasn't on any modern list of the world's seven greatest natural wonders—at least to my knowledge.

Occasionally, Pete assigned me to relieve one of the elevator operators for lunch. It was entertaining to shuttle people up and down between the visitor center and cave and to hear their reactions to the Big Room. I was appalled, however, when one of the elevator operators told me that a ranger who worked at Carlsbad Caverns during the 1930s, and whose last name happened to be the same as mine, had fallen down the elevator shaft. He escaped death by immediately grabbing one of the cables. Completely unfazed, he was back at work the next day.

I spent many tedious hours over the next two weeks—and far beyond—studying such things as cave formations, the geology of the Guadalupe Mountains, the natural history of bats, the chemistry of cave minerals, and the history of Carlsbad Cavern, until I finally began to feel comfortable with the information I had to know. With a minimum of difficulty, I could recite the chemical composition of limestone, state how many insects a Mexican free-tailed bat might consume in one night, tell where stalactites and stalagmites grow—the word "stalactite" contains a "c" for ceiling, while "stalagmite" has a "g" for ground—and explain how each had formed.

Yet that was only the first part of my task. I also had to combine the information in a compelling way for each tour or program, and I had to come up with several major ideas or "themes" that would provide a framework for each one. The theme of Lance's King's Palace tour was "Caves are the ultimate form of wilderness," while that of another interpreter's guided lantern tour through Left Hand Tunnel was "The kind of light we take with us determines how we perceive a cave." The ultimate goal of every theme was to help visitors see the park in a way they might not otherwise have considered.

So what were my themes going to be? After a great deal of thought, I finally selected four ideas that seemed to cover the major attributes of caves. As it turned out, they were good choices: they would not only guide my research and provide structure for my programs, but shape the way I experienced the caves of the Guadalupe Mountains over the coming years.

My first theme was "Caves are places of exploration and discovery." This became self-evident as I read about Jim White and other early explorers of Carlsbad Cavern. White's daring accomplishments were especially noteworthy because he went into the cave all alone and with nothing more than a kerosene lantern and a firm conviction that he would eventually come out. I admired his gumption, and I hoped my involvement in the strenuous caving tours, along with caving and rope climbing in my off-duty hours, would help me appreciate the challenges he faced.

My second theme, "Caves are places of creation," appealed to me because it was so apparent every time I patrolled the Big Room or walked down the Natural Entrance Trail. Carlsbad Cavern was filled with evidence, from its astonishing formations to the immense size of its chambers, that nature is infinitely creative—not just on the earth's surface but underground as well. I never tired of learning about the geologic and chemical processes that had formed the caves of the Guadalupe Mountains, and eventually I came to realize that some of nature's most spectacular creative achievements are found below the earth's surface.

My third theme was an extension of the second: "The same natural processes account for the unusual beauty of caves and the more familiar beauty of the earth's surface." One of my most profound moments at Carlsbad Caverns occurred when I realized a connection between the softness of clouds floating in afternoon sunlight over Guadalupe Peak and the prickliness of aragonite crystals growing in the absolute darkness of Slaughter Canyon Cave. While each was a unique miracle, both had formed through the simple interactions of air and water, processes I had read about and could easily understand. As time passed, I would discover other important links between caves and the world of the surface.

My final theme went in a very different direction: "Caves affect us emotionally and psychologically." A good example is the way some people fear caves, which tend to evoke our most primal emotions about death and the grave. My own experience as a teenager demonstrated this. At the cultural level, caves have influenced our ideas and feelings about the underworld, that legendary realm of darkness thought to exist below the earth's surface. From Judeo-Christian ideas about hell to *sipapu* in traditional Native cultures of the Southwest, human societies have repeatedly imagined a mythical connection between the surface of the earth and what lies beneath—and that surely is relevant to our understanding of caves. The more I thought about this idea, the more it appealed to me, and it ultimately influenced the way I experience caves more than any of my other themes.

With my selections completed, I began working in earnest on the outline for my King's Palace tour, sometimes at my desk or in the park library but usually at one of the Roost's computers. The other interpreters would come and go as I struggled to finish yet another sentence or paragraph. I envied their freedom. They had long since completed their outlines and were giving tours, while I could only see the Roost as a brightly lit, windowless prison. It always amused me how many visitors seemed to think a park ranger's job is perpetually exciting and glamorous, with little or no desk work. That definitely isn't the case.

✐ Because I was most intrigued by the idea that caves affect us emotionally and psychologically, I wanted to develop that theme first. For my King's Palace tour, I concentrated on the idea that caves have influenced our collective imagination. I began to study the mythology of caves. Perhaps I could draw on several myths or legends to illustrate my ideas. (I use the words "myth" and "mythology" to mean traditional stories that convey an important truth about human nature or the world we live in, regardless of whether the stories are literally true.) In Western society, of course, caves have come to symbolize our fear of death and the grave as well as our belief in a spiritual underworld, a place of despair and torment below the earth's surface.

Many years earlier, I had read John Milton's epic poem *Paradise Lost*. Its long, complex sentences and archaic language easily made it the most difficult thing I had ever read, yet its grand scheme and lofty images captured my imagination and carried me into the rigorous spiritual world of Puritan England. Published in 1667, the poem describes the terrifying realm Satan and his angels inherited after their rebellion against God and their fall from heaven. Judging by my own experience of Carlsbad Cavern as a teenager and park ranger, it seemed that Milton's underworld shared a number of characteristics with the cave I worked in every day.

Jim White apparently agreed with me. As he cautiously descended the Main Corridor during his first trips into the cave, he began to name the fantastic things he was discovering in the pervasive darkness: the Devil's Spring, Devil's Den, Devil's Shade Tree, Devil's Easy Chair, Devil's Hump, and Devil's Backbone. We still use those names today, and they seem entirely appropriate because Western mythology tells us that descending into a cave is like descending into the dark realm of Satan. I decided to test this idea when Pete first scheduled me to walk down the Natural Entrance Trail to turn on the lights. I had already made that trip with one of the experienced rangers to learn where the switches were located, but this time I would be alone. What would it be like to walk down the Main Corridor by myself, comparing the things I saw to Milton's vision of the underworld?

On the appointed day, I left the visitor center about ten minutes before the cave opened so I would have plenty of time to make my descent before the first visitors started down the trail. The swallows around the Natural Entrance were flitting back and forth in the warm sunlight, but I didn't stop to notice their antics. Unlocking the barred entrance gate, I pushed it back and locked it against the rock wall, then descended into the shadow of the overhang. The air became cooler, and I could smell the musty odor of bat guano wafting up from the Bat Cave—the area where the Mexican free-tailed bats were roosting—about a quarter mile inside the Natural Entrance. I found the first light switch just before I entered the "twilight zone." (This is the area just inside a cave's entrance, where light from the surface is still visible; the area beyond it is called the "dark zone.") The silence might have seemed oppressive if I hadn't been preoccupied with recalling Milton's imagery. When would I begin to feel Satan's presence? When would I meet the dreadful scenes envisioned in *Paradise Lost*?

As the trail continued its gradual descent, it made an abrupt turn. Instead of going straight ahead in the direction of the Bat Cave, it doubled back on itself, crossed the rubble-strewn floor of the twilight zone, and disappeared into a broad passage that went in the opposite direction, almost directly below the Natural Entrance. I paused to gaze upward into the blinding light of that huge opening and imagined I was peering into the light of heaven itself. That's where Satan and his angels had come from, as Milton tells us at the beginning of his poem:

Him the almighty power
Hurled headlong flaming from the ethereal sky
With hideous ruin and combustion down
To bottomless perdition, there to dwell
In adamantine chains and penal fire,
Who durst defy the omnipotent to arms.

What would Satan's Fall have looked like? If I had been standing in the twilight zone of the underworld as it happened, what would I have seen? Many years earlier, near my home in Tidewater Virginia, I had noticed a rotting log that appeared to be giving off a heavy vapor. When I went over to investigate, I found a huge swarm of winged ants crawling out of a split in the wood and rapidly taking flight. I watched in amazement for several minutes and must have seen many thousands rise in an endless stream that meandered slowly back and forth into the distance, reminding me of those long, serpentine flocks of birds that undulate across the sky in winter. Would Satan and his angels have looked like that?

Peering up at the Natural Entrance, I imagined a vast stream of tiny winged creatures—Satan and his legions in miniature—tumbling out of the blinding light in a firestorm of swirling flames, sulfurous smoke, and crackling lightning, their wings fluttering helplessly as they felt themselves being swept into the utter darkness of the broad passage before me, like leaves in a whirlwind. As they disappeared forever into the terrifying void of the underworld, the firestorm's churning residue of acrid smoke and ash settled across the cave's entrance and into the twilight zone, choking off every vestige of light from above and dimming any memory of their passing.

Yes, it certainly could have looked like that. Continuing down the trail, I flipped the next light switch to dimly illuminate the cave ahead of me. Just beyond the tranquil pool of water known as the Devil's Spring, the trail descended into a massive chamber in another series of steep switchbacks that took me to the brink of the Devil's Den, a deep and sinister-looking pit with nearly vertical walls. Was this where Satan and his angels finally came to rest?

> Nine times the space that measures day and night
> To mortal men, he with his horrid crew
> Lay vanquished, rolling in the fiery gulf,
> Confounded though immortal . . .

I could easily imagine the chamber around me as a place of eternal suffering and torment. Scores of hulking stalagmites, barely visible in the semidarkness, seemed calculated to evoke despair, while mountains of glistening flowstone threatened to surround and overwhelm me. Along the north wall, water dripped dolorously from a line of dark stalactites, and overhead the dimly lit ceiling seemed ponderous and oppressive, as though it might collapse at any moment. Was this what Satan had beheld in Milton's poem?

> A dungeon horrible, on all sides round
> As one great furnace flamed, yet from those flames
> No light, but rather darkness visible
> Served only to discover sights of woe,
> Regions of sorrow, doleful shades . . .
> Such place eternal justice had prepared
> For those rebellious, here their prison ordained
> In utter darkness and their portion set
> As far removed from God and light of Heaven
> As from the center thrice to the utmost pole.

After slowly recovering from the shock of his fall, Satan roused his companions and summoned them to a great consultation to decide how they should respond to their ouster from heaven. They unanimously agreed that surrender was unthinkable and the rebellion should continue.

Peace is despaired,
For who can think submission? War, then, war
Open or understood must be resolved.

This decision marks the beginning of the great cosmic struggle in Judeo-Christian mythology between good and evil, light and darkness, heaven and hell—and perhaps even between the surface of the earth and what lies beneath. Even today those of us raised in the Western tradition tend to think that light and darkness can never be reconciled and that darkness is always bad, as it prevents us from knowing what lies around us and may even conceal danger.

By the time I reached the elevators, I had confirmed my belief that entering a cave is like venturing into the darkness of John Milton's underworld, and I wanted to share that idea with the visitors who went on my King's Palace tours. My outline would ultimately include an abbreviated version of the story of Satan's Fall, to illustrate how caves can affect us emotionally and psychologically. Yet I wanted to do something more.

⌒ Once the human imagination has populated the underworld with the forces of evil, has it run out of ways to interpret the darkness of caves? Not at all, for there are other mythic pathways that can lead us into the dark recesses below the earth's surface. To help visitors realize this, I wanted to compare our Western outlook with the way Native cultures of the Southwest have viewed caves and the underworld.

Like their Paleolithic counterparts in Europe, early Southwestern peoples were drawn to caves. On the limestone walls of the Natural Entrance to Carlsbad Cavern, we still see faded pictographs left by the hunter-gatherers who lived along the escarpment, although we haven't yet found conclusive evidence that they entered the twilight zone, which is separated from the entrance by a sheer drop-off. In Slaughter Canyon Cave, where Dennis and I would be giving tours, there are pictographs well inside the dark zone, about a quarter-mile from the entrance. The small drawings, now only faintly visible, cover a low wall beside an area where there was undoubtedly a pool of water in prehistoric times, and other evidence suggests that the people who made the drawings may have lived in the cave for at least a part of every year.

It's regrettable they didn't leave behind any clues about how they might have viewed the underworld. Traditional pueblo cultures have always seen it in a positive way, as a place of creation and emergence. To illustrate this on my King's Palace tour, I decided to tell a remarkable story from the pueblo of Acoma in northwestern New Mexico. After recounting the myth of Satan's Fall, I suggested that it was possible to experience a different kind of emotional and psychological connection to the darkness of caves. I then asked everyone to imagine a tall, fragrant pine tree growing in the center of the King's Palace, while I related the tale of Ute'tsiti's daughters.

It seems that in the beginning, two female babies were created in the darkness of the underworld, which was called sipapu. It was so dark that the only way they had of knowing about each other's presence was through their sense of touch. After they had grown to womanhood, a spirit named Tsitctinako came to them and said, "I am giving each of you a basket, a gift from your father, who is called Ute'tsiti. In them you will find small images of animals and other things that will be created in the upper world, as well as the seeds of all plants that will grow in the upper world. Take four of the seeds, including the seed of the pine tree, and plant them."

The women did as they were told, and the seeds began to grow, although very slowly. The pine seed, however, grew faster than the others, and in time it became a towering tree that reached all the way to the ceiling of the underworld. Breaking a hole through the ceiling, it continued to grow into the upper world, and for the first time the light of the upper world came streaming into the darkness below.

The hole in the ceiling was too small for the women to climb through. They took the image of a badger out of their baskets, and it came to life. The women said to the badger, "Please climb that pine tree and make that hole in the ceiling bigger, so we can climb into the upper world." When the badger had done this, the women blessed it, and the spirit Tsitctinako said,

It is time for you to go out. . . . When you come to the top, wait for the sun to rise. That direction is called *ha'nami*, east. Pray to the sun with pollen and sacred cornmeal, which you will find in your baskets. Thank it for bringing you to the light. Ask for long life and happiness, and for your success in the purpose for which you were created.

So the women took their baskets and climbed the pine tree into the upper world, and from that beginning came all of the creation we know today. (Visitors on my tours often asked how the two women were able to have children. The answer: when they reached the surface, one of them lay in the rain and conceived by the rainbow.)

There are a number of significant things about this story, the first being that the darkness of the underworld isn't a serious problem for the women. Even though they can't see, they perceive one another, as well as the contents of their baskets, through their sense of touch. Moreover, while the seeds they plant don't grow as fast as they might on the earth's surface, they do grow. Finally, the darkness isn't their ultimate home; it's a place where they wait temporarily, until everything on the surface is ready and they can climb the pine tree into the light of the upper world. The darkness of the underworld is like the darkness of a womb; it's a place of creation and preparation, where all the things we know and love on the earth's surface had their beginning.

This positive view of the underworld has been common among pueblo peoples of the Southwest for many centuries, although the relevant stories vary from culture to culture. A thousand years ago, when the people of Chaco Canyon in northwestern New Mexico were building enormous "great houses" containing hundreds of rooms—unlike any communal structures in Europe—their ceremonial kivas featured a small hole in the floor to represent sipapu and the opening through which their ancestors had emerged from the underworld to populate the earth.

I liked this view. The idea that light and darkness are equally good and desirable brings a sense of harmony and completion to the universe, something missing in Western mythology. In *Paradise Lost*, the darkness of the underworld is evil and needs to be vanquished. Not so among pueblo peoples of the Southwest. I can't say whether the visitors on my tours agreed with me, but at least the story from Acoma shows that we can interpret both the underworld and the darkness of caves in many different ways, whether positively or negatively. I hoped this idea would encourage my audiences to think about their own emotional and psychological connections to Carlsbad Cavern.

When I later began to explore some of the other caves in the Guadalupe Mountains with Lance, Pete, and other friends on the park staff, the idea that caves represent the underworld would have a profound influence on my own thoughts and actions. Every time we went into a new cave, especially if it had a long or difficult entrance drop that made me feel apprehensive about being on rope, I had to remind myself that the darkness of a cave could be anything I imagined it to be, from a place of terror to a place of creation and wonder.

CHAPTER FIVE

Into Tight Spaces

AS I PUT the finishing touches on the outline for my King's Palace tour, I kept thinking about Spider Cave. I hadn't been there and didn't even know its exact location, but it stayed on my mind nonetheless. Dennis said it was at the bottom of a deep ravine near the park's scenic drive, a winding dirt road that took visitors through the arid desert backcountry above the escarpment. Beyond that, I knew only that Pete had already scheduled me to trail Dennis's next tour there. It would be my first involvement with one of the strenuous caving tours, which I would soon be leading myself.

On the weekend before the Spider trip, I accompanied Dennis to Slaughter Canyon Cave, where he gave both the morning and afternoon tours while I served as his trail ranger. (I hadn't yet finished the outline for my own tour.) The cave was located about halfway up the steep western slope of Slaughter Canyon, at the end of a long and difficult climb from the small parking lot in the canyon's mouth. As we ascended the rocky trail, sweating in the early morning sunlight, Dennis mentioned that the canyon was named after Charles Slaughter, who had once owned a ranch near Rattlesnake Springs. He also showed me the fossils of small sea creatures that had flourished along the great Permian reef, including the beautifully coiled shells of ammonoids. At the cave entrance, we had a sweeping view up the broad desert canyon with its rocky dry wash and towering cliffs, and Dennis pointed out the barely visible entrance to Ogle Cave in the distance.

Apart from the trip to Slaughter Canyon, Spider Cave continued to occupy my thoughts during those first two weeks. I was eager to get there. If caves are places of exploration and discovery, as one of my themes stated, I needed to experience it for myself. Besides, my fear of tight spaces was the first challenge I had to overcome if I wanted to reach my goal of becoming an experienced caver. Dennis had said I'd have to squeeze through Spider's cramped, forty-foot-long entrance crawl to reach the first small chamber, and the passage was usually teeming with spiders, which gave the cave its name. Technically, they weren't spiders but daddy long-legs, those funny-looking creatures with long, spindly legs that live in basements and other dark, cool places. Spiders by any other name didn't bother me, though. I was ready for anything.

Then something unexpected happened. I started waking up in the middle of the night and couldn't go back to sleep. Every night it was the same thing: I'd wake up at two or three o'clock and just lie there, staring at the ceiling and thinking about Spider Cave. And I was apprehensive. Sometimes I'd even break out in a cold sweat. After several nights, I was so exhausted that it became a struggle to concentrate on even the simplest task. Whenever I worked at the information desk or trailed another ranger's tour, I was afraid I might fall asleep or even collapse because I felt so tired. Yet that night, I'd wake up again.

By the middle of the week, I was beginning to panic. I certainly couldn't go into Spider Cave in a state of exhaustion, and if I didn't go into Spider, what would Pete think? Was I going to fail my first caving challenge without even trying to squeeze into a tight space? In desperation I finally did the unthinkable: I looked up "Mental Health Services" in the local Yellow Pages and got the number of the mental-health clinic in Carlsbad. When the receptionist answered my call, I told her that I had a personal problem and asked if there was a counselor available who could talk to me about it over the phone. She connected me with a man who seemed very sympathetic as I explained my situation, and he responded as though he knew my problem intimately and had dealt with it many times before.

"So you're afraid of going into the cave?"

"I guess I must be," I replied. "It's what I'm always thinking about when I wake up."

"And why are you afraid?"

"I don't know. I go into the Big Room and Main Corridor almost every day, and it doesn't bother me."

"What's different about this cave?" he asked.

"Well, it's a lot smaller, and it has some really tight crawls."

"Is that what you're afraid of? Tight crawls?"

"I hadn't really thought about it. Maybe." I reflected briefly. "Yeah, I guess it must be."

"And why are you afraid of them?"

"I'm not sure. I suppose because it's so cramped, sort of like being in a coffin or something."

"Why would that bother you?"

"Well, I guess I'm just thinking that maybe the cave will collapse, and I'll be buried alive."

There it was. The same old fear that had kept me from going into Carlsbad Cavern as a teenager, only this time it was associated with tight passages rather than just being underground. *Caves affect us emotionally and psychologically.* What a revelation. I asked the counselor what I should do.

"Let me ask you this: how do you know the cave is going to collapse if you go into it?"

"Well, I don't, really. But it's possible."

"The fact that it's possible doesn't mean it's going to happen," he pointed out. "How old is the cave?"

"Oh, I don't know. Maybe millions of years. I haven't studied that yet."

"So it's been there for millions of years without collapsing, and you think it's going to collapse when you go into it."

"Well, I don't know it for sure, but like I said, it's possible."

"Anything is possible. The next time you drive your car somewhere, it's possible you'll be killed in an accident. The next time you go out your front door, it's possible a meteorite will fall out of the sky and kill you."

"Yes, I guess that's true."

"Let me also ask you this: Where is it written that the cave will collapse?

"Where is it written?" I thought about that. "Well, it isn't."

"That's right. It isn't written anywhere that the cave is going to collapse and kill you."

"No, I guess it isn't."

Everything the counselor said seemed so simple and true, and I began to feel much better. Maybe subconsciously I had just worked myself up over nothing. Maybe all I needed to do was think clearly and recognize the truth of what the counselor was saying. That night when I went to bed, I thought about our conversation and asked myself where it was written that the cave would collapse if I went into it. I slept through the entire night.

⌁ On Sunday morning when I got to work, Pete told me that Dennis had called in sick and Lance would be leading the Spider Cave tour in his place. Uh-oh. I had to feel a little awkward, because Lance knew everything about caves and caving while I knew hardly anything at all. My nervousness only increased as the time for the tour approached and I started helping Lance get things ready. Eight visitors, the maximum number, had signed up. While they were required to bring their own nonabrasive kneepads, heavy-duty gloves, and AA batteries for their head lamps, the park would provide the lamps and helmets.

As Lance and I got out the equipment and made sure everything was in working order, I noticed that he had brought his own helmet, kneepads, and gloves. That made me feel even more awkward, because I didn't own any caving equipment at all. I also noticed that he kept glancing over at me with what seemed to be a skeptical look on his face. Did he think I wouldn't do well on the tour? We didn't know one another yet, and he knew it was my first trip into Spider. Finally, he looked me squarely in the eye and asked, "Are you okay with going into the cave?"

"Me? Sure, I'm okay."

We met our group in the visitor-center lobby, where Lance greeted everyone and checked their reservation receipts. He then led us back into the equipment-storage room, and I helped him distribute the helmets. Although there were no minimal physical requirements for the tour, Lance nonetheless made sure everyone looked capable. He then showed the visitors how to put the batteries into their lamps, and when everyone was ready he went over the tour's basic requirements and rules, stressing that we'd be making a forty-foot-long entrance crawl and warning us that anyone who was claustrophobic shouldn't go into the cave. I felt confident I'd be all right now that I realized the cave wasn't going to collapse and kill me, but I still repeated to myself, "Where is it written?"

Lance emphasized safety in his orientation: the tour, he said, would be hazardous at times, and everyone should pay close attention to his instructions once we were in the cave. Because we'd be moving in single file, he added an important rule.

"Don't go off and leave the person behind you. When we're crawling through a maze of narrow passages, make sure they see where you've gone. If you think we need to slow down, pass word up to me."

He also explained that as a safety precaution we should maintain "three points of contact" whenever we were crawling through difficult or hazardous areas. In other words, we should always be touching the cave with at least three parts of our bodies, such as one hand, one elbow, and one foot; or one knee, one hip, and one hand. However, we shouldn't touch any more of the cave than was absolutely necessary, because one of our goals was to have as little impact on the resource as possible.

With all of that in mind, we started out. I had been on the scenic drive only once before, so the desert scenery held my attention during our brief drive to the small dirt pullover where we parked our vehicles. Lance then led us away from the road and down a rocky trail into a nearby canyon, where the desert vegetation grew so thickly that it was difficult to move without being scratched or punctured by sharp leaves and thorns. The clawlike spines along the edges of sotol leaves were especially treacherous, grabbing our pants legs and not letting go.

At the bottom of the canyon was a typical desert wash with plenty of sand, gravel, and small boulders. On the opposite side and right at the bottom of the slope stood a pile of rocks that for some reason didn't look natural. As we got closer, I realized the rocks had been mortared together to form a small, moundlike structure with an opening at the top, perhaps two feet square, covered by a barred metal gate. Spider Cave. Whatever I had expected, it wasn't that.

Lance climbed onto the rocks and dialed in the lock combination, then lifted the gate and swung it out of the way. It seemed that he had just opened a pathway into the underworld. As we put on our helmets and rechecked our lamps, Lance reached into the entrance and pulled out a long wooden pole with a metal hook on one end. He then started poking it around the rocks just inside the opening, slowly working his way downward. I was about to ask what he was doing when he announced in a loud voice that he was making sure there were no rattlesnakes around before we started down the ladder. *Rattlesnakes?* Was he kidding?

Satisfied with his inspection, Lance sat down beside the opening, put on his helmet, and asked if anyone was feeling claustrophobic. When no one responded, he swung his legs into the opening, mounted the ladder, and slowly descended into the entrance. At his shout of "Off ladder!" the first visitor followed him down. One by one, the others followed until I was alone, gazing into the opening to watch the last person crawl into a low passage that disappeared into the hillside. Taking a deep breath, I asked myself, "Where is it written?" and climbed down the ladder, closing the gate behind me and locking it securely.

When I turned around and crouched onto my hands and knees, I was gazing into a rocky opening whose walls and ceiling were moving up and down, back and forth, up and down. Then it dawned on me: spiders. Or rather: daddy longlegs. There were many hundreds of them swarming over the passage and moving themselves rhythmically up and down, as though they were doing pushups. I would be told later that their odd behavior was a kind of territorial display, but on seeing them I could only feel a little disoriented: up and down, back and forth, up and down.

Turning on my head lamp, I crawled into the opening. Within a few feet, it became so low that I had to stretch out on my stomach and start pulling myself along on my elbows while pushing with the toes of my boots. I immediately thought of the military training I had gone through as a young man, when I had crawled under barbed wire in that very position with an M-16 rifle cradled in my arms. That had been many years earlier, and this wasn't the military, yet the situation felt so familiar that I knew I would be all right. Tight squeezes would no longer be a problem for me.

The passage grew ever smaller as I worked my way forward, until I started to worry that I might inadvertently crush a few daddy longlegs against the ceiling. I even thought I felt one or two drop onto the back of my neck, but that didn't bother me; I was too preoccupied with the thick carpet of painfully sharp rocks covering the floor. When I had gone far enough to think I might be getting near the first chamber, I heard Lance's muffled voice calling out of the darkness just ahead: "Doug, are you coming?"

"Yes, I'm almost there."

The passage finally ended at an opening so impossibly small that I realized I couldn't squeeze through it. Then I heard muffled voices from the other side. Hmm. Positioning the top of my helmet against the opening, I tried to force my head through, but it wouldn't go. The only way I could continue was to turn my head sideways, dig the toes of my boots into the rocky floor, and push with my feet. As I gradually began to slide forward, I could feel the top of the opening pressed tightly against my back and the sharp rocks scraping painfully against my chest. Then my head popped into the first chamber. *Whew!*

Lance was sitting a few feet away with an expectant look on his face, while the visitors hunkered tightly around him, the tops of their helmets only a few inches from the low ceiling. "Where have you been? We thought you'd gotten lost."

"No, I'm here."

What a relief to be able to raise my head. I found a place to sit near the opening, where I tried to make myself comfortable, and then I listened attentively as Lance continued to set the record straight about what it means to be a caver.

"I want you to remember that cavers aren't 'spelunkers,'" he said. "That word was invented by people who don't know the first thing about caving. Call yourself a 'caver.' That's the right word. There's even a saying that goes, 'Cavers rescue spelunkers.'"

He emphasized safety again.

"Any time you go into a cave, remember what we call 'the rule of three.' First, be sure to tell at least three people where you're going and when you'll get back. Second, make sure you go into the cave with at least two other people, for a total of three, in case someone gets hurt. A total of four people is even better. Third, make sure each of you carries at least three independent light sources. And that doesn't mean one helmet lamp with two extra sets of batteries. It means three independent sources, like a helmet lamp and two mini-flashlights, with extra batteries and bulbs for all three."

With those preliminaries out of the way, Lance began to tell us the story of Spider Cave. He said it was a "maze cave" because its narrow passages branched in every direction, doubled back on themselves, twisted and turned, went up and down. A person could easily become lost. To prove his point, Lance told us about a small group of local explorers who were among the first to enter Spider Cave, back in the early 1930s. One of them was Robert Nymeyer, a professional photographer who owned a camera store in the town of Carlsbad. He and his friends had the unusual hobby of exploring local caves in their spare time, and their exploits in the caves of the Guadalupe Mountains had become well-known in the annals of caving. Nymeyer documented their adventures in a book called *Carlsbad, Caves and a Camera*, which included many of the stunning black-and-white photographs he had taken underground. I first learned about the Guadalupe caves by reading Nymeyer's book, and I already knew the names of many, including Black Cave, Hidden Cave, Cottonwood Cave, Hell Below, and Cave of the Madonna.

Nymeyer's journey into Spider Cave began one afternoon in 1933, when he was sitting with Jim White on a bench outside the Natural Entrance to Carlsbad Cavern. He told Jim that he was interested in finding a local cave to explore, and Jim suggested one that wasn't very far away and that had spiders in its entrance. Not long afterward, Nymeyer and several of his friends drove out to Spider Cave on the old dirt road through Walnut Canyon. It was their first caving trip together, and it was the day Nymeyer got bitten by what he later called "the cave bug"—a lifelong desire to go exploring underground. The trip was a big hit with everyone.

Nine months later, Nymeyer went back to Spider Cave with two of his friends and two visitors from Canada. One of the friends, Tommy Futch, had to return to Carlsbad early, so he left the others in the cave at about two o'clock in the afternoon. That night, when Nymeyer and the others failed to return, Tommy knew something must have gone wrong, so he and another friend, Bill Liddell, drove all the way back to Spider Cave to search for the missing men. They found them stranded far from the entrance in a small chamber with a beautifully clear pool of water, which they had named Cactus Spring (sharp aragonite crystals surrounded it like cactus needles). Nymeyer and the others were elated to see Tommy and Bill, because they had spent the entire afternoon and evening trying to find their way back to the entrance, without success. But would they be able to relocate the entrance now that Tommy and Bill had joined them? Fortunately, they were.

When Lance finished his story, the visitors seemed eager to see more of the cave. After he cautioned us to stay inside the brightly colored plastic tape that marked the limits of the trail, they followed him as he started down an adjacent passage, crouching low beneath the irregular ceiling. I dutifully took my place at the back of the group, where I found it was sometimes hard to keep up. After several tight squeezes through a series of small openings, we entered a second, much larger chamber. There we sat for a few moments as Lance told us that Nymeyer had found several sticks of sodden and corroded dynamite in a nearby passage, apparently left behind by some long-forgotten earlier explorer. Because dynamite in that condition is highly unstable, Nymeyer gave it a wide berth. Some time later, the dynamite mysteriously disappeared.

We continued into yet another low passage on our hands and knees and found ourselves in a labyrinth of small tunnels and tight squeezes. We turned so frequently and in so many different directions that I became disoriented and couldn't tell which way was north. That concerned me, because I would have to keep my bearings to lead the tour myself. Yet the farther we crawled, the more confused I became. To my surprise, I would have to make five trips into Spider Cave to learn the tour route, including two with a map of its passages, even though I needed only three trips to qualify as a tour leader.

In one relatively spacious chamber, we found a bulky stalactite about five feet long and three feet wide that was made of pure-white calcite—the name given to limestone after it's been dissolved and redeposited by water. Because of the stalactite's irregularly flowing shape and a large hole through its center, it looked like a one-eyed ghost hanging from the ceiling. As we continued toward the back of the cave, we also came upon the Medusa Room, where the trail ran along one side of a broad and apparently very deep fissure. The wall on the opposite side was covered with hundreds of helictites, the small, delicate formations that twist and turn as they grow, like pigs' tails or baby snakes.

After a long and confusing crawl, we finally arrived at Cactus Spring, where Nymeyer and his friends had been stranded. Lance said we had reached our turnaround point and that we were going to rest for a short while and have a "blackout" by turning off our head lamps. (This was a standard practice for all guided tours, including the King's Palace.) He began by reminding us that light is essential whenever we go into a cave, because we're completely helpless without it. To illustrate, he told another story about Robert Nymeyer, who one day found himself at the bottom of the Main Corridor in Carlsbad Cavern with Ray V. Davis, another professional photographer, whose black-and-white photographs of the cavern have become classics. They had just taken a photo in the King's Palace and were starting up the trail toward the Natural Entrance when the electric lighting system failed. Davis had an appointment to take wedding photographs in Carlsbad that afternoon, so he couldn't afford being stranded in the dark. What to do?

Davis told Nymeyer to feel around in his pack for a box of matches, which he divided equally between them. He then struck a match and told Nymeyer to hurry up the trail until the match burned out. When it did, he told Nymeyer to strike one of his matches so that he—Davis—could hurry up the trail to join him, or possibly go farther. By alternately striking their matches in this way, they slowly made their way back to the surface.

Lance's point was clear: without a reliable source of light, we can't even enter a cave, much less find our way around in it; and if we happen to lose our light sources, we're trapped there. With this thought in mind, Lance instructed us to turn off our head lamps. The resulting darkness was so absolute that it immediately convinced everyone of our vulnerability. Without a doubt, we could never return to the surface without our head lamps, and I resolved never to enter a cave without taking along three independent sources of light and plenty of extra batteries.

After several minutes of darkness, Lance turned his head lamp back on, and the rest of us followed suit. Then it was back to the surface. Lance asked if anyone else wanted to take the lead for our return along the same route. One of the visitors volunteered. I had to admire her eagerness, because I was sure I couldn't find my way back. Until I had more experience, the cave was just too confusing. Yet Spider Cave had captivated me, and once I memorized the route, I never tired of leading tours there.

Eleven years after leaving Carlsbad Caverns, I would learn that Spider Cave is even more complex than I had thought. Park-sponsored survey teams had recently pushed through a series of tight openings to explore 2,164 feet of previously unknown passages, increasing the cave's known length to 4.3 miles. One passage was forty feet wide, fifteen feet high, and over two hundred feet long—the largest known chamber in the cave.

As Lance and I put the helmets away back at the visitor center, he asked for my opinion of the cave, and I replied truthfully that I thought it was outstanding. I didn't mention my initial apprehension, of course, although I suspected he might have guessed the truth even before we reached the cave entrance. All things considered, I was very happy with what I had accomplished. I had taken my first step toward becoming an experienced caver.

The day after our trip into Spider Cave, I phoned the mental-health clinic in Carlsbad and asked to speak to the counselor who had helped me. He recognized my voice right away and said, "I've been thinking about you and wondering what happened. How'd it go over the weekend?"

It was a good question, with a clear answer: I had discovered that I could manage my fear. Having created it by greatly exaggerating the danger of squeezing into tight spaces, I had controlled it by recognizing that it wasn't based on reality. I had learned to do something I was afraid to do.

"Well, it went just great," I replied, "and I want to say thanks a lot."

CHAPTER SIX

Jim and the Giant

IF EVER THERE was a man without fear, it was Jim White, the cowboy and early explorer whose name is almost synonymous with Carlsbad Cavern. I talked about his exploits on my King's Palace tour, when I introduced visitors to the idea that caves are places of exploration and discovery. The tours began in a roped-off area next to the underground lunchroom, with a maximum number of seventy-five visitors for each tour. During the busy summer months, most tours were sold out.

Following my introduction, I would lead each group down the Big Room Trail to the intersection of the Natural Entrance Trail, where we made a right turn and continued through an area of jumbled boulders known as the Boneyard. After passing beneath the manta ray formation that Monty liked to point out to visitors, we arrived at the bottom of Iceberg Rock, an immense block of limestone many stories high that had fallen from the ceiling of the lower Balloon Ballroom. There we turned onto a side trail and passed through the barred metal gate that closed the four scenic chambers to the general public. At the bottom of several steep switchbacks, we came to a small alcove just outside the King's Palace.

This was one of my favorite spots in the cave, because it contained a dazzling array of stalactites, columns, soda straws, and helictites that always captured the visitors' imaginations, as well as my own. Stopping at the bottom of the trail, I would ask everyone to stand along the last switchback, where they had a sweeping view of the alcove. It was a good place to talk about the cave's exploration because of two black marks on the wall. When I asked each group to look around and pick out the alcove's most interesting features, someone invariably spotted the black marks. They had been made by some of the cave's early explorers, who held the flames of their lanterns against the limestone and then scratched the dates 1906 and 1911 into the resulting soot. Additionally, there were three large soot marks on the wall that visitors often didn't see and that I had to point out. They formed the letters "ATL," which were the initials of a man named Abijah Long.

Long was a merchant from the town of Carlsbad who started a guano-mining operation in 1903 about a quarter mile east of the Natural Entrance to Carlsbad Cavern, directly above the Bat Cave. Because guano makes good fertilizer, there was a market for it in the citrus groves of Southern California during the first decades of the twentieth century. After blasting a vertical shaft through the cave ceiling, Long capped it with a wooden hoist and used a large metal bucket powered by a gasoline engine to haul out the bat droppings. When this proved successful, he blasted a second shaft. (The shafts allowed warm air to escape from the Bat Cave ceiling and were detrimental to the bats, so they were filled in after the cave became a national park.) The miners rode the bucket down into the cave every morning, then spent the day loading it with guano and repeatedly hoisting it to the surface.

By the light of their primitive miners' lamps, Long and his men sometimes ventured down the Main Corridor to the scenic chambers, so it wasn't surprising to find his initials in the alcove. A few historic photographs even show some of the miners sitting around the Devil's Spring or perching on top of large stalagmites even deeper in the cave. When Long hired Jim White to work as his mine foreman, Jim often joined the miners' expeditions. However, he had probably entered the cave for the first time at least five years before the guano mining began, so he was already an experienced cave explorer by the time he started working for Long.

The first time Jim White saw the entrance to Carlsbad Cavern, he was an impulsive sixteen-year-old cowboy working for one of the local ranches. He had seen what he called the "great hole" many times, but he didn't pay much attention to it until late one afternoon when he was returning to camp after a hard day of building fences. He happened to notice something in the distance that he had never seen before. It wasn't smoke and it wasn't a whirlwind—or a "whirling dervish," as Jim would have called it—but it nonetheless kept rising into the sky, twisting and turning in a curious way. When he went over to investigate, he found something that would not only challenge his imagination but also change his life. What appeared to be *millions of bats* were swarming out of the huge hole. The sight stirred him so deeply that he decided to climb down into the hole and find out what was there.

But there was a problem. When he descended to the bottom of the entrance slope, he found a sheer drop-off blocking his way into the twilight zone. He decided to come back.

A couple of days later . . . I gathered up a kerosene lantern, several coils of rope, some wire and a hand axe. I got to the cave about mid-afternoon. . . . I got busy with the hand axe, cutting sticks of wood from the shrub growth nearby. When I had a sizable pile, I set about building a ladder by utilizing the rope and wire, with the sticks for steps—like a rope ladder. This I then lowered into the entrance.

Jim made his first trip into the cave alone and without telling anyone where he was going, a practice he would continue throughout his life. Although his rope ladder has long since disappeared, another ladder that he constructed for the eight-story descent into Lower Cave still hangs beside the Big Room Trail near the Jumping-Off Place, a dilapidated reminder of his early exploits.

Visitors frequently asked if Jim White was the first person to enter Carlsbad Cavern, but we'll probably never know who the first explorer was. The early hunter-gatherers may have entered the cave, and there are a number of conflicting stories from other cowboys, miners, and local settlers who claim to have been the first. Nonetheless, the story of exploration has to begin with Jim, simply because he did more than all the others combined. It's even probable that he was the first person to explore most of the cave's known passages.

Visitors also wanted to know how Jim was able to find his way out of such a big cave, so on my tours I challenged each group to name some of the techniques he might have used. Invariably, they came up with three. The first was to carry a ball of string or fishing line and trail it behind him when he went into an unfamiliar area. When he wanted to leave, all he had to do was follow the string out, rolling it up as he went (Robert Nymeyer and his friends also did this). The second technique was to leave some kind of markers along the way, like the soot marks on the wall of the alcove. Jim said that whenever he found a broken formation, he would point it in the direction he should follow back to the surface. The third technique was simply to memorize the cave as he went along, and Jim obviously had a very good memory.

At first Jim thought the cave ended in the four scenic chambers at the bottom of the Main Corridor. Then one day as he was starting back to the surface from the King's Palace, he stumbled onto a passage that led into the darkness on the opposite side of Iceberg Rock. The passage took him through the Boneyard to the north end of the Big Room near today's underground lunchroom, and it began a whole new chapter in Jim's explorations. (A fifteen-year-old Mexican boy whose name has been lost to history probably accompanied Jim on this trip. Jim called him only "Muchacho the Kid.")

The only light sources Jim used were kerosene lanterns. Sometimes he carried a homemade miners' lamp like the ones used in the guano mine, which looked like a coffeepot with a rope or wick sticking out of the spout. But he was using an ordinary lantern when he experienced an accident that every cave explorer particularly dreads. He had become so preoccupied with what he was seeing and doing that he failed to notice when the kerosene in his lantern was getting low. When the flame suddenly flickered out, he was left standing alone in total darkness, far from the cave's entrance.

Fortunately, I had brought with me a small canteen of oil for just such an emergency. But the blackness and the loneliness had got to working under my skin, and when I tried to refill the lantern my fingers shook so much that I fumbled the filler cap and spilled more oil in my lap than I poured into the thing. And I dropped the filler cap when I tried to screw it back on.

Jim survived and went on to create the cave's first trail system—a primitive dirt track with stairs made from sacks of guano, which descended the
Main Corridor—and by the early 1920s he had become a tireless promoter
of the "Bat Cave," as most people called Carlsbad Cavern in those days.
He even led the first guided tours, taking visitors down in the old guano
bucket because there was no trail into the Natural Entrance. In 1928 he
was the logical choice to become the first chief ranger of the newly created Carlsbad Cave National Monument, with a salary of $155 per month.

Jim's appearance throughout his adult life seemed to reflect his love
of caves and his penchant for solitary exploration. His beloved cowboy
hat with its high crown and broad, rolled-up brim—I've never seen a pic-
ture of him without it—along with his work pants and weathered cowboy
boots made him look as worn and craggy as the roughest limestone along
the Guadalupe Escarpment. According to Robert Nymeyer, his "deeply
lined wind-bronzed face and watery, fading grey eyes" were so reminis-
cent of the desert that they seemed to blend into the landscape. What a
character he must have been.

Having told his story many times on my King's Palace tours, there was
one thing I couldn't understand, and probably never will understand,
about Jim White. *What made him do it?* It's true that I wanted to become
a caver with Lance, Pete, and my other new friends. I wanted to go into
as many caves as I could with them, learn how to use the same climbing
equipment, and make the same long rappels on rope. Yet I never had the
desire to go into a big cave all by myself, without telling anyone where I
was going, and with just a burning rope sticking out of a coffeepot to light
my way. *Never.* So why did Jim White do it?

⌒ Because my trip into Spider Cave had quelled my fear of tight spaces,
I didn't have any problem serving as trail ranger for the second strenuous caving tour, which went to the Hall of the White Giant in Carlsbad
Cavern. I now felt completely at home underground, even when I had to
spend relatively long periods in cold, damp passages only a foot high and
not much wider than my shoulders. It was amazing how quickly I had
adapted to tight spaces, and hard to believe I had been so unaware of my
own capabilities.

The White Giant was a massive stalagmite tucked away in one of the most inaccessible areas of the cave, and getting there involved crawls that were longer, tighter, and more difficult than anything Spider Cave had to offer. Yet the route to the White Giant was relatively simple, so I was able to memorize it in just three trips as trail ranger. I had already decided that my tour outline would focus on the idea that caves are places of exploration and discovery, and I finally narrowed it down to a discussion of the problems associated with navigating through a cave.

At the beginning of my tours, I would lead each group down the Natural Entrance Trail to a depth of about forty stories. There we stopped, put on our helmets and gloves, pulled up our knee pads, and crawled into a maze of small openings and boulders that didn't look the least bit inviting and that most visitors probably didn't even notice. When my groups realized where we were going, someone usually said in a low voice, "Oh my God. Are we going in there?"

Jim White might not have wanted to go in there either. When he told Robert Nymeyer about Spider Cave in 1933, he said that he hadn't explored very much of it himself because it was "too small to appeal to me." Interesting. Our initial crawl on the White Giant tour took us through a "corkscrew" turn of almost 360 degrees, in which we were climbing and simultaneously passing over the route we had just covered. A few yards beyond the corkscrew was a small chamber that had been created in part by fallen boulders. That's where I stopped to make sure everyone had found their way through the confusing crawl. When the trail ranger joined us, I started my tour narrative by mentioning Jim White and his peculiar habit of constantly turning around and looking behind him whenever he went into an area of the cave he hadn't visited before.

"Why would he have done that?"

Someone usually guessed correctly that he wanted to see what the cave would look like when he reversed direction and started back out. Many people don't realize that a cave changes dramatically when viewed in opposite directions; if you don't turn around from time to time to see what it looks like behind you, you're increasing your risk of becoming disoriented when you try to leave. That's what happened to Robert Nymeyer and his friends in Spider Cave. (Regrettably, this technique didn't work for me. I envied the way Lance was able to find his way easily through any cave.) Later in the tour, we would talk further about the problems of navigating underground.

Crawling out of the small chamber, we made a right turn into a high-ceilinged, relatively tight passage—often only two or three feet wide—that followed a long, straight crack or "joint" in the rock. The first explorers who entered this area back in 1966—three park rangers named Ben Billings, Gary Matlock, and Lloyd Jacklin—had followed this joint without knowing where it led and without realizing they were about to make the most significant discovery in Carlsbad Cavern since Jim White's earliest explorations. This was partly because the maze of passages they were entering, today called the New Section, happened to contain the Guadalupe Room, the cave's second-largest chamber after the Big Room. This was almost forty years after Carlsbad Cavern became a national park and twenty years after Jim White's death.

Soon we arrived at the bottom of a ten-foot-high, stainless-steel ladder, which the park's cave-resources staff had installed several years earlier. There I instructed everyone to shout "On ladder!" and "Off ladder!" as we made our ascent. At the top of the ladder, we had to crawl on our hands and knees and then drag ourselves along on our elbows until we finally reached Matlock's Pinch—named after first explorer Gary Matlock—the tour's most challenging obstacle. It's a slightly larger opening today than it was when Matlock and his companions squeezed through, because years of traffic have worn away some of the flowstone—calcite deposited by a thin film of flowing water—to expose the silt underneath. In 1966, however, it was so tight that one of the men, Ben Billings, famously snagged his pants on cave popcorn as he wormed through and skinned completely out of them.

Beyond Matlock's Pinch, we had to climb several very slippery flowstone waterfalls. We then emerged from the tight joint into a relatively large chamber known as Sand Passage, which took its name from the huge amounts of silt covering its floor. There we stopped to rest and discuss why it's usually more difficult to navigate in a cave than on the earth's surface. Most groups immediately recognized that tight passages have a tendency to change direction frequently while also going up or down—witness the corkscrew—making it easy to become disoriented. But they often forgot that we can't use the sun's position to help us maintain our bearings and that a cave lacks both a horizon line and landmarks visible over long distances—two things that make navigating on the surface relatively easy.

To prove how disorienting caves can be, I would ask everyone to point toward north, and they invariably pointed in different directions. I then advised them to forget about directions and just keep turning around to study the cave behind them, because most people find that a more reliable way of navigating. When we reached the Hall of the White Giant, I would give one of them the chance to lead us back along the same route.

Following our rest, we continued along the trail through Sand Passage, where the relatively high ceiling allowed us to walk upright. Because a thin crust of cap rock had formed over the silt floor, we made a special effort to stay within the plastic tape marking the trail, so we wouldn't break through the crust and leave footprints. The first explorers didn't have a trail, of course, so they had walked in single file and stepped in one another's footprints to cause as little damage as possible. We could even see a few of their footprints near the trail, more than thirty years after they had been there. This was a good object lesson that any damage we might cause would be around for a long time.

Beyond Sand Passage, we made our way carefully along the edges of several deep pits until we arrived at a large joint passage, perhaps forty feet wide and equally as high, which crossed our route at a ninety-degree angle to create a "T" intersection. A forest of active soda straws hung from its ceiling, the water droplets at their tips sparkling in the glare of our head lamps like fireflies that had become lost underground.

Just within the joint passage, a massive hill of silt and cap rock rose toward the ceiling, and at its apex stood the majestic White Giant formation, gleaming like a bright and very wet apparition. I never tired of seeing the visitors' expressions of amazement when they realized we had finally reached our destination. The White Giant is the second-largest active formation in the cave after Crystal Spring Dome in the Big Room. I always thought the White Giant was more impressive, though, simply because it was less accessible and looked much whiter than any other formation in the cave, due to the purity of its calcite.

After enjoying the White Giant and sharing a long and restful blackout, we retraced our route back to the Natural Entrance Trail, led by a visitor volunteer. If the group had been relatively slow for some reason and the tour had taken longer than the usual three hours, we might find the asphalt trail closed for the day and the electric lights turned off. That was a special treat because it meant we could walk down to the elevators in the dark, by the light of our head lamps.

In time I came to think of the strenuous caving tours as one of the best parts of my job. It was fun to slither along cramped passages and squeeze through tight pinches, just like the early explorers. I began to enjoy the solid feel of the limestone and the way it scraped against my kneepads and helmet, and even my unprotected elbows. The dirtier I got, the more fun I seemed to be having. I also began to understand why Jim White, Robert Nymeyer, and Lance felt so passionately about caves and why they chose to pursue the elusive mysteries hidden beneath the earth's surface. Nymeyer's cave bug had bitten me as well, and I had learned for myself that caves are places of exploration and discovery.

CHAPTER SEVEN

On Rope!

BECAUSE WE'RE MORTALS, we can't go in and out of caves by riding on a firestorm, like Satan and his angels, or climbing up or down a pine tree, like the daughters of Ute'tsiti. We have to rely on other means. This isn't a problem when we want to explore horizontal caves, which have mostly level passages; all we have to do is walk or crawl wherever we want to go. But vertical caves, with their deep pits and dangerous drop-offs, confront us with a serious problem: how are we going to explore them safely? Jim White's solution was to make primitive ladders out of sticks, rope, and wire, but they weren't at all safe: witness the one hanging near the Jumping-Off Place.

The guano miners solved the vertical problem by riding up and down in the metal bucket, but they also constructed a series of wooden ladders down to the floor of the Bat Cave through a small opening in the ground—a second natural entrance to the cave—not far from the mine site. Miners at some of the other guano caves in the Guadalupe Mountains did the same thing, often with amazing results: the ladders at Ogle Cave descended for eighteen stories. This wasn't a safe solution, however: one of the miners fell to his death after being struck by a falling rock. The victim, William Sorrells, was buried on his twenty-fourth birthday.

Robert Nymeyer and his friends were probably the first explorers to make the seven-story entrance drop into a cave in the higher elevations of the Guadalupe Mountains known rather ominously as Hell Below. (Dave Wilson inadvertently came up with that name when he peered over the edge of the drop and exclaimed, "Whoa, boys! This is as far as we go! There's hell below!") For their second visit to the cave, Nymeyer and his friends made a climbing rope from "some 150 feet of manila stake line," which they doubled and then knotted at three-foot intervals. After anchoring it around a thick column just inside the cave entrance, they tossed it over the edge of the drop, only to find it wasn't long enough. So they pulled it up, tied a lariat to the end, and tossed it back in again.

Nymeyer was the first to go down, but the knots got in his way and made his descent both awkward and tiresome. At the bottom of the manila stake line, he couldn't get a secure handhold on the lariat and fell about ten feet, "like a plunging meteor," to the cave floor, where he collided with the electric lantern he and his friends had previously lowered. When he recovered from the impact, he found himself lying on the wet floor in absolute darkness. Turning on his flashlight and peering upward, he was horrified to see that the rope "seemed to dwindle to a mere string before disappearing into the hole far above in the darkness."

After Dave Wilson and Ted Fullerton joined him at the bottom, all three men realized their makeshift climbing rope was useless. They were already exhausted, and the knots undoubtedly would be an even greater hindrance if they tried to climb out. Because three other friends remained overhead, Nymeyer shouted up and told them to go for help. Several hours later, they returned with Seth McCollum's father and three thirty-foot lariats tied together.

The men on top dropped one end of the lariats to those stranded below. One at a time, the stranded men tied it around their chests just under their arms, and as each took his turn struggling doggedly up the knotted rope, the men above pulled up the slack in the lariats to keep him from falling. During Nymeyer's ascent, the knotted rope and lariats became fouled when he began spinning around in midair, but with perseverance he eventually got them untangled. By the end of the day, after long and torturous hand-over-hand ascents, Nymeyer and his two friends finally reached safety.

⌒ Nymeyer's experience in Hell Below was a grim reminder that bad things can happen in caves and that we might be justified in thinking them sinister places. This is the view of Western mythology, of course, as shown by the myth of Satan's Fall. To illustrate how deeply this idea is engrained in our collective psyche, I asked the visitors on my King's Palace tours to name other traditional stories that portray caves in a negative way, and they always responded with a variety of myths and folktales.

Most said that all sorts of evil creatures are supposed to live in caves, from goblins and ogres to the dragon that battled St. George in medieval folklore, whose fiery breath invokes the fires of hell. They also mentioned Homer's epic poem *The Odyssey*, in which Odysseus, wandering across the ancient Mediterranean world after the Trojan War, encounters the one-eyed Cyclops Polyphemus living in a cave on the island of Cyclopes. Some audiences recalled Hades, the ancient Greek underworld, as a darkened realm below the earth's surface where the dead wander as mere shades of their former selves. Occasionally, someone even cited *Inferno*, the opening section of Dante Alighieri's epic fourteenth-century poem *The Divine Comedy*, which describes the hell of Christian mythology with its nine circles of suffering, hidden deep in the earth.

Because I had overcome my fear of caves and tight spaces, these myths would no longer shape my feelings about venturing underground. However, I had been into just three horizontal caves—Carlsbad Cavern, Slaughter Canyon Cave, and Spider Cave—and they hadn't tested my fear of heights. I didn't really know how I would react to a deep vertical cave like Hell Below. Would the myth of Satan's Fall now haunt me because it portrays the act of falling? I had exaggerated the dangers involved in my previous fears, but the fact that Robert Nymeyer had fallen while descending into Hell Below wasn't an exaggeration. It was real.

In Gustave Doré's 1866 engraving, Satan tumbles backward into the dark abyss as the archangel Michael, poised above him in a blaze of light, thrusts his sword downward in condemnation. It looked to me as though Satan had just lost his grip on a knotted manila stake line. Yet he was no Robert Nymeyer. According to *Paradise Lost*, legions of Satan's cohorts fell with him, and at the end of nine days he recovered to begin plotting perpetual war against heaven. If Nymeyer had fallen seven stories into Hell Below, he would have been completely alone, and his broken body would have lain on cold, wet limestone until his friends could find a way to haul it out of the cave.

Despite such troublesome thoughts, I had cause for hope. My rope training was about to reveal that caving technology has come a long way since Nymeyer's time and that today's ropes and climbing devices, when used properly, are not only efficient and easy to use but also completely safe.

⌒ I had my introduction to rope climbing in the underground lunchroom, where the interpretive division had set up a climbing-demonstration area at the far end of a broad expanse of picnic tables. Behind it loomed the dark reaches of Left Hand Tunnel, a fairly large passage that ran due east for almost half a mile before descending to the Lake of the Clouds, the deepest known point in Carlsbad Cavern. We conducted guided lantern tours along a dirt path through Left Hand Tunnel but didn't take visitors to the Lake of the Clouds because it would involve using ropes and so was off-limits.

Along with Lance and Pete, a number of other interpretive staff members already knew how to climb rope, including my desk partner Dennis, another permanent interpreter named Barb, and seasonal interpreters Kenny and Becky. Because Lance, Barb, and Kenny had been certified to give climbing demonstrations, Pete suggested I ask each of them if I could help out by tending rope in exchange for some instruction on the basics of climbing. They agreed, and I became something of an apprentice in the underground lunchroom, managing the anchor and later climbing for short distances while Lance, Barb, or Kenny explained to the audience what I was doing. At first I was thoroughly confused by the unfamiliar climbing terms and intimidated by the equipment, which seemed perplexing despite its simplicity. And when I tried to climb, my movements felt awkward and unnatural.

Lance was a true perfectionist and a demanding instructor. The first time I assisted him, he patiently explained the difference between a "croll" and a "safety"—I'll describe both shortly—and showed me how to use each one. For some reason, I found it hard to remember the word "croll," so I kept repeating it to myself out loud—"croll, croll, croll"—hoping it would somehow stick in my mind. A short time later, when I made a mistake on rope, Lance came over and started repeating in a loud voice, "croll,

croll, croll," something he would continue to do for months. Every time I forgot a caving term or lost my concentration on rope, I'd hear "croll, croll, croll." It didn't bother me, though, because I knew he harassed only his friends—he once told me, "Hey, if I didn't like you, I wouldn't do it"—and it inspired me to try harder. I also managed to redeem myself to some extent that first day by climbing about twenty feet to the cave ceiling, after which Lance loosened the rope at its anchor and lowered me to the floor.

The first time I worked with Barb, she showed me how to do a maneuver called a "changeover," which allows a climber to reverse direction while in mid-climb or mid-descent. In other words, he or she stops going up the rope, changes over to a different type of equipment, then goes down the rope, or vice versa. The steps were relatively simple, but I wasn't sure I could remember the correct sequence once I got started. Barb told me to try it anyway while she and the visitors watched, so I clipped onto the rope, climbed a short distance, and started doing just that. Within minutes I was dangling helplessly with my feet above the level of my head—I still don't know how I did it—struggling to right myself as I heard Barb tell the visitors, "He's just learning."

About a week later, while assisting Kenny with one of his demonstrations, I completed a changeover on my first attempt and even did a repeat performance, to the visitors' applause. I felt quite satisfied, and Kenny was so pleased by my accomplishment that he offered to give me some additional training after-hours. Kenny was always good about things like that. He even took me into Spider Cave with two other staff members after-hours to help me learn the tour route.

Despite the challenges involved, I worked hard to become proficient on rope, and I made steady progress. Within a week or two, I understood how the various pieces of equipment functioned and how they would help me accomplish things that Nymeyer and his friends had never dreamed of doing. From the very beginning, I could see that the ropes and climbing devices I was using, for all their simplicity, were impressive technological achievements.

⌁ Vertical caving became feasible with the development of nylon ropes in the mid-1940s, about ten years after Robert Nymeyer and his friends courted disaster in Hell Below. Two characteristics made nylon ropes ideal for caving. First, they can support extremely heavy weights: each of the ropes we used could hold about six thousand pounds. Second, they can stretch, which is important if a climber happens to fall; the stretch will absorb much of the shock and make it less likely that he or she will be seriously injured. High-stretch nylon ropes are called "dynamic," while low-stretch ropes are "static."

Stretching can sometimes be a drawback, as I discovered during my first long climb—about eighteen stories—out of a vertical cave. When I clipped onto the rope and placed my weight on it, it stretched halfway to the cave floor, and I began flailing awkwardly back and forth on my knees, like a pendulum. Whenever I went on rope after that, I always pulled the rope repeatedly through my ascending device until all the slack was taken up and it was completely tight. Yet I would still bounce to some extent whenever I began a long climb. When I eventually made a climb of about forty-four stories, I kept bouncing three or four feet during the first half of the ascent, and when Lance made his 109-story climb out of Sotano de las Golondrinas in Mexico, he bounced about twenty feet.

Lance introduced me to the term "kern-mantle," which refers to the fact that a nylon rope consists of a "kern," or core, and a "mantle," a sheath of woven cords surrounding the core. Not long after I started learning how to climb, I found a short length of discarded rope and cut away part of its sheath to expose the core inside. I was amazed to find that it consisted of many thousands of microscopically thin fibers, each one no thicker than a single strand in a spider's web. The mantle was made up of sixteen nylon cords, each about an eighth of an inch thick, woven around the core in the same pattern children create when they wind colorful ribbons around a Maypole. This is significant because the sharp metal teeth on a climber's ascending devices are forced between the interwoven cords as he or she ascends.

For our demonstrations in the underground lunchroom, most of us used a type of personal climbing system called the "frog"—so named because it requires a climber to alternately pull his or her legs up and then extend them, the way a frog kicks its way along through water. The frog system consists of two harnesses: a "seat harness" around the climber's waist and thighs and a second around his or her chest. Lance always stressed that both harnesses should be unbearably tight when I put them on, especially after I hunched over and clipped them together with a cara-biner, a type of metal connector with a spring-loaded gate. The tightness would help me maintain the correct posture when I was on rope. I under-stood his reasoning, and the tightness did feel relatively comfortable once I started climbing, but until I rested my weight on the rope I had to move around awkwardly in a stooped-over position. I felt like a crab going out for a walk.

The seat harness is held together in front by a metal connector called a D-ring. I once made a potentially life-threatening mistake with the one on my harness. I was doing some practice climbing after-hours with Lance and several other staff members in the visitor center lobby when Lance came over and pointed at my D-ring. "Bad!" he said, loudly enough for everyone to hear. "Bad! Bad! That's bad!" I had no idea what he was talking about, but when I looked down at my D-ring, I realized I hadn't screwed the lock shut. If I had been climbing or making a long drop in a cave, that mistake would have compromised my safety, and I might have fallen if the front of my seat harness had come apart. "Bad!" Lance repeated. "That's very, very bad!" It was the last time I ever failed to lock my D-ring. Because Lance had always stressed that we should have another person check our gear for safety before we went on rope, I started doing that reli-giously after this incident.

The frog system has two ascending devices, which the climber uses simultaneously and which enable him or her to move up a rope, but not down. They are the croll—yes, the infamous croll—which is fitted directly onto the D-ring, and the hand ascender, or "safety," which is attached to the D-ring by a short length of rope and which the climber holds in his or her hand. The frog also features a descending device attached to the D-ring, which enables the climber to descend a rope at a safe speed by regulating the amount of friction on the rope. When not in use, the descender is removed from the D-ring and hung from a belt loop on the climber's seat harness.

In the underground lunchroom, we used a type of descender called a "rack" to anchor the climbing rope. Lance had tied it to a thick limestone projection on the cave floor, with the rope passing through the rack and then through a pulley tied to another limestone projection on the ceil-ing. After locking the rack securely so the rope couldn't move, we would climb on the rope's free-hanging end below the pulley. If a climber had to be lowered to the floor, the rope-tender simply loosened the rack and then controlled the speed of the rope as it passed through.

When used properly with nylon ropes, modern climbing devices solve all the problems associated with the ladders and ropes of early cave explorers: they allow a climber to rest safely on rope whenever necessary, they make it impossible for him or her to slip, and they prevent falls.

⌒ After several weeks of training in the underground lunchroom, Lance told me he was going to conduct an after-hours rope-training course in the visitor center lobby for anyone interested in learning to climb rope. That was exactly what I needed, so I graduated into Lance's training course. The setup in the lobby was identical to the one in the underground lunchroom, with a rack anchored near the bottom of one wall and a pulley bolted to the ceiling. Following each session of Lance's instruction, we took turns climbing three hundred feet of rope—thirty stories—while timing one another. As one person was climbing, another person would tend the rope by feeding it through the rack at a steady rate, so the climber remained suspended halfway between the ceiling and floor. It seemed strange at first to keep climbing the rope without going anywhere.

Initially, it took me almost twenty minutes to climb thirty stories, which was a little discouraging, because Lance could do it in only six minutes. I kept at it, though, and as the weeks and months passed my time steadily improved until it was just less than twelve minutes. My goal was ten minutes flat, but as hard as I tried I never got it below ten minutes, five seconds. My time improved, of course, because I was becoming more proficient with the equipment. It now felt like second nature to clip onto the rope and start climbing. Once I set a steady pace, I thoroughly enjoyed using the frog system—especially after I bought my own equipment and adjusted the rope tethers to the lengths of my arms and legs. After a great deal of practice, I climbed seventy-four stories continuously in one session, almost equivalent to climbing the elevator shaft out of Carlsbad Cavern.

Lance constantly emphasized what he called "gear management," which meant keeping our equipment properly organized, both on our persons and when working on rope. Without proper management, the various pieces of equipment and their tethers might become fouled, or it might otherwise become difficult to perform a maneuver. Our goal was to handle every piece of gear efficiently, to minimize our movements and conserve energy. Lance was flawless in this respect, and I never tired of watching him whenever he was on rope. I envied both the way he managed his equipment and the way he appeared to move without any effort.

Lance also emphasized the importance of knots. I had never paid much attention to knots before I started climbing; learning to tie anything beyond a simple bow had seemed pointless and boring. As long as I could tie my shoelaces, I was satisfied. Vertical caving changed that. I now had to tie my safety and my "cow's tail"—a short safety tether—to my D-ring, and I had to tie a foot loop to my safety. I also had to know how to tie a carabiner to one end of a climbing rope so I could anchor it with a "friction wrap"—I'll explain what that is shortly—and how to tie two ropes together to make a longer rope. In short, I needed to learn about knots.

Once I got started, I was surprised to find that knots are quite interesting. Each one has its own logic and beauty, and each turn or twist in a knot has a purpose. I liked the symmetry of the figure eight, the asymmetry of the mountaineer bowline, and the feel of the rope between my fingers as I twisted it here or looped it there. My favorite knots were the figure eight on a bight, the butterfly, and the double fisherman's knot, because they were the most fun to tie.

At Lance's suggestion, I started carrying around a short length of rope so I could practice the knots I was learning in my spare time. I practiced diligently every day and felt guilty if I neglected to bring my rope to work with me in the morning. During my study time, I would sit at my desk or in the library and tie one knot after another, until I could tie the most essential knots with my eyes closed, and even behind my back (Lance had pointed out that a caving emergency might someday force me to tie knots in the dark). When I worked at the Natural Entrance and there were no visitors around, I would tie my rope repeatedly around the metal railing beside the trail. I also learned how to "dress" each knot properly to remove kinks, decrease the amount of strain it placed on the rope, and make it easier to inspect (and also enhance its beauty, which I thought was important).

With Lance's training course under my belt and several months of climbing practice in the visitor center lobby, I began to feel ready for a trip into one of the deep vertical caves of the Guadalupe Mountains. But which one? There were several nearby caves with relatively short entrance drops, including Chimney Cave at about seven stories and Little Manhole Cave at about five, but I had my heart set on something deeper. I kept hearing about the eighteen-story drop into Ogle Cave, and that certainly was a possibility. Lance had recently taken part in a rescue operation there after a caver became exhausted during the long climb out. I asked Lance what he thought about the drop into Ogle, and he said it was one of the best in the Guadalupe Mountains. He also suggested I ask around to see if anyone was planning a trip into Ogle anytime soon. That settled it: Ogle it was.

Ogle Cave

ONE OF THE other staff members who attended Lance's training course and practiced climbing in the visitor center lobby was a seasonal interpreter named Dave. He was in his early thirties and a student at the University of Northern Arizona at Flagstaff, where he was majoring in park and recreation management. Dave was no stranger to Carlsbad Caverns: he had worked previously as a park volunteer under the university's internship program. His dream was to become a permanent employee of the National Park Service, and he was doing everything he could to broaden his experience and develop skills that might help him achieve his goal. Because Dave and I were at about the same level of rope training, we often partnered during climbing practice, checking one another's gear for safety and timing each other on rope. Dave told me that he also wanted to make a rope descent into a deep vertical cave.

Dave had grown up in Alaska, and while he was thoroughly acclimated to the deserts of the Southwest, I couldn't help feeling that his heart was still in the far north. He almost exuded snow and cold weather, and every June, at the beginning of the salmon run, he migrated north to Alaska's Bristol Bay—a drive of four thousand miles in three and a half days—where he worked on a small skiff with three other men, netting salmon in the mouth of the Naknek River.

Dave was also an avid hunter. He had killed his first mountain goat at the age of nine and never tired of lamenting that its horns would have made the record book if the required length hadn't been upped by an eighth of an inch just before his hunt. He went on to bring down a moose at the age of twelve, a Dall sheep when he was fourteen, a caribou just after he graduated from high school, and a black bear at the age of twenty-one. While working at Carlsbad Caverns, he had hunted Barbary sheep—an exotic species that has replaced the native mountain sheep—and killed a mule deer in the foothills north of the Guadalupe Mountains. He frequently vented his frustration over the fact that someone had stolen the deer's carcass after he went to fetch his pickup truck. I came to think of Dave as "the Hunter," and I wasn't surprised to find that he kept a tall stack of hunting magazines in his bathroom.

Dave was relatively short and fairly muscular, with a stocky build. After wrestling in high school, he had gone on to earn a black belt in judo, and he seemed to enjoy all physical activity. He was definitely a fast walker. Even though his legs were shorter than mine, he could easily outpace me on a hike, or even on a short walk across the visitor center lobby. It always seemed to me that he was in a perpetual hurry to get somewhere. He was strong, too. One afternoon when I was helping him clean out his garage, he showed me his compound hunting bow. It was strung so tightly that I couldn't draw it back, yet he effortlessly pulled it taut and held it that way for over a minute.

Because Dave was an open and friendly person, he got along well with park visitors, who liked his informality and quirky humor as much as I did. He had an endless repertoire of comical facial expressions, and I had to laugh every time he raised his eyebrows and flashed a broad grin. Sometimes I even thought he communicated more through his facial expressions than through his words. Yet he was a talented conversationalist and loved to talk incessantly about any subject that was practical rather than philosophical.

During my first summer at Carlsbad Caverns, I started hosting a "movie night" at my apartment every other weekend. Everyone on the park staff was invited, and usually a significant number of people from the housing area and a few from town would come over to watch a video, eat popcorn, and drink beer. When the movie was over, a few of us would sit around talking and drinking until well after midnight, while Dave entertained us with bizarre stories about his youth or his misadventures while working on the custodial staff at Walt Disney World in Florida: "So it's raining, and I'm cleaning the women's restroom in Fantasyland, and this woman comes in and asks if I have a plastic bag she can put over her head so her hair won't get wet . . ."

When Dave faltered, Lance would take over with fantastic tales about caving in Mexico or searching for undiscovered caves along the highest ridges of the Guadalupe Mountains—he called it "ridge walking"—or even about the sprites and spirits said to hide in caves, waiting to harry unsuspecting cavers by tangling their ropes or making their equipment disappear. He called them "hodags," and he associated them with the ghostly lights he and a few others had seen occasionally in the dark recesses of Chimney Cave.

I looked forward to spending time with Lance and Dave, and I began to think of them as friends, people I could hang out with and get to know personally as well as professionally. Because I had been in charge at Gila Cliff Dwellings and hadn't been able to develop very close friendships with other staff members, it was easy to gravitate toward Lance and Dave whenever I was off duty. We would talk and joke endlessly with one another, bouncing mock insults back and forth like Ping-Pong balls and otherwise honing our skills in the art of friendly verbal harassment. I thought it would be great fun to go on a caving trip with them, and I noted that Dave also hadn't made the drop into Ogle Cave.

⌒ Just before the end of my first summer at Carlsbad Caverns, Lance went on an extended trip to the state of Oaxaca in southern Mexico, where he took part in the continuing exploration of Sistema Cheve, a complex cave system that had been discovered only ten years earlier, in the mid-1980s. Cheve was then the deepest known cave in the Western Hemisphere, at 4,869 feet—almost a mile—and its most remote terminus was 5.8 miles from the nearest entrance. Lance spent eleven consecutive days and nights underground, climbing or descending hundreds of feet at a time, rappelling through waterfalls, and helping to "push," or extend the length of the cave's known passages. In the process, he discovered Cheve's largest known chamber, Harbanger Hall. When he returned to Carlsbad Caverns after eight weeks, he had lost about twenty pounds and looked like a scarecrow.

⌒ That fall—my second at Carlsbad Caverns—I took part in my first rope-climbing demonstration at the Natural Entrance with Lance, Kenny, Becky, and Clarence, another permanent interpreter. We gave it late in the afternoon after the Natural Entrance Trail had closed for the day, for an audience of about fifty visitors in the bat flight amphitheater, which faced the entrance. I remember thinking we couldn't have had a more magnificent setting: there was very little haze that afternoon and we could see the entire sweep of the Guadalupe Mountains stretching into the distance.

The drop from the top of the rock overhang down to the Natural Entrance Trail was over six stories. Because I had previously been only four or five feet above the floor of the underground lunchroom or visitor center lobby, this would be the first long rappel of my short climbing career and the first challenge to my fear of heights. I couldn't help noticing that we were almost directly above the cave's twilight zone, where I had paused a year earlier to imagine Satan and his angels tumbling out of heaven in a swirling firestorm. I was also acutely aware that the drop I was about to make was only ten feet shorter than the one Robert Nymeyer and his friends had made into Hell Below.

Lance started anchoring the rope to a large boulder about fifteen paces from the edge of the overhang, while I watched intently so I could learn the correct way to set up an anchor. He explained that because any kind of knot inevitably places a strain on the rope, it's best to make an anchor by using a "friction wrap," which keeps the strain to a minimum. He demonstrated by wrapping one end of the rope around the boulder three times. The friction between the boulder and the rope would hold the rope securely throughout the demonstration. To finish off the anchor, he tied a carabiner to the shorter "working" end of the rope, then loosely clipped it onto the longer "running" end—the end we would be climbing—within a few feet of the boulder.

After completing the anchor, Lance clipped onto the running end with his safety and worked it down the rope to the overhang, where he dropped the remainder of the rope over the edge. To keep it from fraying against the limestone, he placed several rope pads over the sharpest edges. (During later caving trips, I would learn that shirts and caving packs can serve as rope pads.) When everything was ready, he came back to the anchor and clipped off the rope.

Because Lance was the lead climber and in charge of the demonstration, he decided that I would go down the rope first, followed by Becky and then Kenny. Clarence would remain with the visitors in the amphitheater to interpret what we were doing. While we were putting on our equipment, Lance walked back to the amphitheater and down the Natural Entrance Trail to the bottom of the rope, where he would "belay" me during my descent. This means he would hold the rope loosely and be ready to pull down on it as hard as he could if I lost control of my descender and started to fall. That would increase the friction between my descender and the rope and slow me down, if not bring me to a complete stop.

After squirming into my harnesses, I asked Kenny to check them for safety. When he gave me a thumbs-up, I attached my descender to the rope, shouted "On rope!" and waited. Despite my fear of heights, I was ready—even eager—to make my first long drop. Yet what would it be like to ease myself over the lip of that overhang? I tried to imagine myself standing on top of a six-story building, peering over the edge, but because I had never done that I couldn't get a clear impression of how high I would be. After a short wait, I heard Lance shout, "On belay!" and I gamely started backing toward the edge of the overhang, feeding the rope slowly through my descender as the visitors in the amphitheater watched expectantly.

When I reached the edge, I planted my boots firmly against the limestone, leaned cautiously backward, and peered between my legs to see Lance staring up at me—a tiny figure far below, holding the rope. That's when my fear of heights vanished. The tautness of the working end and the obvious strength of the anchor were so reassuring that my apprehension melted and my confidence began to soar. Easing over the edge, I started down the face of the overhang, pushing myself away from the rock with my feet and carefully replacing the rope over the pads. The heaviness of the rope as I fed it through my descender surprised me, but it wasn't a problem. I was feeling the same elation I had felt in Spider Cave when I realized that tight squeezes would no longer bother me.

Dropping free at the bottom of the overhang, I was poised in midair with scores of cave swallows circling, swooping, and chirping around me, like noisy children on a playground. I felt as light as the downy feathers floating nearby, and I could have locked off my descender and stayed there for the rest of the afternoon, enjoying the swallows and their antics. However, Lance shouted that he was going to demonstrate a belay by pulling down on the rope as I descended. When he did, I came to a complete stop. When he released his grip, I began to move again. Cool.

A few moments later, my boots landed firmly on the trail, and Lance congratulated me for completing my first drop. I felt happy with what I had accomplished and gratified to know my fear of heights wasn't going to be a problem. What a relief. I had come a long way since my first walk around the Big Room Trail, when I stared into the Bottomless Pit and wondered what it would be like to descend on a nylon rope using technical equipment. Now I knew, and I was eager for the challenge of Ogle Cave.

Without giving me a break, Lance told me to climb back up and demonstrate a changeover for the audience. As I removed my descender from the rope, he walked back up the trail to rejoin Kenny and Becky above the entrance. I set a moderate pace as I started up, relishing the familiar sensation of raising my legs and extending them repeatedly, like a frog kicking itself along through water. At last I was using my new climbing skills in an actual cave setting. Just before I reached the bottom of the overhang, Clarence shouted from the amphitheater that I should stop and let go of the rope, then lean backward and dangle there so the visitors could see how my equipment held me securely in place. As I did, I could hear a woman in the audience saying repeatedly, "Oh my God!" She would obviously never be a caver.

After completing the changeover, I lowered myself to the trail a second time, removed my descender from the rope, and moved a few paces out of the way so I could belay Becky's descent. I had never belayed anyone before, but how difficult could it be? All I had to do was pull down on the rope, just as Lance had done. After shouting "Off rope!" and "On belay!" as loudly as I could, I gripped the rope loosely and looked up at the overhang, waiting for Becky. She soon appeared at the edge and cautiously began to descend the face of the overhang, but she seemed to be having a problem with her descender, and Lance apparently was coaching her as she struggled along. I couldn't imagine what the problem was.

Then Becky fell against the overhang, lost control of her descender, and started plunging down the rope. Screams erupted from the audience. I pulled on the rope as hard as I could, but it didn't do any good: down she came, rocketing like the proverbial bat out of hell. In desperation, I threw my entire weight onto the rope, trying to slow her down. She hit me with so much force that it knocked me onto the trail, leaving me sprawled on my back with Becky flailing on top of me.

As we slowly helped one another up, Lance shouted, "Doug! Get her off rope!" and we began fumbling to unclip Becky's descender. When I called back that we were clear, Lance came gliding down to join us. Becky kept insisting she was all right, but when she took off her leather gloves we found she had blistered both hands. She was also beginning to feel pain in one of her ankles, although she could still walk. Lance was visibly shaken by what might have been a very serious accident, while I felt completely dejected.

"Lance, my entire weight was on the rope," I stammered, "but it didn't do any good. Did I do something wrong?"

"No, you did okay, Doug," he replied, slowly regaining his composure. "A belay isn't going to stop someone who's already in a free fall. About the best it can do is slow the person down. You did as much as you could, and it was enough to keep Becky from being seriously hurt. Don't worry about it."

Lance's reassurance made me feel better, but I was still trembling as he and Becky started walking slowly up the trail together, to the sound of the visitors' applause. I was left to struggle alone with the chilling lesson of Becky's mishap: even with modern climbing equipment, it's possible to fall when descending. I had always known this in an offhand way, but now I had lived the nightmare, and I realized that control was infinitely important. As long as I controlled my descender, I would drop at a safe speed; but if I somehow lost control, I would plummet like Satan into the dark abyss of the underworld.

⌐ My long-awaited rappel into Ogle Cave took place the following summer. It began with a conversation about "burrito bags" as Lance and I were driving into the town of Carlsbad in his Ford pickup. He had agreed to lead a trip into Ogle so Dave, Kenny, another seasonal interpreter named Mike, and I could go along. After working for a year and a half at Carlsbad Caverns, I was finally going to explore a deep vertical cave. Lance had already picked up our caving permit from the park's Cave Resources Office, but there was something I wanted to ask him before the trip. I knew about pee bottles, and I carried one in my caving pack when I took visitors into Spider Cave or led them to the Hall of the White Giant. But what if . . .

"Hey, Lance, what if we get into Ogle Cave and I need to use something more than a pee bottle? What do I do?"

"What do you do? You wait until you're out of the cave."

"Come on, I'm serious."

"So am I." He paused to catch my reaction. "Get a life, Doug. Haven't you ever heard of a burrito bag?"

"No."

"Damn, you don't know anything," he scoffed. "You carry two large Ziploc plastic bags in your pack along with a big, square sheet of tinfoil and a scoop of kitty litter. If you need to use the restroom in a cave, you find a private spot and spread the sheet of tinfoil on the trail. That's your restroom. After you use it, you fold the tinfoil into a little packet, like one of those foil-wrapped burritos you see in convenience stores. You put the packet into one of the Ziploc bags, zip it up, then put it inside the second Ziploc bag along with the kitty litter. Zip it up again, and there's your burrito bag. When you're finished, you pack it out of the cave."

"Oh, okay. That makes sense."

Unable to resist sarcasm, he replied, "I can't believe you want to take a burrito bag into Ogle for just a one-day trip. What a loser."

"Well, Mother Nature isn't always our friend, you know."

"What a loser."

"Keep it up, Lance. If you take chances, one of these days you're going to learn an important lesson the hard way."

"Loser."

That weekend our group of five drove in Lance and Dave's pickup trucks to the small parking lot at the mouth of Slaughter Canyon. We were getting an early start because the temperature was going to be over one hundred degrees that afternoon, and we didn't want to hike out of the canyon after the relentless desert sun had turned it into an inferno. Each of us carried a caving pack containing extra light sources, our climbing gear, food, and water. Lance carried the rope draped over one shoulder like a bandolier, neatly coiled, wrapped, and tied off with a square knot. It was the most important piece of gear we were taking with us because our lives would depend on it.

The trail from the parking lot meandered up the canyon along the sandy floodplain until it finally disappeared in the rocky dry wash. Lance then struck off toward the opposite side of the canyon, where he began climbing a steep draw, picking his way through dense brush and prickly sotols toward the cave entrance. It was a brutal climb, and I was relieved when we finally arrived, panting and sweating, at a narrow terrace adjoining a huge pit, perhaps forty feet across, about halfway up the draw. Ogle Cave. It didn't look like much of a cave, though, because we couldn't see anything beyond the bottom of the steep slope that descended to the pit's edge. The opposite side of the pit was a sheer limestone cliff rising three or four stories above the level of the terrace. For some reason, the whole setting made me feel uneasy. I thought about the guano miner who had fallen from the wooden ladders to his death in this very cave.

At the top of the slope stood the remains of a massive winch, which the miners had used to hoist guano out of the cave. Lance dropped his pack down beside it, then started untying the rope, and I realized the winch was going to serve as our anchor. He wrapped one end of the rope six or seven times around the axle to create a friction wrap, then finished it off with a locking carabiner, which he clipped to another part of the winch. He then began "flaking" the remainder of the rope—the running end— starting at the anchor and using one hand to pull several feet at a time through the fist of his other hand, while letting it fall into a jumbled pile at his feet. I was surprised to learn that flaking the rope in this way would keep it from tangling when he threw it into the pit. When he finished, he picked up the last twenty feet or so in a shapeless mass and tossed it as hard as he could over the far edge of the steep slope. Its weight began pulling the rest of the rope behind it, starting at the top of the pile and continuing to the bottom. I watched in amazement as the pile grew smaller, until it finally disappeared and the rope hung tautly from the anchor.

I began to feel uneasy again as I put on my harnesses and checked my helmet lamp. The rappel was going to be three times longer than the drop at the Natural Entrance, and if I lost control of my descender on the way down, a belay wouldn't help me. All I could do was trust my equipment and my own ability to use the skills I had developed over the past months. I wondered how Dave felt, but I didn't ask him. He seemed as relaxed and outgoing as he always did. That's one of the things I liked about Dave: he was consistently steady and reliable, and when he did feel uncertain about something his sense of humor would carry him through. I was always glad to be around him in a situation like this.

Because Lance was the trip leader, he would go down first. He had already attached himself to the rope before I could even get my seat harness clipped together. With a shout of "On rope!" he started backing down the slope. I had to envy his self-assurance; I suspected I wouldn't look as confident when it was my turn. Reaching the edge of the pit, he paused for a moment to look down, then anchored several rope pads against the rock and placed the rope over them as he lowered himself out of sight. The rest of us stood or crouched around the winch, watching the rope vibrate as he descended and wondering what it would be like when we went down. After several minutes, the vibrating stopped and we heard a faint cry of "Off rope!" echoing from the cliff on the opposite side of the pit.

Dave rappelled next, apparently without any problem, and then it was my turn. When I began threading the rope through my descender, its extreme weight shocked me. Being three times longer than the rope at the Natural Entrance made it three times heavier, and it would be far more difficult to control. I hoped that wouldn't be a problem. After locking my descender, I shouted "On rope!" and started backing down the slope, managing the rope with great difficulty. It was so heavy that I had to lift it with both hands. How would that affect my descent once I started down the vertical wall of the pit? The image of Becky hurtling downward at the Natural Entrance passed briefly through my mind.

When I reached the edge of the slope, I peered cautiously into the semidarkness below. *Holy hodag!* I was poised over an abyss so appallingly deep that Lance and Dave had been transformed into minuscule ants. I could barely see them as they ducked under an overhang to protect themselves from falling rocks. Tightening my grip, I began lowering myself into the pit, lifting the rope above my descender with both hands so I could feed it downward. Already my arms were getting tired, and I could see why my type of descender—we called it a "simple"—wasn't at all practical for drops much longer than the one we were making. However, I was relieved that the rope became lighter as I went deeper, and by the time I reached a broad ledge about halfway down, I could manage it fairly easily. Looking up I saw a circle of blue sky, but Kenny and Mike remained out of sight at the winch.

After backing across the ledge, I continued down the wall, and eventually my feet touched the dirt-covered floor. *Hallelujah!* I had descended eighteen stories and completed my first drop into a deep cave. Running enough rope through my descender to create some slack, I quickly disengaged. When I shouted "Off rope!" I could hear my voice echoing in the dark recesses of the cave off to my left, but I ignored that and joined Lance and Dave under a nearby overhang. I didn't want to complete my first long drop and then be killed by a falling rock.

After Kenny and Mike joined us, we took off our climbing equipment and headed into the darkness of the cave, following the colorful plastic tape that marked the trail. The main chamber was enormous and much deeper than the bottom of the pit, so we had to descend a steep slope of rubble before the trail leveled off. Within about fifty yards we confronted a massive wall of limestone draperies that extended to the ceiling, their folds curling back and forth along the trail like a giant curtain on the stage of a theater. Just beyond them the trail forked. Lance guided us to the left, toward a gigantic formation that rose all the way to the ceiling from an immense mound of "breakdown"—small rocks and boulders that had fallen from the ceiling long ago. Lance said the formation was called the Bicentennial Column and that it was almost eleven stories tall. As far as anyone knew, it was the tallest column in the Western Hemisphere, and it dwarfed the huge formations I saw almost every day in the Hall of Giants in Carlsbad Cavern.

Although bats no longer roosted in Ogle Cave, there were sizable deposits of guano beyond the Bicentennial Column, stretching all the way to the back wall. Much of it was crusted with a thin layer of cap rock, and there were more large areas of breakdown. In a level area, we found that the cave-resources staff had arranged a display of tools and lanterns left by the guano miners, and we stopped to sign our names in the cave register, which was folded up in a waterproof container. When we finally reached the back wall, we saw graffiti from the early 1900s, including a few names I recognized from my reading about the cave's history. This was where we ate our lunch, sitting along a wide part of the trail and using our packs and extra shirts as tablecloths. (It's always best not to eat in a cave, because food particles promote the growth of mold. However, on trips lasting a day or more it's often necessary. Our "tablecloths" would prevent crumbs from falling onto the cave floor.)

Retracing our steps, we returned to the fork in the trail and took the route we had bypassed earlier, which led into a side chamber decorated with many imposing stalagmites. We eventually arrived at a small alcove where the guano miners had tried to blast a horizontal tunnel. Their goal was to create an opening in the side of Slaughter Canyon; if they had succeeded they could have removed guano from the cave relatively easily. However, they had stopped after going only a short distance. The only notable thing in the tunnel was a tiny drapery formation that had started to grow on the inclined ceiling. It was about four inches long, and when we directed our helmet lamps against its back side we found that its translucence glowed beautifully in the semidarkness.

After spending the entire morning in the cave, we made our way back to the pit, where we put on our climbing equipment and began the long ascent to the surface. I remember standing against the opposite wall and watching Kenny as he worked his way up the rugged limestone. By the time he reached the top he was a tiny figure barely visible against the darkly shadowed rock. When I finally started up, I have to admit that I clipped onto the rope reluctantly. The cave had been so fascinating that I didn't want to leave. Yet it was time, so I shouted "On rope!" and began climbing toward the surface, pushing myself away from the wall with one foot.

The temperature in the cave had been in the mid-fifties, but the canyon was already approaching meltdown by the time I arrived at the winch. After clipping off the rope, I stood nearby to remove my equipment, then gazed toward the broad panorama of open desert beyond the canyon's mouth. There wasn't a cloud in the sky, and the drab vegetation that stretched to the horizon was shimmering in the midday heat. Across the canyon, I could see the entrance to Slaughter Canyon Cave and the steep trail leading up to it, and I realized how fortunate I was to be living and working among the caves of the Guadalupe Mountains. As far as I was concerned, I could have stayed there forever.

When everyone was out of the cave and we had stowed our equipment in our packs, and after Lance had coiled and tied the rope, we started down the steep slope toward the dry wash and the trail. Because Dave and Mike would be driving back together in Dave's pickup, they didn't try to keep up with the rest of us, and Lance, Kenny, and I arrived back at the parking lot before they did. After stowing our gear in the back of Lance's pickup, we climbed into the cab and began the long drive back to the highway, churning thick clouds of dust into the summer air as we went.

Although I would make the drop into Ogle Cave four more times while working at Carlsbad Caverns, this trip was by far the most significant because it culminated my initial training as a caver. While there would always be new climbing techniques to master, I had proven that I could control my descender during a long rappel and otherwise use technical equipment safely. However, I hadn't fully overcome my fear of heights. When I first stared into that pit, and even as I was climbing out, I felt a queasy, tingling sensation in my stomach. Yet it was obvious that my fear of heights and even the myth of Satan's Fall wouldn't deter me from exploring vertical caves, and I looked forward to more caving trips with Lance and Dave.

As I watched Slaughter Canyon recede in the side rearview mirror, I thought of Robert Nymeyer and his friends. Had they ever stood at the brink of the drop-off into Ogle Cave, wondering what lay at the bottom? I mentioned Nymeyer to Lance and Kenny, and Lance began an animated retelling of the legendary trip into Hell Below. Soon we were caught up in the drama of those early days, trying to imagine what it must have been like to face the darkness of hell with only 150 feet of manila stake line and a lariat. I think Lance already knew, judging by the wistful tone of his voice as he gazed intently at the road ahead and murmured, "Wouldn't it have been a hoot to go caving with those guys?"

Salt Basin and Guadalupe Mountains.

El Capitán, Guadalupe Mountains National Park.

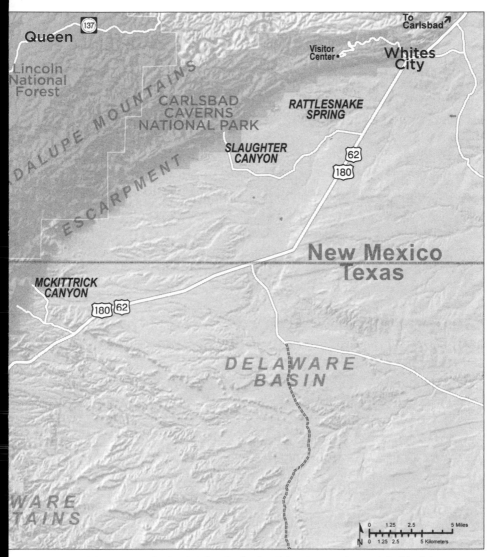

Guadalupe Mountains National Park, the Guadalupe Mountains, and Carlsbad Caverns National Park. Map prepared by Red Paw Technologies, Albuquerque, New Mexico.

Guadalupe Escarpment and Slaughter Canyon.

Natural Entrance to Carlsbad Cavern and bat flight amphitheater.

Devil's Spring, Carlsbad Cavern.

Hall of Giants, Carlsbad Cavern.

Trail to Spider Cave.

Spider Cave entrance crawl.

Doug in Spider Cave.

Aragonite crystals spanning about ten inches, Spider Cave.

White calcite soda straws and columns, Spider Cave.

Helictites three to twelve inches tall, Spider Cave.

White calcite flowstone and cave popcorn, Ogle Cave.

Dave viewing a small drapery formation in Ogle Cave.

Doug in Fort Stanton–Snowy River Cave, New Mexico.

Iffy in the High Guads, Guadalupe Mountains National Park.

Lance in Fort Stanton–Snowy River Cave, New Mexico.

Iffy on rope at Gunsight Cave, Lincoln National Forest.

Slaughter Canyon Trail.

Delaware Basin as seen from the Guadalupe Escarpment.

McKittrick Canyon, Guadalupe Mountains National Park.

Permian Reef Trail, Guadalupe Mountains National Park.

Lance at one of his recent park assignments.

Dave at his current park. Photograph by Allison Thomas.

Iffy as a protection ranger at his current park.

Part Two

EXPLORING

Kokopelli

THE DROP INTO Ogle Cave proved I was well on my way toward achieving two of the goals I had set for myself: learning everything I could about Carlsbad Cavern and the other caves of the Guadalupe Mountains, and becoming an experienced caver. But I also had a third goal: exploring and learning about the Chihuahuan Desert.

I had known from the beginning that I would spend a significant amount of time interpreting the desert to park visitors, and that was definitely proving to be the case. Hardly a day passed when I didn't get questions about rattlesnakes, scorpions, vultures, prickly pears, or the desert's arid climate. The park, after all, contained more than forty-six thousand acres of desert, and many visitors were just as curious about the things they were seeing aboveground as they were about the park's caves. Over the coming years, my hikes and other adventures in the desert would become an enjoyable alternative to the often-hectic pace of work and the excitement and hazards of caving trips. I didn't have to be concerned about tight spaces, heights, nylon ropes, technical equipment, or the rule of three. I could hike alone, move at my own pace, and wander wherever I wanted to go. All I had to do was take along plenty of water.

In time I would come to appreciate how intimately the desert and its caves are related, but at first I could only marvel at their obvious differences: Caves are dark, silent, and confined, while the desert is a realm of brilliant sunlight, cacophonous sounds—the cicadas chirp endlessly throughout the summer—and broad vistas. Caves change at an unbelievably slow pace, while the desert can change dramatically within the timespan of a single thunderstorm. Caves support only microorganisms and a few insects and animals that are very small and hard to detect, while the desert teems with a wide variety of amazing creatures running the gamut from small and timid to huge and threatening. I would be exploring two fundamentally different worlds during those six years. Yet I would discover that the desert and its caves are linked in ways I hadn't imagined.

   ⌒ I began to learn about the desert shortly after my arrival at Carlsbad Caverns, when I walked around the park's nature trail to become familiar with the local desert plants. Some were entirely new to me, like agarita—also known as desert holly—with its small, prickly leaves, tiny yellow flowers, and red berries. I also hiked the five-mile trail that ran east from the visitor center along the top of the escarpment, following the route of the old dirt road from Whites City to the guano mine. Along the way, I saw turret-like mounds of strawberry cactus, some three feet wide and two feet high, and clusters of spiky lechuguilla plants—the name is Spanish, pronounced leh-choo-*ghee*-uh—the nemesis of every Chihuahuan Desert hiker with an aversion to being stabbed painfully in the leg. I even walked around the ten-mile scenic drive and completed a number of cross-country hikes along the escarpment and into several canyons in the park's rugged backcountry.

I had arrived at Carlsbad Caverns near the end of the summer rainy season, when the desert was just beginning to curl up and go to sleep for the winter. I had to wait until the following spring to see it come to life again. That winter we had an uncommonly heavy snowfall that lasted for several days, covering the landscape with a downy-white blanket and the cliffs along Walnut Canyon with lacy patterns of ice and frost. Standing at the side door of the visitor center one snowy morning, Lance pointed out to anyone who was interested the distant column of steam rising from the cave's second natural entrance near the old guano-mine site. He explained that the cold air on the surface was sinking into the Bat Cave, while the relatively warm air in the cave was simultaneously rising. It was a phenomenon that made spotting undiscovered caves fairly easy, and that's why snowy weather was the best time to go ridge walking.

Hiking to Spider Cave in the snow became an otherworldly adventure. A bitterly cold wind blowing across the escarpment sent clouds of snow billowing into the canyon as the lead ranger, eight visitors, and I made our way cautiously down the trail, surrounded by the ghostly shapes of snow-covered yuccas and ocotillos. The lead ranger and I were bundled in our winter uniform coats with woolen scarves and stocking caps for the cold hike, but when we took them off and stored them at the bottom of the entrance ladder, then crawled into the cave's relatively warm and moist sixty-two degrees, it felt as though we were entering a sauna. The hike out of the canyon after the tour was even more captivating: the wind had stopped, it was beginning to get dark, and the snow fell as languidly as the blossoms that had long since dropped from the yuccas.

Spring announced itself with a burst of vivid colors that migrated across the desert and into the canyons well before the first summer rains appeared: yellow tinged with orange and sometimes deep red on the prickly pears, blazing red at the tips of the ocotillos, waxy white on the sumptuous plumes of the soaptree yuccas, a mixture of brilliant orange and vermilion on the claret cups and Indian paintbrush, blushing pink on the desert willows—which liked to hide in canyons and along dry washes— and deep magenta on the strawberry hedgehogs. An expansive yellow carpet of tiny creosote blossoms converged around the mouth of Slaughter Canyon and surged like waves against the base of the escarpment.

That spring I began riding my bicycle down the road to Whites City and back again—about fourteen miles round trip—once or twice each week, something I would continue to do throughout my years at Carlsbad Caverns. After coasting down the short drive from the housing area to the main road, I would make a right turn, pedal as hard as I could for a few hundred yards, then begin coasting down the steep, mile-long decline to the bottom of Walnut Canyon. Hunkering over the handlebars with my T-shirt flapping against my back, I would squint into the onrushing desert air and sing one of the choruses from Haydn's mighty oratorio *The Creation*—performed in the Big Room of Carlsbad Cavern in 1933—to the ravens and cave swallows circling overhead: "Sing to God, ye myriad hosts! Thank him for his new creation!"

Down I would go, leaning to the left as I swept around the first broad curve, gradually righting myself for the quick descent along the gently curving face of the cliff, then leaning steeply to the right as I entered the sharp turn at the bottom. When I finally emerged onto the straightaway below the canyon's far wall, I would be traveling thirty-five miles per hour and almost shouting at the passing cliffs: "Awake, ye heavenly harps and choirs! Resound the praise of God on high!" It was the only way I could express the joy I felt at being surrounded by the incomparable beauty of the Chihuahuan Desert.

One afternoon at the beginning of the rainy season, I rounded the curve at the top of the steep decline to find a small, ephemeral rain shower emerging from the upper part of the canyon and beginning to envelop the road and dry wash below. The rain was so gentle that I could barely distinguish it from the wisp of cloud overhead, and both reflected the late-afternoon sunlight so softly that they seemed more imaginary than real. Nevertheless, I applied my brakes and began to slow down before I reached the wet pavement.

I entered the rain at the beginning of the sharp curve—a mist so refreshingly soft that I stopped singing and just coasted through it as though it were a beautiful dream. The wonderful smell of rain on dust permeated the air, and I seemed to be savoring it for the first time. When had the desert landscape ever felt so fresh and vigorous, and when had it ever been so new? Surely not since the creation itself. When I emerged on the far side of the shower and continued down the canyon, I was barely wet, and within a short distance I had dried completely. I've recalled that shower many times over the years, and when I compare it to the others I've known throughout my life, it's the one I would most want to relive. The desert had shown a kind and gentle face to me, and I haven't forgotten.

⌒ My research in the park library introduced me to a variety of desert nature guides, from James MacMahon's classic *Deserts* to Steve West's *Northern Chihuahuan Desert Wildflowers*. It also introduced me to Kokopelli, the humpbacked flute player who first appeared in southwestern ceramic and rock art more than a thousand years ago. Given my penchant for mythology, I realized that Kokopelli had something important to tell me about the desert, just as Satan's Fall and the daughters of Ute'tsiti had informed me about the darkness of caves.

Anyone who goes into a southwestern gift shop knows what Kokopelli looks like, because his image is everywhere: on T-shirts, scarves, mugs, drinking glasses, wallets, wind chimes, greeting cards—you name it. He's usually a simple stick figure with a pronounced curve to his back, a flute in his hands, and several lines protruding from his head to represent the feathers of a headdress. Sometimes he wears a short skirt, but not always. Kokopelli's image may initially have represented one of the prehistoric traders from northern Mexico who regularly visited southwestern pueblos, and who may have played flutes to announce their peaceful intentions from a distance. If so, Kokopelli's hump probably represented a trader's backpack.

Because the cultures that first embraced Kokopelli depended on agriculture, it's not surprising that in his final, supernatural form he's a benign figure associated with fertility. Often he's thought to chase away the winter cold while ushering in the spring. He can also summon the clouds, bring rain, and assure success in the hunt. Invariably, he bestows fertility—his most important function—and for that reason unmarried women of childbearing age try to avoid him and will even hide when they think he's near. In a few traditions, he distributes babies from his backpack, just as the stork delivers babies in Western mythology. Even today Kokopelli is an important figure in Native cultures across the Southwest, including the Hopi of Arizona and the Zuni of New Mexico.

The thing that intrigued me most about Kokopelli was his flute, which he apparently used to summon the clouds. It must have been a remarkable instrument. I liked to imagine him sitting on the edge of a desert cliff playing a simple yet haunting melody, with clouds gathering overhead like sheep harkening to their shepherd. It was an important ritual because without it the desert would remain barren. Performed properly it would bring the colorful blossoms that appeared along the escarpment every spring, the emerald-green pools of water in the canyons, the bright-red or purple fruit on the prickly pears, and the fat tarantulas I saw walking across the road whenever it rained. Kokopelli's flute symbolized his benign powers because it made the desert bountiful. The kind and gentle face I had seen in Walnut Canyon was Kokopelli's doing.

⌒ It occurred to me that the little humpback had a big job on his hands. The Chihuahuan Desert needs very little water to prosper, but its huge size—it extends six hundred miles into Mexico—means that "very little" is a staggering amount. Where is it going to come from, and how is it going to get to where it's needed? The closest oceans are many hundreds of miles away, and the only way to transport their water to the desert is to have it evaporate and then moved across the continent by way of air currents. That takes a tremendous amount of energy. And if it's going to be a good year, the rains will have to continue for at least two consecutive months, preferably three. Quite an assignment for one small flute.

I decided that the air currents must be Kokopelli's most pressing concern, simply because of the Chihuahuan Desert's size. There's a lot of air out there. So I began to notice how the atmosphere moved over the desert landscape, assuming Kokopelli had a hand in it. The most obvious movement occurred every spring, just before the summer rainy season arrived, when violent winds howled relentlessly through the canyons and across the open desert for weeks at a time. No one looked forward to it, and it was the only thing I didn't like about living in the Chihuahuan Desert.

I'll always remember one March day, when a woman who obviously had never experienced the spring winds of southeastern New Mexico came up to me in the visitor center lobby. It had been windy for several weeks already, with tumbleweeds bobbing across the roads as though they were spring-loaded and the sky brown with dust that had blown all the way from who knows where. I could imagine her lying sleepless the night before, listening in abject terror as the shrieking wind shook the motel where she and her husband were staying and the windows rattled as if they were going to implode. With a haggard expression on her face and a tone in her voice that fairly pleaded for some kind—*any kind*—of blessed relief, she looked me in the eye and asked, "When is this going to *end*?" It was difficult to return her gaze as I tried to answer gently, "Well, ma'am, probably this summer."

One of the best places to experience the spring winds without being blown away was the entrance to Slaughter Canyon Cave. We took our lunch breaks on a small ledge nearby, which gave us an unobstructed view of the entire canyon. On the opposite slope stood a huge limestone fin, a narrow projection of rock many hundreds of feet high that extended all the way up the slope and looked like a fin on the back of a giant fish. We were relatively protected from the wind on our ledge, but the fin received a massive and sustained broadside every spring. The steady roar it created as the air spilled over the top and whipped around the sides is one of my most vivid memories of the Chihuahuan Desert. Some of the other interpreters likened it to the whoosh of a jet or the muted sound of a freight train.

Often the winds would stop for a short time and then begin again. This happened in an unusual way during an overnight hike I made into Big Canyon with Lance and Tammy, one of the seasonal interpreters. The canyons of the Guadalupe Mountains are narrow and twisted in their upper reaches and unbelievably rugged, with sheer cliffs on both sides and long, trackless stretches where massive boulders have fallen to fill the bottoms, often making it necessary to travel by means of "boulder-hopping." We had hiked well up the right fork of Big Canyon that afternoon, until we came to a sheer cliff that prevented us from going any further. Calling it a day, we started back down the canyon, looking for a place to camp.

That's when it happened. We began to hear a strange sound coming down the canyon behind us, like the rushing of a waterfall, and when we turned around we saw the distant cottonwood trees beginning to thrash around violently in a strong wind. The movement spread rapidly down the canyon from tree to tree, coming ever closer as the sound grew louder, until the wind overtook us and the trees and brush around us joined the melee, jerking and gyrating as though they were animated puppets on invisible strings. Then, as suddenly as it had come, the wind passed and everything became still again. If you've ever taken part in a "human wave" at a ballpark, you know exactly what we experienced.

We found a place to camp that night at a sharp bend in the canyon, just upstream from several large and beautifully tranquil pools of water. Shortly after bedding down in our sleeping bags, we watched the full moon rise silently over the canyon walls and flood our camp with pale light. Then it began again. A gust of wind moved down the canyon from its uppermost reaches, the first of many that would continue intermittently throughout the night. Each would begin far away and grow increasingly louder as it approached, until the nearby trees and vegetation began their exuberant dancing. After only a few seconds, the gusts would pass and everything would become peaceful again.

The springtime atmosphere didn't always move in such a spirited way, of course, and I can recall times when it came or went slowly and with great subtlety. Late one afternoon at the beginning of the rainy season, as I drove toward Whites City on my way home from the town of Carlsbad, I found the top of the escarpment covered with a shallow and exceptionally beautiful sea of clouds that was spilling over the edge and slowly cascading down the rocky slope to the desert below, where it quickly evaporated. Down it came, as stealthily and as beautifully as the moonlight that had spilled into Big Canyon on that night when the wind blew so erratically. I've seldom seen a lovelier or more unusual sight, and I've always remembered it as evidence that Kokopelli has a well-developed aesthetic sensibility.

⌒ For all their ferocity, the spring winds were a warm-up of sorts, a precursor to the thunderstorms of summer, when moisture transported from the Gulf of Mexico fell on the Chihuahuan Desert in sudden and often cataclysmic downpours. Once the first storms arrived, the air no longer moved in windy unison but instead lay sultry and still as clouds gathered over the mountains or distant sand hills, built themselves into darkly ominous towers of water vapor and air, then moved slowly and ponderously across the desert. Often in the evenings, I would sit on one of the picnic tables next to the visitor center parking lot, where I had an unobstructed view of the southeastern horizon, watching distant thunderstorms at work. I always felt a sense of loss and disappointment when a storm exhausted itself and slowly dissipated, but the grandeur of the ever-changing display made even that worthwhile. Sometimes there would be two or even three storms at once, many miles apart and perhaps moving in different directions.

Thunderstorms had an immediate and profound impact on the desert. They seldom lasted more than a few minutes, yet they dropped tremendous amounts of water, which obviously had to go somewhere. Some of it percolated into the sandy soil to sustain the sparse vegetation, but much of it quickly evaporated, which made the atmosphere seem excessively humid and uncomfortable, in my opinion. In canyons and dry washes, the water frequently accumulated in flash floods and surged rapidly downstream, carrying with it tons of sand and rock and sculpting the canyon bottoms into their familiar serpentine form. It worked relentlessly on the limestone cliffs as well, streaking them with dark mineral stains known as "desert varnish" and eroding them into whimsical shapes.

The most amazing aspect of thunderstorms, however, was their cooling effect. One afternoon as I drove across the desert from Carlsbad Caverns toward the small Texas crossroads community of Orla—a post office, a feed store, and several abandoned buildings—I noticed a huge and exceptionally dark thunderstorm moving up from the south and crossing the highway several miles ahead of me. My car's external thermometer indicated that the temperature was hovering around 102 degrees. When I entered the thunderstorm and its massive raindrops began impacting violently against my windshield, the temperature dropped to 72 degrees. A few miles later, when I emerged on the other side of the storm, it immediately shot back up to 102—a change of thirty degrees within several minutes.

As much as I liked the practical aspects of thunderstorms, I admired their aesthetics even more, and I saw the rainy season as the most enchanting time of year because of all the wonderful things that happened to the sky. The mountainous cloud formations gleamed with the purest and brightest white I had ever seen, although they were most stunning just before sunset, when they fractured the sunlight in ways that reflected its loveliest pastel shades of yellow, orange, red, pink, blue, and purple. And the rainbows were perfect. I once saw three distant and exceptionally dark thunderstorms covering more than half the horizon, and two of them reflected rainbows that were mirror images of one another.

Lightning was by far the most awe-inspiring and memorable part of any thunderstorm, although it could be a serious threat when hiking during the rainy season, especially in the higher elevations of the mountains. I once ran from the top of Guadalupe Peak down to the trailhead in Pine Canyon—a distance of over four miles—to escape a violent thunderstorm that suddenly developed over the salt basin and began moving in my direction. I wasn't afraid of getting wet, though; several weeks earlier, a visitor at Carlsbad Caverns had been killed by a lightning strike while walking across the visitor center parking lot.

Occasionally I would sit at the picnic tables after dark to enjoy the magnificent lightning displays on the horizon, which often lit the entire sky. Sometimes I wouldn't even know a storm was there until lightning began flickering silently in its clouds, like a lamp with an electrical short flickering in the dark, intermittently illuminating its lampshade. But what a lampshade: mountains of billowing clouds with brightly glittering peaks and ridges, dark canyons, and glowing foothills—a celestial landscape to rival the Guadalupe Mountains—alternately appearing and disappearing in the darkness.

One night at the picnic tables, I witnessed what had to be the most spectacular of all lightning displays. I knew the sky was overcast, but it was so dark that I couldn't see anything overhead—until lightning began streaking from one horizon to the other. It started below the southern horizon and darted through the clouds silently and almost instantaneously in one long bolt, traveling all the way to the northern horizon, where it disappeared. I had never seen anything like it, and I sat transfixed as successive bolts traced different routes across the sky, as though they were following one another to some prearranged destination: south to north, silently, instantaneously.

Despite its beauty, lightning did serve a practical function, because it occasionally started grass fires that renewed the desert's scant vegetation. Yet I couldn't help feeling that its primary purpose was to make the desert grand and glorious, and I came to see it as Kokopelli's ultimate aesthetic display. Once a bolt of lightning had burst from the clouds and sent its thundering reverberations into the farthest reaches of every canyon along the escarpment, when the last, rumbling echo had faded to insignificance over the broad desert landscape, nothing more was possible. Yet that burst had been enough. And it sometimes led me to ask: Does Kokopelli ride the lightning? Does he jump astride those great bolts and go hurtling across the sky from one horizon to the other? Does he summon the clouds whenever he needs to travel?

CHAPTER TEN

Old Man Coyote

AFTER THE RAINY season, or whenever the rains failed to appear, the desert became far less bountiful and showed a decidedly less friendly face. I generally saw the Chihuahuan Desert as a place where bounty and beauty went hand in hand with austerity and hardship, and where danger and death were common. But that's the way Old Man Coyote intended it.

I began reading about Coyote in the park library shortly after I discovered Kokopelli. Sometimes known simply as Old Man outside the Southwest, he was one of the First People, those mythical beings who climbed out of the underworld in the beginning and used their magical powers to create the world and populate it with human beings. Coyote did many things to help humans, such as teaching men and women their cultural roles and showing them how to plant crops and use fire. Yet at heart he was a trickster and spoiler who continually took advantage of others, even though his schemes often backfired and got him into trouble. He was also a glutton, a lecher, a liar, and a thief—qualities that certainly made him more intriguing than respectable.

It was Old Man Coyote who brought disorder and imperfection into the world. That's why he interested me; anyone could see that the Chihuahuan Desert was a disorderly and imperfect place, despite Kokopelli's efforts to the contrary. The seemingly impregnable limestone of the Guadalupe Escarpment was slowly crumbling and eroding away, while the open desert was a vast and trackless waste where distances invariably proved to be much longer than they appeared; virtually every plant bristled with painfully sharp thorns or prickly leaves; springs were rare and often unreliable, even in the rainy season; and the summer heat was all but unbearable.

Coyote's disorderly meddling had even spoiled the magnificent night sky that captivated me at the picnic tables, as explained in a traditional Hopi story called "Coyote Places the Stars." It seems that when the First People created stars, they gave them to a pair of cosmic deities known as the War Twins, who took them into the sky and started arranging them in an orderly fashion. Regrettably, Coyote accompanied the twins and watched as they created the perfectly formed constellations we see today. This went on for a very long time, and Coyote became increasingly impatient. Finally, he told the twins that placing the stars properly was taking too long, and he grabbed the remainder and threw them haphazardly across the sky. That night when the constellations began to appear, the First People were pleased with their beauty, but when the improperly placed stars also began to appear, they knew whom to blame: "Bad Coyote! Why did you go into the sky with the War Twins? Now most of the stars are jumbled, without any order at all." Coyote responded, "Who cares? Trying to make the night sky perfect was too much trouble. The stars are fine just as they are."

Sometimes the imperfections Coyote brought into the world make life more difficult for human beings. In a story called "Coyote Lays Down the Law," we're told that rivers were perfect in the beginning because they flowed downstream on one side and upstream on the other, so people in canoes could drift along easily in either direction, without having to paddle. Yet Coyote decided to interfere, saying, "That shouldn't be! Let the water flow only downstream, so people will have to paddle when they go upstream." Also, at one time, when women filled their baskets with heavy loads of firewood, the baskets would stand up and walk by themselves, so the women didn't have to carry the loads home. Coyote again interfered, saying, "That shouldn't be! Just let the young wives carry those loads." By challenging humans with such hardships, Coyote made the world an imperfect place, and people didn't become lazy.

After reading only a few tales about Old Man Coyote, I began to see him as a likable rogue, and I realized that he and his bumbling antics play a far different role in Native stories than does Satan in Western mythology. In most ways, the two are complete opposites: Coyote emerged from the underworld as a part of nature's creative spirit, while Satan was cast into the underworld as an embodiment of the most destructive aspects of human nature. Coyote is a benefactor who teaches human beings the skills they need to survive, while Satan is the sworn enemy of humans and engineers their downfall. Coyote shapes the world through his laziness, meddling, and trickery, while Satan is motivated by pride, hatred, and malevolence.

The most important difference, however, is that Coyote's imperfections make the world a more suitable home for human beings, who also are imperfect. Such flaws are necessary and even desirable because they complete the world and make it what it ought to be. Satan's evil, on the other hand, spoils God's perfect creation and makes the world a place of travail and torment for human beings. His evil is alien, unwanted, and subverts the natural order.

Perhaps the best summary of Coyote's motives and influence comes from a Thompson River Native who noted that "Coyote did a great deal of good, but he did not finish everything properly. Sometimes he made mistakes, and although he was wise and powerful, he did many foolish things. He was too fond of playing tricks for his own amusement."

⌐ Whenever I went hiking along the escarpment or into the higher elevations of the Guadalupe Mountains, I couldn't help feeling that life must have been difficult for the earliest inhabitants of the Chihuahuan Desert, at least by today's standards. My hikes lasted only a day or two, and afterward I could go home to my swamp cooler, water faucets, and refrigerator. The hunter-gatherers who lived along the escarpment, on the other hand, and the Mescalero Apaches who followed them, had little respite from the challenges that Old Man Coyote embedded in the desert landscape.

Just walking across those deceptively long distances could be hazardous, because every plant along the way seemed carefully designed to draw blood or induce pain. The most threatening, in my opinion, was lechuguilla, the smallest species of agave. Each of its upturned leaves ended in a slender, needle-sharp spike, and one plant could easily cripple a hiker or a horse or puncture an automobile tire. It also had the annoying habit of spreading itself densely over large areas, and I often had to pick my way through lechuguilla obstacle courses whenever I hiked cross-country. Being stabbed was extremely painful, as I discovered on several occasions, and the wounds took a surprisingly long time to heal—sometimes up to three weeks.

Another formidable adversary was catclaw, a deciduous shrub with small leaflets whose curved thorns looked and scratched like the claws of a malevolent cat. It often choked the canyons along the escarpment so thickly that it was impossible to hike through them without being scratched repeatedly. Once when Lance and I were hiking up Black Canyon wearing our usual hiking shorts, we had to force our way through an exceptionally thick swath of catclaw. Lance raised both arms over his head and kept rotating his body as he forged ahead, yet I still heard a continuous stream of "Ouch! Ouch! Ooh! Ouch!" until he reached the other side. For my part, it was one of the worst ordeals I ever experienced while hiking.

Then there was prickly pear cactus, which was especially threatening on steep or rocky slopes where it was difficult to keep a solid footing. One morning when Lance, Dave, and I were hiking to Gunsight Cave with our friend Iffy, one of the seasonal interpreters, I suddenly lost traction on a slope of loose talus and fell on my side—right on top of a small and pitifully desiccated prickly pear. When I managed to stand up, I found that one of its needles had gone into my upper leg at a shallow angle just under the skin. When I pinched the quarter-inch stub and slowly pulled it out, it was almost two inches long.

Such experiences led me to believe that thorny and spiny plants were the most inventive and pernicious of Old Man Coyote's desert challenges. I could almost hear him saying, "That shouldn't be! Let the plants grow thorns and needles, so people will be scratched and jabbed when they go hiking." I still think that's true, but in the years since my introduction to desert plants, I've come to realize that there's another, equally valid way of looking at them.

Like human beings, plants have had to adapt to the desert's harsh conditions, especially prolonged drought and the blistering heat of summer.

So they've developed small leaves, thorns, and needles to help them survive. This is because water evaporates through leaf surfaces. Plants with big leaves ordinarily won't do well in a desert, but those with very small leaves, like catclaw and other acacias, lose less water and so have a better chance of surviving. Plants that shed their leaves altogether and grow needles instead, like prickly pear and other cactus, may have an even better chance. Also, if plants are unable to give up their big leaves for some reason, those with leaf surfaces that are thick and waxy will conserve water more efficiently than their less-thick, less-waxy competitors. That's why lechuguilla and other agaves do so well in the desert.

By the time the first hunter-gatherers appeared along the Guadalupe Escarpment, desert plants had already set the example they needed to follow: let go of the old, take on the new, and develop a thick skin. In other words, adapt. It was the only way to elude the carefully set snares of Old Man Coyote.

The hunter-gatherers adapted, in part, by learning how to use those very plants for a variety of purposes. They harvested yucca, agave fibers, bear grass, and sotol to make baskets, mats, and sandals, and they gathered pine pitch and mesquite gum to render them waterproof. They also used grass for bedding and the sharp tip of the lechuguilla, with its attached fibers, as a needle and thread. Most importantly they adjusted their diet to use whatever plants were both edible and in-season. One of the other permanent interpreters occasionally gave a program in the visitor center lobby about the various plant foods used by the hunter-gatherers. I once tasted the prickly pear jelly and other items she had prepared herself. It was a bland and uninviting diet by today's standards—but then, perhaps we're just too finicky in our tastes.

The hunter-gatherers' most important plant food was the agave, also known as mescal, which grew abundantly along the escarpment. When hiking, I would often come upon one or more of the large rings of piled-up rocks, called middens, where they had roasted the nutritious mescal hearts and other plant foods. There was even a midden next to the bat flight amphitheater at the entrance to Carlsbad Cavern. In historic times, the Mescalero Apaches may also have used some of these middens; the people's name derives from the word "mescal."

The hunter-gatherers also learned how to adjust to the desert's heat and aridity. During the hottest part of the day, they found shade in small caves and rock shelters along the escarpment—one is near the park's entrance drive in Walnut Canyon—often leaving pictographs behind as evidence of their passing. Through patient exploration, they learned where the most reliable springs and pools were located, and they developed ways to carry water over long distances. (Hunter-gatherers in the Big Bend region of West Texas were known to carry water in long sections of tied-off horse intestine.) Finally, the hunter-gatherers learned how to travel safely over unstable limestone and found the best routes to follow when climbing between canyon bottoms and the top of the escarpment. Through foresight, tremendous stamina, and the kind of knowledge that can only be gained by trial and error over many generations, they slowly came to terms with the desert's most persistent challenges. In other words, they made a tenuous peace with Old Man Coyote.

⌁ Whenever park visitors hiked into the desert and had to be rescued, it was because they either forgot or didn't know about the lessons its earliest inhabitants had learned. One hot summer morning when I was working in the visitor center, a young couple asked for directions to the trailhead near the old guano-mine site. They were going to hike the five-mile trail to Whites City and then return by the same route. When I reminded them to take plenty of water, one of them held up a one-liter bottle. That wasn't nearly enough, so I took a few minutes to explain the four most basic rules for surviving in the desert:

◇ Carry plenty of water with you—at least one gallon per person, per day.
◇ Wear a hat and clothing that will protect you from the sun.
◇ Recognize your own limitations and never exceed them.
◇ Never underestimate the harshness of desert conditions.

The couple said they would get more water, but their lack of preparation was typical. Many visitors didn't realize that hiking into the desert without understanding its challenges or being adequately prepared to meet them could be dangerous at best and perhaps fatal. (I'd even guess that most of them had never heard of Old Man Coyote.) That's why I always emphasized the four basic rules; they summarized the most important lessons the desert's native inhabitants had learned in order to survive.

I took part in one search-and-rescue operation while working at Carlsbad Caverns, and it came about because a visitor didn't understand how to interact safely with the desert. One morning in March during my second year at the park, Pete informed me that a search was underway at Guadalupe Mountains National Park for a twenty-year-old woman who had disappeared the previous afternoon. Several staff members from Carlsbad Caverns were needed to help with the operation. After signing out one of the park's portable radios, I went home to get my overnight backpack, my sleeping bag, and all of my water containers. Within an hour, we were on our way to the Guadalupe Mountains visitor center.

There we learned that the woman had signed a trail register the previous afternoon, indicating that she was going to hike the Tejas Trail—"Téjas" is the Spanish name for Texas, pronounced *tay*-haas—from the bottom of Pine Canyon to the crest of the mountains. It was a long and tedious climb, even for experienced hikers. Unfortunately, search teams hadn't been able to find her along that route or on any of the park's other trails. For the rest of the day, my friend Clarence and I were part of a search team that scoured the areas north of the visitor center and between the visitor center and highway, without finding any trace of the woman.

That night our team searched the bottom of Pine Canyon with flashlights and glow sticks, using the dry wash as a baseline for our sweep. By nine o'clock we had been fighting our way through catclaw and other prickly desert plants for almost twelve hours with only a twenty-minute break, and we were dead tired. Then the command center unexpectedly recalled our team for a rest, with two exceptions: Clarence and I were to hike up the Tejas Trail and relieve the volunteer who had been monitoring the trail intersection at the crest. This was discouraging news for me, because we would have to hike almost three miles and climb more than two thousand feet to reach the intersection. I wondered if I'd have enough energy to make it that far.

It took us almost two hours to reach the summit, taking one plodding step after another. By the time we arrived at the halfway point, a bitterly cold wind was blowing and the sky had become so clear that the stars were exceptionally resplendent. I think I could have appreciated their beauty if

I hadn't been so tired. Gradually we began to hear the clatter of hooves just ahead, and then we could make out obscure figures approaching in the darkness. One of the park's packers was coming down the trail, riding a horse and leading a pack mule. Stopping briefly, he told us that he had just delivered supplies to a team of searchers who were spending the night at the Pine Top ranger cabin. As he continued down the trail, Clarence and I moved well out of the way so we wouldn't spook the animals, and the clatter gradually faded away in the darkness. Lacking experience with horses and mules, I was amazed that they could make their way down such a treacherous trail in the dark.

We arrived at the intersection just before midnight, and the volunteer was glad to see us. After he started back down the trail, we decided that Clarence would monitor the radio for three hours while I slept, and I would then take over until sunrise. However, because I was only able to sleep for about an hour, I mostly lay bundled in my sleeping bag, listening to the wind in the ponderosas and the sound of deer moving nearby, or looking up at the magnificent, starry sky. From time to time, I wondered how the lost woman was spending the night.

Shortly after sunrise, another packer came up the trail with hot break-fasts for Clarence, me, and the search team at the Pine Top cabin. A little later, the command center instructed Clarence to hike to the top of Bear Canyon and monitor the trail intersection there, while I was to remain at the top of the Tejas Trail. As I listened to my radio throughout the day, it appeared that the focus of the search was shifting. Search teams in the canyon below were being reassigned to sectors south of the visitor center, in the direction of El Capitán. I even heard that a "clothing item" had been found, apparently belonging to the missing woman.

At the end of the day, the command center instructed me to return to the park-maintenance area, and I hiked down the Tejas Trail with the search team from Pine Top. When we reached the bottom, we heard over our radios that the woman had at last been found. That night, over a hot meal in the maintenance area, we learned what had happened. Instead of hiking up the Tejas Trail, as the trail register indicated, she had taken another trail that ran south from the same trailhead toward the desert slopes around the base of El Capitán. After reaching the salt basin over-look, she apparently decided to leave the trail and hike down a rugged talus slope to the highway, which she could see in the distance. It was a costly mistake. Overcome by fatigue, she spent the first night in a small cave on the talus slope and the second under a large boulder. On the third day, a motorist happened to spot her from the highway.

This was an unfortunate incident, but it provides two important lessons. First, if you say you're going to hike a certain trail, be sure to hike that trail and not another. Second, don't take what may seem to be an easy shortcut if you become fatigued. Stay on the trail, because that's the first place searchers will look for you. At the time of her rescue, the young woman was suffering from exhaustion, dehydration, and multiple bruises from several falls, but at least she had survived. Not all hikers who become lost in the desert are that lucky.

⌇ It was Old Man Coyote who brought death into the world. In a long and complex story called "Sex, Fingers and Death," three of the First People—Cottontail, Lizard, and Gray Squirrel—create human beings, who multiply rapidly because there is no death. Coyote notices the resulting overpopulation and tells the three creators, "The world is becoming crowded. People need to die when they get old, to make room for all the new people." Lizard agrees that people should die, but he insists they should also come back to life and rise from the grave. Coyote will have none of that. When the first human dies and later begins to rise from his grave, Coyote jumps on the man and pushes him back into the earth, exclaiming, "What do you think you're doing? You need to die! Get back in your grave and stay there!" When none of the other First People object, Coyote says with appropriate finality, "Now he's gone for good, and we won't see him anymore." Coyote's action brought a momentous change to the world: ever since that day, death has taken not only human beings but animals and plants at the end of their appointed time.

When I first read this story, I was struck by the difference between Coyote and Satan's motives concerning death. By tempting Eve in the Garden of Eden, Satan provoked God to ordain death as a punishment for human frailty. Coyote, on the other hand, created death as a practical solution to overpopulation. By recognizing that death is a necessary part of life, Coyote was simply giving to the earth its greatest imperfection: all of us must die.

⌒ Late one hot afternoon in August, as I emerged from Spider Cave at the end of my guided tour, I immediately noticed the sound of a helicopter. A few moments later, as the visitors and the trail ranger were climbing the ladder to join me, a US Army Blackhawk passed overhead, flying low and heading west toward Rattlesnake Canyon. Something was wrong: a helicopter wouldn't be flying over the park unless there was an emergency. What had happened?

On our way back to the visitor center, we found one of the seasonal interpreters stationed at the beginning of the scenic drive to prevent visitors from entering. I asked her what was going on, and she said a search-and-rescue operation was underway in Rattlesnake Canyon. A visitor death had been reported. That was all she knew. When we arrived at the visitor center, we learned that protection rangers at the scene were making only guarded statements, so there was no further information. We didn't learn the entire story until the next day.

Five days earlier, two young men from Massachusetts had parked their car at a trailhead on the scenic drive and hiked into Rattlesnake Canyon, where they planned to camp overnight. They carried a tent, a few camping supplies, and only three pints of water, which they had purchased that afternoon at the visitor center. The next morning, when they couldn't relocate the trail they had followed into the canyon, they began wandering up and down the dry wash, looking for a way out but finding only treacherously rocky slopes and unscalable cliffs. By morning of the fourth day, both men were seriously dehydrated and apparently in great pain. One of them, fearing a prolonged death, begged his friend to kill him with their knife, and his friend complied by stabbing him twice in the heart. When one of the park's protection rangers discovered their makeshift camp later that morning, the men were only a short distance away from the rock cairn that marked the trail they were seeking.

It was an appalling story, and some of us couldn't help questioning the men's actions. Why hadn't they taken more water with them, especially after being told about the one-gallon-per-person requirement at the visitor center? Also, why hadn't they recognized the location of the trail? It ascended the only prominent side canyon on the east side of the dry wash. Why couldn't they have just looked at the terrain around them and realized where they were? While it was true that they were unfamiliar with the park's rugged backcountry and apparently had little experience with topographic maps, that didn't change the fact that one of them had suffered a needless death. At his trial, the surviving young man would be sentenced to fifteen years in prison, which the judge reduced to two years.

I thought a lot about this incident over the following weeks, and as tragic as it was, I had to feel that the outcome wasn't surprising. The desert seldom forgives human error, and the men had made serious mistakes. Moreover, human death had been a part of the Chihuahuan Desert since the first hunter-gatherers walked across its arid terrain in search of water. They certainly hadn't learned to adapt without succumbing on occasion to the desert's most serious challenges, and the same was true of plants and animals. Every time I went hiking along the escarpment and saw the decaying remains of a strawberry cactus or the sun-bleached bones of a deer, I was reminded that death isn't a mysterious unknown in the desert. It's an ever-present reality.

One evening about a month after the incident in Rattlesnake Canyon, I was sitting on one of the picnic tables watching an exceptionally imposing thunderstorm over the higher elevations of the Guadalupe Mountains. A second storm appeared to be gathering on the southeastern horizon near the community of Orla. Because it was late September, it occurred to me that this might be Kokopelli's last chance of the season to bestow fertility on the desert's plants and animals.

Gradually I became aware that something was moving under the bench where I was resting my feet. When I looked down, I saw an animal—and froze. *Skunk!* I had been so engrossed in watching the storm that I hadn't even seen it approach, yet there it was, directly below me. Despite my surprise, I didn't feel too concerned after that first moment of recognition. The skunk had already walked right up to me, which meant it didn't see me as a threat, and if I continued to sit just as I was, without moving, I wouldn't give it any reason to see me otherwise. I was safe. It was a hog-nosed skunk, the most common of the three skunk species in the park, and I watched intently as it poked around under the bench. After sniffing and scratching the dirt for several minutes, it ambled over to a nearby trash can, sniffed and scratched again, then disappeared into the sotols and mesquite at the edge of the picnic area.

I could hardly believe it. How likely was it that a wild skunk would approach a human being that way, especially without becoming aggressive? I was lucky it hadn't sprayed me, just to prove I wasn't immune to Old Man Coyote's trickery. But the skunk was merely an emissary—a gentle reminder that the desert, in spite of its beauty and the relative bounty of its rainy season, is a dangerously imperfect place. Kokopelli may well bestow fertility, but Coyote will always have his way.

Because I didn't want to be around if the skunk decided to come back, I got up from the picnic table and headed across the parking lot toward the visitor center. The storm over the mountains was beginning to abate, and as I started down the trail into Bat Cave Draw, taking my time and enjoying the serenity of the evening, I could almost hear the faint chuckling of Old Man Coyote echoing in the distant canyons.

Places of Creation

TRADITIONAL NATIVE CULTURES of the Southwest seemed to know intuitively that caves are places of creation. Their stories tell us repeatedly how nature's creative impulse emerged from sipapu, the mythical realm below the earth's surface, as the First People or, in the story from Acoma, the daughters of Ute'tsiti, who climbed a pine tree into the upper world.

Yet subterranean creativity was a new idea for me. Because I had never been around caves or thought much about them before working at Carlsbad Caverns, it hadn't occurred to me that they might be places where nature expends a great deal of creative effort. Yet they were—as I discovered when I walked around the Big Room Trail for the first time. When I began my library research, my first goal was to learn how caves form, and I became engrossed in an amazing story. A host of cave geologists, including Carol Hill, Harvey DuChene, Victor Polyak, David and Rebecca Jagnow, and Michael Queen, became my constant study companions, guiding me through a labyrinth of unfamiliar terms and ideas. Hill's monumental *Geology of Carlsbad Cavern and Other Caves in the Guadalupe Mountains* became my fountainhead, and words like "speleothem," "helictite," and "coralloid" were soon embedded in my vocabulary. I even began discussing convection currents, ambient temperatures, and the creation of hydrogen sulfide gas with my fellow interpreters. A whole new world had opened up to me.

On my King's Palace tour, I introduced park visitors to the idea of underground creativity by briefly describing the unusual process that had created Carlsbad Cavern and more than three hundred other caves in the Guadalupe Mountains. If you're familiar with other limestone caves— Mammoth Cave in Kentucky, for example—you know they usually form when water seeps or flows into the rock along preexisting cracks, called "joints." Because limestone dissolves fairly easily, the water gradually enlarges the joints to create cave passages, some of which may eventually contain underground streams or rivers. Yet the limestone caves of the Guadalupe Mountains didn't form that way. Instead, they were created by sulfuric acid—the kind of acid found in car batteries.

The story began in Permian times, around 265 million years ago, when the open desert that now lies southeast of the escarpment was a shallow ocean and today's Guadalupe Mountains were a barrier reef growing along its shore. As the ocean gradually receded, the algae, sponges, and other small creatures that had comprised the reef were transformed into limestone. About twenty million years ago, mountain-building forces began to lift the old reef above the surrounding terrain to create the mountains we know today. Sulfuric acid came into play because the bed of the former ocean, now called the Delaware Basin, contained significant deposits of oil. Over millions of years, hydrogen sulfide gas from those deposits seeped into the mountains, where it combined with oxygenated water to form sulfuric acid. The acid then dissolved the limestone to create caves.

This method of formation has given the caves of the Guadalupe Mountains a number of distinctive characteristics, all of which can have an impact on caving trips. Most significantly they tend to have exceptionally large chambers—the Big Room of Carlsbad Cavern is the most notable example—because the sulfuric acid formed at the water table, where it could dissolve massive voids whenever the aquifer remained stationary over long periods.

Guadalupe caves also tend to have deep vertical fissures and pits— think of the Bottomless Pit in the Big Room of Carlsbad Cavern—which geologists believe were entry points for much of the hydrogen sulfide gas that produced the sulfuric acid. Because of their large chambers or deep pits, many of the caves require extremely long rappels and climbs, like the eighteen-story drop we made into Ogle Cave and the twenty-six-story drop I would make in Cave of the Madonna with Lance and several other friends. In time I would even make a thirty-story climb into an area of Carlsbad Cavern known as Chocolate High.

Another distinctive feature of Guadalupe caves is their huge deposits of gypsum, a sparkling-white mineral that forms as a by-product whenever sulfuric acid dissolves limestone. The deposits were a major reason why geologists concluded that the caves had been formed by sulfuric acid. I was already familiar with the massive gypsum blocks in the Big Room of Carlsbad Cavern, and I would find extensive gypsum deposits or formations in many of the other caves I visited, particularly Lechuguilla Cave. On almost every caving trip, I found plenty of evidence, from massive chambers to delicate gypsum crystals, that sulfuric acid can be highly creative.

How old are the caves of the Guadalupe Mountains? Geologists have found the answer to that question in a clay mineral called alunite, which is another by-product of the reaction between sulfuric acid and limestone. The age of alunite can be determined radiometrically, and careful testing has shown that the ages of Guadalupe caves decrease with their elevation. Caves in the highest elevations are the oldest, having formed about twelve million years ago, while caves in the lowest elevations—including Carlsbad Cavern—are the youngest, having formed between four and six million years ago. This means the water table has dropped almost seven-tenths of a mile over the last twelve million years, creating progressively younger caves in its descent. (It's important to remember that the decline of the water table and the lifting of the mountains occurred simultaneously.) The higher the cave, the greater its age. This rule even applies to the four horizontal levels in Carlsbad Cavern. Because the Bat Cave is the highest level, it's also the oldest, followed by the New Section, then the Big Room, and finally Lower Cave, which is the lowest and youngest level. The water table now rests several hundred feet below the Lake of the Clouds, the cave's deepest known feature.

I had already experienced the creative wonders of several lower and therefore younger caves in the Guadalupe Mountains: I had seen the White Giant formation, Crystal Spring Dome, and the scenic chambers in Carlsbad Cavern; Cactus Spring and the Medusa Room in Spider Cave; the Mushroom formation and the sparkling calcite crystals of the Christmas Tree formation in Slaughter Canyon Cave; and the massive Bicentennial Column in Ogle Cave. Now I wanted to see the wonders that existed in some of the highest and oldest caves in the mountains, to prove to myself yet again that caves are places of creation. I wanted to go caving in the High Guads.

⌁ Lance was the first person I heard using the name "High Guads" to refer to the higher elevations of the Guadalupe Mountains. Essentially the southern half of the escarpment, the High Guads included its deepest and most impressive canyons—Pine Canyon, McKittrick Canyon, Big Canyon, and Black Canyon—as well as the highest peaks and ridges in Guadalupe Mountains National Park and the Lincoln National Forest. By any standard, the High Guads were a vast and rugged wilderness, extreme in their austerity and permeated with an acute sense of isolation and loneliness. There was just something about them that made a person long for human companionship.

The ruins of the old Butterfield stage station still nestled in the mouth of Pine Canyon, an almost-forgotten reminder of the time when southeastern New Mexico was part of the frontier. The High Guads had been an important landmark on the Butterfield route during the late 1850s, when a trip by stagecoach from St. Louis to San Francisco took twenty-five days, much of it through the upper Chihuahuan Desert. The stop at Pine Springs provided only a brief rest and a change of mules before the stage began its treacherous descent into Guadalupe Pass. In 1869, almost ten years after the Butterfield route had faded into history, a detachment of US cavalry troops all but annihilated a sizable encampment of Mescalero Apaches near the Butterfield station, irrevocably ending centuries of Mescalero dominance in the area. That same year, Captain Felix McKittrick settled beneath the eastern slopes of the High Guads in the mouth of the canyon that still bears his name.

Not surprisingly, tall tales and legends had gathered around the High Guads like dark clouds before a summer storm. A few stories centered on lost gold mines, the most notorious being the mine that "Old Ben" Sublett was supposed to have found in the early 1880s, and a few people still stubbornly believed that a treasure of some sort lay hidden in the High Guads, just waiting to be discovered. My favorite stories, though, were about ghostly apparitions, like the tale of the B-24 Liberator bomber that had crashed in the High Guads during World War II. Over the years, many hikers claimed to have heard the faint sound of a propeller-driven aircraft, followed by an explosion, and a few had even reported seeing an illusive figure wearing a green flight suit near the crash site—supposedly the ghost of the only crew member whose body was never recovered. Although I took most of these stories with a grain of salt, I nonetheless saw them as an important part of the mountains' colorful history.

I experienced the High Guads for the first time shortly after my arrival at Carlsbad Caverns, when I began hiking the trails in Guadalupe Mountains National Park, one of which took me to the top of Guadalupe Peak, the highest point in Texas. The view was so incredible that I seemed to be standing, however trite it may sound, on the very top of the world. I was captivated by the contrast between the parched desert stretching below me toward El Paso and the ponderosa forest covering the peaks and canyons to the north. I loved the High Guads, in part because of the gradual transition between the tough and thorny desert plants of the lower elevations and the stately conifers, oaks, maples, and aspens of the higher elevations and peaks. In McKittrick Canyon, I couldn't get enough of seeing prickly pear cactus growing in the shade of maple trees.

Most of the caves in the High Guads were hidden in remote canyons that could only be accessed from the northwest side of the mountains, which was a long way from Carlsbad Caverns. Lance said a caving trip to the High Guads required driving halfway to the town of Carlsbad, then around the mountains' northern foothills by way of Dark Canyon Road and Highway 137. Beyond the small mountain community of Queen lay a network of rugged dirt roads that led to Guadalupe Ridge and other popular caving areas. I checked a map and found that the fire tower on Guadalupe Ridge was less than twenty miles away from the park's housing area as the crow flies, while it was a tedious seventy-mile drive by the route Lance described. Distance didn't bother me, though, if it meant reaching those caves.

⌒ One spring morning Lance and I hiked up Black Canyon with our friend Jake, one of the seasonal interpreters, to visit the entrances of two caves in the High Guads that could be reached from our side of the mountains: Frank's Cave and Vanishing River Cave. Jake was a likable fellow in his early twenties with a short, jet-black beard, a stocky build, and the odd habit of walking around with his bootlaces untied whenever he was off duty. We drove to the mouth of the canyon in Lance's pickup truck over rough dirt roads that gave us a sweeping view of the Guadalupe Escarpment. Because the open desert was cattle country, we encountered barbed-wire fences along the way and had to stop repeatedly to open gates and close them behind us. I learned that the best place to sit in the cab of a pickup truck is in the middle, because the person who sits there doesn't have to drive or get out to open and close gates. (This was before I heard the popular southwestern riddle that asks the uninitiated, "If three men are riding in the cab of a pickup truck, which one is the cowboy?")

We parked near an isolated stock-watering tank in the mouth of the canyon, where Jake and I noticed a huge opening in the cliffs just above the high talus slope. Lance said it was the entrance to Frank's Cave, our initial destination. Thinking it would be a fairly easy climb, we started up the slope, only to find that it was steeper than we had expected and that the talus was treacherously unstable. However, the view from the cave into the open desert beyond the canyon's mouth made the effort worthwhile.

The entrance was far bigger and more impressive than it had looked from down below. We estimated it to be about ten stories high—six stories higher than the Natural Entrance to Carlsbad Cavern. Because we didn't have a permit to enter, we sat on a nearby boulder to eat our lunch, where Lance broke the stillness with an uncanny statement.

"I don't like it here."

"You don't? Why not?"

"I don't know, but I feel like we shouldn't be here, and we shouldn't get too close to the cave entrance."

"For what reason?"

"I don't know, but I think we ought to leave right away when we finish eating. There's just something about the cave entrance I don't like."

"Are you sure?"

"Yeah."

I had heard him make similar statements before. I found it amusing that he was mildly superstitious about caves, given that he spent so much time in them. I didn't give him a hard time about it, though. I had plenty of idiosyncrasies myself and didn't want to provoke Lance into retaliating when they came to light—which he definitely would.

After lunch we carefully made our way back down the slope, trying not to dislodge the unstable rocks. In an especially treacherous area, Lance stepped onto a flat boulder that suddenly gave way and began carrying him down the slope like a surfboard. Jake and I could only watch as he disappeared behind a copse of scrub oaks in a cloud of dust, balancing himself upright and hooting like a cowboy. Catching up with him, we found that he had traveled about twenty yards and had enjoyed the ride. Shortly afterward our descent became even more memorable when we noticed a large bird of prey circling above the cliffs on the opposite side of the canyon. Lance's binoculars revealed that it was a golden eagle.

We had to continue up the canyon another two miles to reach Vanishing River Cave, which meant a strenuous hike with plenty of boulder hopping and many painful encounters with catclaw. We even had to free-climb a cliff that was over two stories high—something I had never done before. The cave entrance turned out to be a yawning pit in the bottom of a narrow side canyon, right against the base of a massive cliff. Jake and I noticed a deep cut in the rocks above the cave, and Lance said that whenever it rained, a waterfall formed there and tumbled into the entrance, giving the cave its name.

We sat under a nearby tree to rest and have a snack, and Lance told Jake about the cave as I finished off a granola bar and an apple. He began ominously: "Vanishing River has a pretty bad reputation. A caver was killed in it a few years ago."

"Really? What happened?"

"He was climbing out, and when he reached the steep slope at the top of the entrance drop, he clipped off the rope too soon and lost his footing."

"No way."

"He fell about ten stories back into the cave."

"Wow. I guess they recovered his body, right?"

"Yeah, and it wasn't pretty."

Unable to keep quiet any longer, I had to interrupt.

"My gosh, Lance, why did you tell us that? I'm gonna remember it every time I rappel into a vertical cave."

"Well, it's what happened."

"I know, but, geez! Now I'm gonna remember it."

"In that case, here's something else." Lance was warming to his subject. "Vanishing River's got what they call 'bad air.'"

"Bad air? What the heck is that?"

"Every time it rains, the waterfall carries a lot of dead vegetation into the cave, and it slowly decays and produces dangerous levels of carbon dioxide. If you go in, you have to be really careful or you might lose consciousness and die."

"My God," I said. "Remind me never to go into this cave."

"Some people recommend taking a lighted candle along so you can tell if the oxygen is getting low, but that seems pretty risky to me."

"Like I said, remind me never to go into this cave."

It was almost dark when we started back to Lance's truck, so we had to use our head lamps during the return hike, even after the moon rose and filled the canyon with its silvery light. I had a hard time keeping up with Lance because of his *very* long stride, but I did manage, and as we neared the canyon mouth we were far ahead of Jake. I asked Lance if he was walking at his normal pace, and he replied that if he had been alone, he would already be back at his pickup.

⌒ As much as I appreciated the hike into Black Canyon, I kept hoping Lance would invite me along on one of his caving trips to the northwest side of the High Guads. Because the trip into Ogle Cave had shown that I had the necessary caving and climbing skills, I was eager to start learning more about the mountains' deep vertical caves by visiting them in person. I had already explored several small caves near Carlsbad Cavern with Lance and other park staff members, including Chimney Cave, Helen's Cave, and Little Manhole Cave, but their entrance drops were only a few stories, insignificant compared to the twenty- and thirty-story drops in the High Guads. I also wanted to become more involved with Lance, Pete, and other serious cavers on the park staff, to strengthen our friendships and develop a greater sense of belonging. Yet it didn't seem right to hint for an invitation.

Lance was doing most of his caving then with Pete, Jake, and two of his other friends: Tracey, a young seasonal interpreter with an outgoing personality and a remarkably raucous laugh; and Beth, who was in her early thirties and a volunteer from England, where she had learned most of her caving skills. Lance and his four caving friends got along exceptionally well and always seemed to be going places and doing things together— one spring they even went on an extended road trip into Baja California— and for that reason I came to think of them as "the Gang of Five."

While waiting for a caving opportunity to come along, I continued to explore the High Guads by way of the trails in Guadalupe Mountains National Park and by hiking cross-country along some of the more prominent ridges. "Climb the mountains," John Muir had said, "and get their good tidings. Nature's peace will flow into you as sunshine flows into trees. The winds will blow their freshness into you, and the storms their energy." I took Muir at his word, and the High Guads delivered.

⟅ At about this time, I began to develop a new interpretive program for the visitor center lobby about the creative actions of water—the most obvious link between the Chihuahuan Desert and the Guadalupe caves. By explaining how water produces cave formations, I hoped to show park visitors that caves are places of creation and that their unique beauty results from the same natural processes that account for the beauty of the earth's surface.

Carol Hill's book on cave geology had impressed me with the idea that water does the same things underground that it does on the earth's surface: it seeps, drips, flows, pools, evaporates, and condenses. In the mountains and open desert, these six processes account for cloud formations, thunderstorms, rainbows, dewdrops, the shapes of limestone cliffs, the configurations of dry washes, the sizes and shapes of boulders, and the patterns of vegetation in a canyon. In caves that lie hidden within the mountains, on the other hand, they produce wonders we never see on the surface, from drapery formations to soda straws, totem poles, helictites, cave popcorn, aragonite crystals, and sparkling gypsum crusts. Identical processes, different results.

This is primarily because water moves at a much slower pace in caves than it does on the surface. Just to reach a cave in the Guadalupe

Mountains, rainwater has to seep downward for many months, mostly through joints in the rock. This gives it plenty of time to dissolve small amounts of limestone—called "calcite" in its dissolved form—as it descends. Upon reaching a cave, the water either drips from the ceiling or flows as a thin layer of moisture over the walls and other surfaces. The slowness of these actions now allows the water to deposit its calcite as stalactites, stalagmites, columns, draperies, and flowstone through a process called "degassing," in which it releases excess carbon dioxide into the air. When the water pools, it may create cave rafts, shelfstone, or cave pearls. Yet even as it drips or flows into a pool from above, it slowly seeps from the bottom of the pool to continue its journey toward the aquifer. As a rule, these changes occur so slowly that they're seldom measurable within the scope of a human lifetime, while on the earth's surface the changes caused by water occur as rapidly as the blowing of winds, the gathering of storms, and the surging of flash floods.

Evaporation and condensation also take place in caves and are linked to air circulation, which follows the same principles that govern air circulation on the surface. In my interpretive program, I emphasized the tendency for warmer air to rise and cooler air to sink. On the surface, this leads to the formation of cumulonimbus clouds and the settling of cooler air in canyon bottoms during the night. In caves it produces convection currents, like the one that forms every year in Carlsbad Cavern. During the winter months, air on the surface is usually colder and thus heavier than air in the cave, so it sinks into the natural entrances and circulates along the floor, while the warmer air of the cave is flushed out through the natural entrances, moving along the ceiling. This accounts for the column of steam that rises out of the Bat Cave during snowy weather.

Because winter air from the surface also tends to be drier than air in the cave, it promotes evaporation as it circulates and contributes to the creation of cave popcorn. The calcite accumulates on small bumps and other irregularities on the surface of the limestone, and as the bumps grow larger they begin to look like popcorn. This explains the "popcorn line" in the Big Room and several other areas of Carlsbad Cavern; the popcorn has formed only on the lower two-thirds of the wall, where the drier air has been circulating.

Condensation also affects the shapes of formations and other cave features. One of the best examples in Carlsbad Cavern is the so-called New York City Skyline near the underground lunchroom, where acidic water has condensed on the ceiling and dripped onto several immense boulders below, corroding their top surfaces into a city of miniature skyscrapers. Sculpted formations like this are known as "rillenkarren."

Through these and other examples, park visitors learned that the creative processes we find underground are the same that occur every day on the earth's surface. Because water behaves in six predictable ways and moves at a slower pace underground, caves are places of creation, and their features are as different from surface features as night is different from day.

This brings up an important difference between caves and the earth's surface that wasn't apparent in my interpretive program: caves are perpetually dark. As amazed as I was by nature's underground wonders, it was even more amazing that they had been created in absolute darkness. What sort of creative genius would make such things and then keep them hidden?

My most memorable experience with the darkness of a cave occurred during one of my Spider Cave tours. The visitors were exceptionally friendly that day, and because they had done well on the most difficult crawls, I decided to reward them with a longer-than-usual blackout. As we sat in a loose circle at Cactus Spring, I asked them to turn off their helmet lamps, while I kept my own lamp turned on and extinguished it gradually. When it finally blinked out, the darkness closed around us as softly and completely as the proverbial blanket around a newborn baby. Not a sound came from the visitors; they were as still and quiet as grubs in their cocoons, waiting expectantly for something to happen, their senses straining to detect anything familiar in our surroundings. Yet there was nothing—just absolute darkness and silence.

We sat for perhaps seven or eight minutes, and then: *kerplunk!* A drop of water hit the pool. There wasn't even an echo—just the sound of impact followed by silence. We waited breathlessly for something more, but the interminable silence continued as though nothing had happened. Five minutes passed, then six. Silence. Nature had made its statement and had nothing more to say. Yet that statement spoke volumes. The drop of water had carried an infinitesimally small amount of calcite from the ceiling into the pool, completing one brief step in a process of creation that had extended over millions of years. And there was no end in sight. Like sipapu, the cave was in a state of becoming, its darkness saturated with nature's creative spirit. What could be more astonishing than that, or more beautiful? "Descend into the earth," John Muir might have said, "and get its good tidings. Nature's peace will flow into you as water flows into clefts in the rock. The darkness will breathe its freshness into you, and the silence its energy."

⌒ One morning in mid-December, Lance came up to me in the temporary building as I was studying Carol Hill's chapter on mineralogy.

"Are you interested in going on a caving trip to the High Guads this weekend?"

"I sure am," I quickly replied. "Are you going?"

"Yeah, Pete and I are taking Jake, Beth, and Tracey into one of the caves up there. You can come along if you want."

"Hey, that would be great, Lance. I'm definitely interested."

"Okay, then," he said. "We'll leave Friday evening right after work, so get your caving pack and equipment ready the night before. We'll camp out in the High Guads Friday night and go into the cave Saturday morning, so bring along enough food and water for an all-day trip."

"Thanks, Lance. I'll definitely be ready."

It was exactly what I had been waiting for.

The High Guads

IT WAS A beautiful name: "Cave of the Madonna." I repeated it to myself as we drove along the highway through Dark Canyon in Lance and Pete's pickup trucks, heading for the dirt roads on the northwest side of the High Guads. Our destination was Guadalupe Ridge, where we were going to camp. Because the night was overcast and exceptionally cold with a chance of snow in the forecast, I wasn't looking forward to camping, but I was eager to take on the cave. Lance said we would be making two long drops—the first almost twenty-six stories and the second almost seventeen—to reach an area of the cave known as the Wine Cellar, which contained some of the finest and most imposing formations in the Guadalupe Mountains.

By the time we reached the isolated community of Queen—a US Forest Service office, a small restaurant, and several houses scattered among the junipers above Gilson Canyon—we were encountering light rain and occasional snow flurries. The canyon took its name from G. B. Gilson, a forty-three-year-old homesteader who was murdered by unknown assailants in 1883. His barely legible tombstone can still be seen near the canyon's dry wash and the crumbling remains of what was apparently his small rock home.

A few miles beyond Queen, we turned off the highway onto the first of several dirt roads that would take us into the higher elevations and suddenly found ourselves churning through a quagmire of thick mud. The next hour was a tedious and seemingly endless trial of bone-knocking jolts as our pickups lurched along muddy ruts and scraped across boulder-choked washes toward the steep climb that would take us to the top of Guadalupe Ridge.

When we finally slid to a stop in the murky darkness, the rain had stopped, but it was so cold that we decided to bed down quickly. Unloading our gear from the trucks, we crawled into our sleeping bags in a small clearing on the north side of the road. During the night—I think it was around three o'clock—we awoke to find ourselves covered with almost an inch of very wet snow. I found it difficult to fall asleep again after getting up to shake off my sleeping bag, but on the positive side it soon stopped snowing.

Morning light brought my first glimpse of the High Guads from Guadalupe Ridge. There was indeed a deserted fire tower several hundred yards back along the road, and a sweeping view toward the open desert to the southeast. Our isolation was palpable: Queen was a grueling hour's drive away, and the nearest gas station and hospital were another hour beyond that. The area confirmed my belief that the High Guads must be one of the loneliest places in the Southwest, even when you're with friends. After a hasty breakfast, we piled into Lance's pickup and drove another couple of bone-knocking miles along the crest of the ridge until Lance finally pulled over and stopped. Because the cave was located in the side of a rocky canyon, we had to hike along a secondary ridge and then down a steep limestone slope for about a mile to reach the entrance. The trail gradually became so indistinct that I had to wonder how Lance was able to find his way, but eventually we arrived at a nondescript opening in the rocks.

The cave took its name from a small formation just inside the entrance that was supposed to look like the Madonna and her sleeping child. I thought that was a stretch of the imagination; it didn't look like much of anything to me. Beyond the formation, we got down on our hands and knees and followed Lance into a low, cramped passage that made a series of confusing turns before bringing us to the first drop—an innocuous vertical joint running across the floor with a short slope leading to its edge. Despite its benign appearance, I was beginning to feel apprehensive again; at twenty-six stories, this would be my longest rappel yet and my first in complete darkness. Most of my concern centered on the weight of the rope. The drop would be eight stories longer than the drop into Ogle Cave, and I was using my "simple" again because I didn't own a "rack," a type of descender better suited for long rappels. That meant I'd have to lift the rope with both hands during the first part of the drop, which seemed intimidating.

Because Lance was training Pete to become a trip leader, they worked on the anchor together while the rest of us put on our climbing gear. With the anchor secured, Pete attached himself to the rope and went down first, followed by Lance and Beth. I had already clipped onto the rope with my safety and was waiting for Beth's cry of "Off Rope!" when I suddenly heard her screaming at the top of her lungs far below— apparently just to create an echo. When she finally touched down and shouted that she was clear, I threaded the running end into my descender and locked it in, then backed down the short slope on my knees while controlling the rope with both hands. Reaching the edge, I slowly eased over. When I felt my weight resting safely on the rope, my apprehension vanished. The running end was heavy, but not a serious problem. I was beginning to realize that most of my long rappels would follow the same pattern: I'd feel nervous and uneasy until I went over the edge, and then I'd be fine, although I usually had to keep telling myself to "trust the rope" on the way down.

I descended the narrow joint for what seemed like a long time—that part of the drop was about ten stories—using my feet to push myself away from the wall. When I finally emerged at the bottom of the joint, I was hanging freely above a massive chamber with nothing below but absolute darkness. Pete, Lance, and Beth were waiting about sixteen stories down, but because I couldn't see their helmet lamps I guessed they had turned them off. The darkness was astounding. It had been there for millions of years, waiting for just that moment. It was the darkness of the underworld, out of which the First People and daughters of Ute'tsiti had emerged in the beginning. That made it the source of nature's creative impulse. Who could say what wonders it might conceal?

⌒ At the bottom of the second drop—almost seventeen stories down a narrow chimney—the Wine Cellar sloped away from us at a steep angle. Lance said almost everyone called it the "Whine Cellar" because it took so much effort to get there. It appeared to be a large chamber with a relatively low ceiling, and I was eager to start exploring. Heading down the marked trail, we began to encounter "totem poles"—stalagmites so fantastically tall and slender that they looked like boney fingers pointing toward the upper world. We seemed to be walking through a forest of giant toothpicks. When stalagmites have no corresponding stalactites overhead—like the totem poles—it often means the water has been dripping fairly rapidly; because it stays on the ceiling for only a short time, it carries most of its calcite to the floor, where it creates stalagmites. The reverse also is true: if water drips slowly and stays on the ceiling for a relatively long time, stalactites tend to form.

When we reached the end of the trail, we found the amazing formations Lance had mentioned. An elegant ledge of thick "shelfstone" protruded from the walls all around the chamber, indicating that a large pool of water had once covered the floor; the shelfstone had formed along its edges at the waterline. Yet the pool hadn't been there initially. Many thick columns connected the floor to the ceiling, showing that the floor had been dry when they formed, and each column displayed a graceful ledge of shelfstone around its middle, at the waterline of the later pool. Imagine sticking a pencil through the center of a disc of cardboard about two inches in diameter, then holding the pencil upright with the cardboard disc positioned about a third of the way up from the bottom. That's what the columns looked like, and that's why they were called "candlestick" formations. They told an obvious story—the entire history of that part of the cave.

Why had the pool disappeared? Probably because the caves of the Guadalupe Mountains are relatively dry now, or "dormant," compared to what they were like at the end of the last Ice Age, about seven to ten thousand years ago. Because the climate then was milder and much wetter than it is today, there was more rainwater seeping into the caves, and that's when most of the formations were created. If the climate should happen to become mild again, the Guadalupe caves would become active and the pool at the bottom of the Wine Cellar might reappear.

We spent the entire day in the cave. When we finally emerged from the entrance after saying good-bye to the Madonna and her child, we discovered a bitterly cold night and a brilliant half-moon that flooded the canyon with its light. I carried one of the ropes slung over my shoulder as we hiked back to the truck, because I wanted to do my share of the work after someone else had carried it down to the cave. The view back into the canyon by moonlight was one of the loveliest I had ever seen, with pale-blue limestone cliffs and slopes rising starkly above dark cottonwood trees in the canyon bottoms. It was my first night exit from a cave, and it couldn't have been more beautiful. When we finally reached the top of the ridge, I had fallen well behind the others and was breathing heavily, but the hard climb and cold wind had been worth it.

⌒ I went on to visit a number of other caves in the High Guads over the next few years, including Black Cave, Cave of the Bell—which I helped survey for the US Forest Service—Cottonwood Cave, Gunsight Cave, Hell Below, Hidden Cave, Red Lake Cave, and Virgin Cave. The trip into Virgin was especially memorable because cave geologist Michael Queen was a member of our group. A slender middle-aged man with graying hair, he had spent a good portion of his adult life studying the Guadalupe caves and seemed to know everything there was to know about them. Interestingly, he didn't care for high climbs. Even though he had helped set up the rope for the historic first ascent into the Spirit World in Carlsbad Cavern, he had chosen not to make the climb himself.

The Virgin Cave trip was also noteworthy because we were able to see the amazing "snake dancer" helictites I had heard so much about. They really did look like dancing snakes, twisting and gyrating to a melody only they could hear. However, the most memorable part of the trip occurred at the top of the eleven-story exit climb, when I failed to recognize the spot where I should have clipped off the rope. Continuing to climb, I followed the working end into an exceptionally tight squeeze, where I became stuck. It wasn't a serious problem, because my friends were there to help me if I needed them, and after a brief struggle I was able to free myself. Nonetheless, Lance and Dave never let me forget it.

The trip into Hidden Cave disclosed a series of sinuous rimstone dams covering the floor near the four-story entrance drop, their innumerable folds creating an extravagant maze that twisted and turned in every direction. Although most were only a few inches high, the largest rose almost six feet above the floor. Such dams form when very shallow water flows slowly over a cave floor; as calcite builds up along small ridges in the limestone, it gradually creates miniature dams that impound the water, forming shallow pools.

At the beginning of a tight squeeze in a narrow side passage of Black Cave, our head lamps disclosed an eerie sight: the skeleton of a ringtail encased in flowstone. Ringtails are similar to raccoons, although they're smaller, sleeker, and lack the raccoons' distinctive black mask. The little animal had somehow wandered into the cave's dark zone and become trapped, and now its remains were perfectly preserved within a limestone crust. We had no way of knowing how long it had been there, although we certainly were curious. Animal remains have also been found in the dark zones of several other caves in the Guadalupe Mountains, including Musk Ox Cave, which contains the bones of an extinct species of ox, and even Carlsbad Cavern, where the bones of an extinct species of ground sloth were found near the bottom of the Devil's Den. Bat remains are the most common, including a flowstone-encased skeleton beside the Big Room Trail in Carlsbad Cavern, near the Top of the Cross. I often pointed it out to visitors when I was in that part of the cave.

On almost every caving trip, we came upon handsome displays of aragonite crystals, which often form instead of cave popcorn when water evaporates. Most cave geologists believe the amount of magnesium dissolved in the water, relative to the amount of calcite, determines whether popcorn or aragonite will form—although other factors also may play a role. A high proportion of magnesium apparently serves as a catalyst, bonding the molecules of calcite in a way that reproduces their needlelike shape in the long, thin aragonite crystals.

Of all the wonders I saw in the caves of the High Guads, the most unique and creative wasn't a formation at all, and it was so unobtrusive that at first I didn't even know it was there. It was tucked away in a narrow joint deep within a cave I had heard a great deal about and knew I would have to visit. Yet when I finally got there, it turned out to be my first and only negative caving experience, when the myth of Satan's Fall came back to haunt me relentlessly.

⌒ I suspected there might be a problem because of the name "Hell Below." My old nemesis. It reminded me of John Milton's underworld—a place of unmitigated evil and everlasting torment—and any cave with a name like that had to be malevolent, or at least unlucky. Robert Nymeyer and his friends had discovered as much when they found themselves trapped at the bottom of their knotted climbing rope. If their experience in Hell Below had turned into a nightmare, why couldn't ours as well? There were four of us—Lance, Dave, Ruth (one of the seasonal interpreters), and me—and we had camped overnight beside the dirt road that ran east from the fire tower along the crest of Guadalupe Ridge. Hell Below was our objective.

Ruth was a slender middle-aged woman with straight, grayish-blonde hair and plenty of caving experience. She had worked as a volunteer for the park's Cave Resources Office as well as for the US Forest Service, and she had taken part in numerous cave surveys and cave-restoration projects throughout the Guadalupe Mountains. She and Lance had already been into Hell Below several times. Dave and I, on the other hand, were making our first trip, and while Dave seemed eager to get started, I was struggling with that name. As I watched Ruth consume a huge breakfast even by Lance and Dave's standards, Hell Below's seven-story entrance drop kept preying on my mind. I had to admit I was feeling more apprehensive than usual, even though I knew it would be a simple rappel.

After securing our camping equipment in Lance and Dave's pickup trucks, we began the two-mile hike to the cave entrance, with Lance and Ruth leading the way up a nearby dirt road and then along a faint trail through the ubiquitous juniper and piñon pines. On the steeper slopes, we began to come across scrub oaks and even some ponderosas. The entrance turned out to be an oppressively small opening hidden in the side of a prominent ridge, and given my apprehension I couldn't help thinking it might start belching sulfurous smoke at any moment. As Lance dialed in the lock combination and swung open the barred metal gate, my foreboding turned into a cold and relentless dread. It seemed that something very bad was going to happen in this cave.

After crouching through the low entrance, we descended a slope of loose rubble into a sinister-looking joint passage that burrowed straight into the ridge. Lance anchored our rope around a large stalagmite near the entrance and dropped the running end into a narrow vertical crevice on the left side of the passage. He then clipped on and descended about two stories to the bottom of the crevice, where a short crawl would take him to the infamous seven-story drop. There he would anchor the lower part of the rope using two metal bolts fastened permanently to the wall. (When it isn't possible to anchor a rope using cave formations and a friction wrap, a cave's administering agency may install permanent anchor bolts. This makes a less desirable anchor, however, because it requires the use of knots that place a strain on the rope.)

While Lance was working on the lower anchor, I clipped onto the rope and went down to join him. That's when things started to go bad. As I eased into the crevice, I could see that it became extremely narrow directly below me and that I would have to move farther to my right, where it opened up slightly. I didn't move far enough, though, and immediately became wedged between the walls with my legs flailing uselessly below me. For the first time in my climbing career, I began to panic, and instead of being patient and trying to free myself, I started calling to Lance for help.

"Hey, Lance, I'm stuck. I need some help."

"Don't get excited. Just relax and try to work yourself loose."

"That's not going to happen. I need some help."

"I'm busy setting up the anchor."

"Seriously, Lance, I need help."

"Doug, you can work yourself loose if you try. What if I wasn't here? What would you do then?"

"I need help, Lance. I really do."

"I don't believe this."

Lance stopped what he was doing and crawled back along the joint until he was directly below me. Standing up, he grabbed my ankles and positioned my feet against his shoulders, giving me the leverage I needed to free myself. For the first time, I was glad he had long legs.

That fiasco was only the beginning. The seven-story drop seemed so intimidating that I was afraid to clip onto the rope, and throughout the descent I felt certain I was going to lose control of my descender and suffer the fate that had engulfed Satan in Milton's epic poem.

Him the almighty power
Hurled headlong flaming from the ethereal sky
With hideous ruin and combustion down
To bottomless perdition . . .

It was a long and fearful descent, yet somehow I made it to the bottom, where I suddenly realized we had reached the spot where Nymeyer and his friends had been trapped. That thought became so unnerving as we continued into the cave that I began to panic whenever we moved precariously along the edge of a deep pit, thinking I was going to slip and fall to my death. I kept pestering Lance and Ruth about how deep the pits were. At one point, overcome by fear, I momentarily refused to go any farther. A short time later, when we had to jump across a narrow pit onto a large boulder with a treacherous slope, I couldn't bring myself to do it, and Lance had to send Dave back to help me.

Things eventually became so stressful that I was ashamed to have my friends see how frightened I was. They were patient with me and tried to joke about it, but that made everything seem even more hopeless. My worst nightmare was coming true, and I could feel the terrifying darkness of hell closing in around me.

A dungeon horrible, on all sides round
As one great furnace flamed, yet from those flames
No light, but rather darkness visible
Served only to discover sights of woe,
Regions of sorrow, doleful shades . . .

After exploring the cave for almost eleven hours, we finally started back to the surface. Yet for me, the nightmare continued. At the top of the seven-story climb, I managed to become stuck just below the anchor and couldn't pull myself over the lip for several minutes, even though it shouldn't have been difficult. All I could do was curse and flail, until I began to feel my struggle was in vain, and I was destined to remain in Hell Below forever.

Here their prison ordained
In utter darkness, and their portion set
As far removed from God and light of Heaven
As from the center thrice to the utmost pole.

I was greatly relieved when we finally emerged from the cave late that
afternoon. Yet the experience had been so disheartening that I talked with
Lance about it several days later. If I was serious about caving, I couldn't
let something like that hold me back. He reassured me that almost everyone involved in caving eventually has some kind of freak-out experience
in a cave—he had even had one himself—and he advised me not to worry
about it. It was encouraging to hear him say that. When I took part in
two other caving trips in the High Guads about a month later, each with
a challenging drop, I didn't have any problem.

This episode proved yet again that my attitude could determine the
way I experience a cave. If I expect to meet only terror and the malevolence of hell underground, that's probably what I'll find. But if I challenge
my fear and remain open to the limitless possibilities of discovery, I may
experience the type of joy that can only be found in the all-encompassing
beauty of the natural world.

⌒ And what was the creative wonder hidden in the depths of Hell
Below? It was a simple yet highly unusual result of something called
hydrostatic pressure. Because limestone is porous, it absorbs water relatively easily, like a sponge, which means the limestone in a cave may contain varying amounts of absorbed water. Like water in a sponge, which
seeps outward when the sponge is squeezed, the water contained in limestone may also seep out under certain conditions. Most commonly it
occurs when a tiny pore in the surface of the rock provides an outlet. The
weight of the water—its hydrostatic pressure—causes it to seep outward
through the pore.

This helps explain the creation of helictites, the small formations that
twist and turn as they grow, like pigs' tails or snakes. As the water seeps out,
it deposits calcite around the pore, and as more calcite accumulates it forms
a small projection with a tiny capillary tube running through its center. The
water now seeps through the capillary tube toward the helictite's growing

tip, and because gravity doesn't play a role in the helictite's creation, it's free to grow in any direction. It's a simple yet highly creative process.

However, the wonder in Hell Below wasn't a helictite. Despite my fear and reluctance, we finally arrived at the end of a long, relatively high passage deep in the cave. Cleaving the wall before us was a narrow vertical joint about two and a half feet wide, its floor a steep slope of very slippery flowstone. Ruth said the goal of our trip was hidden in the joint and that we would have to crawl up the flowstone one at a time to see it, because the joint was so narrow. Dave and I couldn't imagine what it was, and Lance and Ruth wouldn't say.

Lance crawled into the joint first, and when he came back Ruth went up. Then it was Dave's turn. A few minutes after he disappeared up the slope, Lance called after him to ask how he was doing, and Dave shouted back that he couldn't figure out how to get past a single strand of spider web stretched across his path. It was so unusual that he didn't want to break it. I was about to ask how a spider could have gotten that far into the cave's dark zone when Dave suddenly exclaimed, "Holy moly! That's unbelievable!"

When Dave emerged from the joint, I eagerly headed up the slope. After climbing about twenty yards, I came to a shallow pool of water. Because I couldn't go any farther, Dave's strand of spider web had to be nearby, so I crouched low and began bobbing my head around to scan the area with my helmet lamp. I spotted it about a foot above the floor, then did a double take. Was that what I thought it was? Slowly moving the palm of my hand through the spider web, I found it didn't break. Instead, I felt a momentary coolness against my skin. When I passed my hand through it a second time, the same thing happened.

It wasn't a strand of spider web at all. It was a microscopically thin jet of water shooting all the way across the joint from one wall to the other. Hydrostatic pressure was forcing it out of the limestone so rapidly that no helictite could form, through a pore so tiny I couldn't even see it. It was one of the most amazing things I had ever seen, and I now understood why Lance and Ruth had called it "the Squirt."

Many months earlier, after cutting away the sheath of a discarded section of climbing rope, I had discovered thousands of nylon fibers, each one no thicker than a single strand in a spider's web. Now I had found something even more amazing: a single strand of spider web that was *made of water*. Challenged by human inventiveness, nature had simply upped the ante: "You think you've topped one of my creations? All right, then, top this." And there it was, hidden in the dark zone of a cave.

In *Pilgrim at Tinker Creek*—a must-read for anyone who loves the natural world—Annie Dillard quotes a sixteenth-century alchemist who wrote of the philosopher's stone, "One finds it in the open country, in the village and in the town. It is in everything which God created. Maids throw it in the street. Children play with it." The same is true of nature's creative spirit. If we climb the mountains like John Muir, we find it in the sunshine, the trees, and the blowing winds. If we descend into the earth, we find it there as well, hidden in the darkness and silence of caves, waiting to speak to us.

Turning to Live with Animals

THE TARANTULA PADDED methodically across pebbly sand and small rocks toward the far side of a dry wash. I watched intently as its legs rose and fell in perfect sequence, like slowly moving pistons in a tiny machine, carrying the furry creature to whatever destination it had in mind. Its unassuming gait created graceful patterns of movement that repeated themselves endlessly, just as a dancer creates patterns of movement when she performs a long series of pirouettes. I had never thought of tarantulas as being creative, but this one was. Unintentionally creative, perhaps, but creative.

This simple event reminded me not only that animals can mimic human creativity but also that the Chihuahuan Desert is a place of creation—as shown by the beauty of sculpted limestone cliffs or the perfect symmetry of tiny acacia leaves. It's also a place of exploration and discovery, as I learned each time I hiked into one of the escarpment's rugged canyons or noticed pictographs near a rock shelter. It affected me emotionally and psychologically whenever I read a story about the First People or sat at the picnic tables to watch an evening thunderstorm. It had finally occurred to me that my four interpretive themes applied to the desert as well as to caves; there are links between the two other than the creative actions of water, and I was beginning to notice them.

The tarantula was a case in point: it created a link simply by being alive. Nature distributes its living creatures both below and above the earth's surface in an endless profusion of forms, sizes, and behaviors, just as it distributes water, air, light, and sound. Every desert animal has a distant relative living underground. That's one reason why I liked working at Carlsbad Caverns: I had always loved animals, and now I could see them in the darkness of caves as well as in the light of day. They surprised me, amused me, fascinated me, irritated me, and occasionally even threatened me, and I couldn't begin to imagine my life without them. Seeing an animal, especially at close range, was nature's greatest gift.

⟿ Although most of the animals I saw in caves were small and inconspicuous, cave swallows and bats were noisy, relatively large, and flew back and forth through the Natural Entrance every day from early spring through early fall—bats, of course, only in the evening and early morning hours. Yet they weren't true cave dwellers, because they spent a significant part of their lives aboveground. That's why books in the park library called them *trogloxenes*, a Greek word that means "cave visitors." The daddy longlegs of Spider Cave were also trogloxenes because they clustered only near the cave entrance and didn't spend their entire life cycle in complete darkness.

Cave crickets were fairly common in Carlsbad Cavern, and I often saw them when patrolling the trails. Although often classified as trogloxenes, those in the Big Room were so deep in the cave that they never saw the light of day. Some of the other staff members speculated that the cave's lighting system and underground lunchroom had lured the crickets much deeper into the cave than they otherwise would have gone.

True cave dwellers live their entire lives in the dark and are known as *troglobites*. Rhadine beetles are a good example; we often saw them in Sand Passage during my caving tours to the Hall of the White Giant. Similar in size, shape, and color to large red ants, they wandered in perpetual darkness, locating and eating the eggs of cave crickets, which we also saw from time to time. On one tour, we even spotted a three-inch-long centipede that had lost its coloring because it lived in total darkness. It was completely transparent and appeared to be made of spun glass. Another troglobite beetle, the species *Dermestes carnivora*, lived in the Bat Cave's massive guano pile, feeding on sickly or unlucky bat pups that happened to fall from the ceiling before they were old enough to fly. Because the pups couldn't fend off the beetles or otherwise save themselves, they regrettably were doomed to a tragic end.

Many troglobites were invisible to the naked eye, like the thousands of astonishing microbe species being studied under research permits in several of the park's caves. Some bacteria in Lechuguilla Cave were already known to be naturally resistant to antibiotics and so held great promise for medical research. Others produced chemicals that killed human cancer cells under laboratory conditions without harming normal cells. There were even microbes that oxidized magnesium and iron and apparently contributed to the corrosion of formations and other cave features. Yet they never absorbed sunlight and functioned in absolute darkness, suggesting that if life exists on other planets, it may consist of similar microbes living deep underground.

⌒ While it was always entertaining to see trogloxenes and troglobites at work and on caving trips, my favorite animals lived their entire lives aboveground. The desert had its share of crickets and microbes, but it also had deer, elk, skunks, raccoons, rattlesnakes, and eagles—large and exuberant animals that nonetheless flourished on a diet of meagerness and aridity. I could even imagine them with personalities, which added to the desert's own unique character. They were so different from the tiny creatures I saw in caves that I was almost tempted to rethink my belief that animals are a link between caves and the desert. Was a jackrabbit really connected to caves in a meaningful way?

William Bright convinced me it was. In his preface to *A Coyote Reader*, Bright tells us that when the First People emerged from the darkness of the underworld, they could change their shape at will and so were neither animal nor human but a curious blend of both—which explains why Native storytellers often refer to the mythic period as "the time when animals were people." Bright also says that after they created human beings, the First People transformed themselves into the animals we see around us today—which means, quite obviously, that animals are an important mythical link to the creative darkness of caves.

Bright's point encouraged me to learn more about traditional Native attitudes toward desert animals. I already knew about Old Man Coyote, but what other creatures figured prominently in southwestern mythology, and what ideas did they represent? As I set about this task in the library, I continued to watch for animals whenever I was outdoors, both at work and while hiking in the desert.

⌒ Lizards were among my favorite sightings. They roamed between the housing area and visitor center in great numbers. I was amazed by the intricate patterns on their necks, backs, and tails, and by the variety of their colors: bright red, emerald green, slate gray, ebony, an amazingly iridescent blue, garish yellow. I learned to identify the most common species, including collared lizards and the various whiptails, and I never tired of watching them sprint along the ground on their hind legs at amazing speeds, like professional athletes.

Scorpions were among my least favorite sightings because I usually saw them inside my apartment. About two inches long and always looking eager for a fight, they would suddenly materialize under my dining-room tablecloth, in the bathtub, in closets, in storage boxes, in the kitchen and bathroom wastebaskets, under the sofa, on walls, and in the ceiling light fixture directly over my bed. One morning I even discovered one walking brazenly down the middle of the hallway with its stinger cocked defiantly over its head and a look in its eye that said, "Get the hell out of my way!" I always captured these pint-sized intruders in a tin can and released them outside, and they definitely kept me busy; during my first summer at Carlsbad Caverns, I relocated twenty-nine of them (most summers I caught only five or six). Although their stings were far from lethal—Pete told me from experience that they were similar to bee stings—I nonetheless began checking inside my shoes before putting them on and underneath the sheets before going to bed.

If scorpions looked perpetually feisty, giant centipedes looked downright malevolent. The only redeeming thing about them was that they generally stayed outdoors; I found only one in my apartment during the six years I lived there. Yet one was enough. I happened to spot it running across the kitchen floor one afternoon: eight inches long and an inch wide with shiny, dark segments, vicious-looking antennae, and scores of orange legs undulating in unison along both sides of its body. One of the seasonal interpreters had recently been stung by a giant centipede at the Natural Entrance and been rushed to the hospital when she went into anaphylactic shock. Yikes! I didn't want one creeping around my apartment. Unfortunately, it disappeared under the stove before I had a chance to corner it, and I didn't see it again until the following morning, when I captured it on the living-room rug.

Not all animal sightings around the housing area were harrowing, of course. My good friend Craig, one of the seasonal interpreters, once pulled out the oven broiler in his dorm kitchen and discovered a nest of tiny field mice. Even I had some entertaining visitors. One night I happened to be in my bedroom with the venetian blinds pulled up—the window covered a large part of one wall down to about eighteen inches above the floor—when I decided to retrieve a book from my dining-room table. Because my apartment was built in an "L" shape, the outside of my bedroom window was visible through the dining room's sliding glass doors, which I happened to glance through as I retrieved the book. There they were: three large raccoons standing side by side on their hind legs outside my bedroom window, peering inquisitively through the screen and wondering where the human being had gone.

I shared many animal sightings with Dave, especially during our frequent trips in my Jeep along the rugged dirt roads in the northwestern foothills of the High Guads. Two were especially memorable. The first occurred early one fall, when Dave and I spent an entire day hiking up Horse Canyon from a place called Horse Well. Dave wanted to scout for signs of deer before the upcoming hunting season—we were in the Lincoln National Forest, where hunting was permitted—but regrettably, we didn't find any. However, as we came around a hairpin turn in the narrow upper canyon, we surprised a golden eagle that was standing in the middle of the dry wash about ten yards in front of us. It immediately took off, flapping its broad wings vigorously as it retreated up the canyon just a few feet above the ground. Its wingspan was enormous. I'll never forget how regal it looked at close range and how its wing tips brushed against the scrubby vegetation as it hurried away.

The second sighting occurred on a trip through upper Dark Canyon, when we stopped for lunch near the old corral at Spring Canyon Ranch. We sat within a foot of one another on the decaying skeleton of a ponderosa log that sagged pitifully under our weight, talking and joking as we ate our lunch. When we finished and stood up to leave, I noticed something at the base of the log, right between the spots where we had just been sitting. *Tarantula!* It was a big one with typical black legs and a brown, hairy torso, and throughout lunch it had been crouched within six inches of our bottoms. As you might guess, we were careful about where we sat down after that.

As engaging as these encounters were, they didn't top my list of memorable animal sightings. That position was held by two creatures that seemed to typify the desert more appropriately than any other, and whose reputations among park visitors had achieved mythic proportions, judging from the questions and comments I received every day. One of them was fairly common—Dave and I often saw them around the housing area or in Bat Cave Draw—while the other was elusive at best. I'm referring, of course, to rattlesnakes and mountain lions.

⟶ My library research informed me that snakes are the most important animals in pueblo mythology, which sees them as guardian spirits having supernatural powers, including the ability to cure illnesses. Because they move in zigzag patterns similar to lightning, they're also linked with rain and the fertility of fields, and their association with the ground gives them direct access to the underworld and its vast reservoirs of water. Following the performance of a snake ceremony, the dancers release their snakes to carry a request for rain to the waters of the underworld or, among the Hopi, to the spirits of the four directions. The snakes become communicators and mediators between the pueblo people and the spiritual forces that govern their world.

The most intriguing and powerful of all snakes is the Horned Water Serpent, who rules the waters of the underworld and replenishes the waters of the surface by sending rain and causing streams to flow. Because he's also associated with fertility, he's usually seen as a benevolent spirit who genuinely cares for people and answers their prayers for rain. Knowing his story encouraged me to think of snakes—especially rattlesnakes—as benevolent creatures with an essential role to play in the desert's ecosystem.

Three species of rattlesnake inhabited our neck of the Chihuahuan Desert: the western diamondback, the mottled rock rattlesnake, and the northern black-tail. Although western diamondbacks were the largest—over six feet long in some cases—and probably the best known, I saw very few of them, and the only time I saw a mottled rock rattlesnake was at Slaughter Canyon Cave, when my desk partner Dennis and I found one curled up on the ledge where we usually ate our lunch. It was surprisingly small, which was typical for its species, and its dull-gray color blended almost perfectly into the surrounding limestone. I did see many northern black-tails, on the other hand, and they were my favorites because of their striking pale-green color and the bold pattern of their brown-and-black markings. Their name, of course, derives from their solid-black tails. I once read in a field guide that black-tails are relatively nonaggressive, but I never felt inclined to test that observation.

Dave was a big fan of rattlesnakes and voluntarily developed an interpretive program about them, which he presented in the visitor center lobby. Whenever I had a question about rattlesnakes, I went to Dave, because he invariably had the answer. Occasionally, when someone on the park staff found a dead rattlesnake along a road outside the park, they would bring it to Dave, and if it was in fairly good condition he would remove the hide, spread it out on a board, tack it down, and tan it. I once helped him scrape the flesh off a western diamondback hide and was surprised to find it a fairly riveting project. Dave was quick to point out that the number of segments in the snake's rattle—contrary to popular belief—*doesn't* indicate the number of years it has lived, because rattlesnakes can gain or lose more than one segment each year. He also explained that rattlesnakes are known as "pit vipers" because they have a pair of heat-detecting indentations or pits between their eyes and nostrils, which allow them to detect warm-blooded prey. Most rattlesnakes feed primarily on mice, kangaroo rats, and other small mammals—although rock rattlers tend to prefer lizards—and some large western diamondbacks have even been known to swallow cottontail rabbits.

Late one afternoon, several park visitors reported seeing a rattlesnake just inside the Natural Entrance to Carlsbad Cavern, along the trail switchbacks leading from the surface into the twilight zone. After work Dave and I hiked down the trail to see if we could find it. We spotted it on a ledge between two of the switchbacks, and it was a beauty: a western diamondback we estimated to be over four feet long. It had apparently crawled into the entrance through a concealed water drain. Because it was extremely lethargic and swollen around the middle, we thought it might be sick or digesting a meal, but Dave finally concluded it had to be pregnant. We reported this diagnosis to the park's Surface Resources Office, and the next morning one of its staff members captured the snake and released it on the surface. Regrettably, we never found out if it had a successful delivery.

My closest encounter with a rattlesnake—dangerously close—occurred on a caving trip with Lance and Ryan, one of the seasonal interpreters. I had just bought a 140-foot climbing rope from Ryan and was eager to use it for the first time, so Lance suggested we visit Red Lake Cave on the northwest side of the Guadalupe Mountains near the small community of Queen. With an entrance drop of only four stories, it would be ideal for trying out my new rope.

We took Lance's pickup truck, and after making the long drive through Dark Canyon into the foothills of the High Guads, we turned off the highway onto a dirt road that Dave and I had already explored on one of our scouting trips. A short, bumpy drive through mixed juniper and piñon pines brought us to a fairly open area, where Lance pulled over and stopped. He had been to Red Lake Cave twice but couldn't remember its exact location, so we would have to scout around for the entrance, which he said was just a small opening in the ground.

We separated and began looking, and after several minutes Ryan called out that he had found something. When Lance and I joined him, he pointed to a narrow crevice in the limestone, about eighteen inches wide and five or six feet long, at the base of a large and very-gnarled juniper tree. Because the tree had insinuated its thick roots into cracks in the rock, it formed one side of the cave's entrance, with several of its lowest branches extending precariously over the void below. We anchored my rope to the thickest one, using a friction wrap.

I was the first to go down, and I had a difficult time forcing my way through the tight crevice, but within about five feet it opened up into a spacious chamber. Lance had called Red Lake a "joint cave" because it consisted of only one room that had been enlarged out of a single joint in the rock, and I could see that clearly as I swept my helmet lamp back and forth through the darkness below. The rope was hanging about two feet away from one wall, all the way down to the floor. Red Lake Cave was noteworthy for being the home of a small population of salamanders—a type of amphibian with stubby legs and a long tail—and our permit had advised us to watch out for them and not disturb them in any way. I could already see two or three lying motionless against the wall on the far side of the chamber, and I paid close attention to the floor directly below me so I wouldn't land on any others unexpectedly.

When my feet were within six inches of touching down, an angry and sickening *whirrrrr* came out of the darkness just below me. *Rattlesnake!* I immediately froze, and my heart sank. Where was it? How far away? And why hadn't I seen it when I swept my light around the floor? Moving my head lamp v-e-r-y slowly in the direction of the sound, I found myself gazing down at the bottom of the adjacent wall, and there it was: a northern black-tail stretched out full-length within two feet of the spot where my feet would have landed. All I could think was *Oh, God!*

I felt relieved that it wasn't poised to strike, but nonetheless it was within striking distance and obviously saw me as a threat. If I made a wrong move, it could easily become aggressive. The best thing to do was remain perfectly still and hope it would soon forget I was there and decide to crawl away. However, I was slowly rotating on the rope, and my boots were moving closer to the snake, prompting it to *whirrrrr* its tail furiously again. What to do?

The snake made that decision for me. Almost imperceptibly, it began to move along the bottom of the wall, apparently wanting to put some distance between us. After moving only a few inches, it stopped. Then it started again, traveling so slowly I could barely tell it was moving. If I waited long enough, it would eventually be out of striking distance. Was it safe to attempt a changeover? Perhaps if I moved slowly and quietly enough, I could start back up the rope while the snake was preoccupied with moving away. It had gone about a foot now, the muscles of its pale-green body undulating slowly in that characteristic way that seems so beautiful when viewed from a safe distance. Then Lance's voice came booming through the eerie silence: "What the hell's going on down there? What's taking you so long?"

Talk about bad timing.

"Are you off rope yet?"

If I didn't respond, he'd yell even louder, so I called out weakly, "There's a rattlesnake down here!"

Without missing a beat, Lance came back with one word: "Sweet!"—the only sympathy I was going to get. By now the snake was gradually increasing its speed and had moved a couple of feet along the base of the wall, so I decided to drop to the floor and get off rope quickly. In less than a heartbeat, I was in the middle of the chamber, shouting with relief that I was off rope. Moments later Lance came gliding down to join me, followed by Ryan.

Red Lake turned out to be a fairly engrossing cave, and we did see a number of salamanders along the walls—I think Lance counted seven—but the only thing I could think about was the rattlesnake. After several minutes, it started climbing the wall, using crevices and small ledges to push itself along, and when we left the cave it was about five feet above the floor. I wondered how it had gotten into the cave. Did it live there, like the salamanders, feeding on cave crickets and whatever small creatures happened to fall through the entrance? Or was it just a visitor, like us, who happened to be there at an inopportune time? Either way I was glad to say good-bye to it, and on later trips into caves with dark entrance drops, I tried not to be the first person down the rope.

⌐ Like most animals in pueblo mythology, mountain lions are helpers and mediators, especially during the hunt. Although earlier pueblo peoples depended mostly on agriculture, they also hunted, and the mountain lion was known to conjure game animals and make them appear where they could be taken easily. He did this by simply willing it to happen, without using spoken incantations.

Chiricahua Apaches also recognized the special nature of mountain lions, as shown by Geronimo's fascinating description of a visit to the underworld: "Once when living in San Carlos Reservation an Indian told me that while lying unconscious on the battlefield he had actually been dead, and had passed into the spirit land." The man's journey took him into a cave deep in the earth, which was guarded by a variety of creatures, including a human warrior at the entrance and two huge serpents, two grizzly bears, and two mountain lions within its narrow passages. They let the man pass when he showed no fear. According to Frederick Turner, this type of dream or vision was common among nineteenth-century Chiricahua Apaches. The special status of snakes, bears, and mountain lions is apparent.

Because of their elusiveness, I saw mountain lions as the Holy Grail of animal sightings. Solitary and nocturnal to begin with, their position at the top of the food chain also meant there were very few of them. Moreover, they tended to range over extremely large areas, especially the males, so they came and went with frustrating inconsistency. On a scale of one to ten, spotting a mountain lion was definitely a ten.

Because of his interest in mountain lions, Dennis occasionally helped with the park's population surveys by scouring the remote backcountry canyons for tracks and scat, and he often told me about his findings. He could say which areas and water sources the lions were frequenting, and occasionally he would know about their kills. Dennis explained that the local mountain lions usually hunted mule deer and often hid the carcasses by covering them with leaves or other vegetation, returning to feed on them intermittently over the course of several days or weeks. Dennis also taught me how to recognize the mountain lions' distinctive, three-lobed paw prints, but despite looking for them, I never saw any on my hikes along the escarpment.

One summer a mountain lion began stalking mule deer in the area around the Natural Entrance, and several visitors reported seeing it near the bat flight amphitheater or along the nature trail. One of the protection rangers even discovered a mule-deer kill in upper Bat Cave Draw. Because the lion was doing most of its hunting at night, the protection rangers began closing the trails near the visitor center at dusk and reopening them every morning. One evening a visitor who was attending the bat flight program unknowingly caught the lion on videotape. He was filming a small herd of mule deer on the far side of the draw, and when he looked at the tape afterward, there was the mountain lion, stalking the deer. The protection rangers who saw the tape said it was fascinating.

Lance, Dave, and I often talked about the possibility of seeing a mountain lion on one of our hikes or caving trips, if not up close then at least from a distance. Lance and I finally got lucky during our last year together at the park, and it was an experience neither of us will ever forget. We had camped overnight on a ridge above McKittrick Canyon in the High Guads, with me sleeping in my one-person tent and Lance in the back of his pickup truck with Chance, his big German shepherd. I mention this because the wind battered my tent so relentlessly during the night that I didn't get much sleep and was tired the next day. Nonetheless, everything was calm by the time we ate breakfast, and we eagerly took in the spectacular view of the canyon as the sun came up.

By midmorning we were driving back toward Carlsbad Caverns along the Rim Road, which skirted the western edge of the High Guads above Dog Canyon. We had gone only a few miles when Lance asked if I would like to visit the entrance to a nearby cave known as Robbers' Loot, which had a thirty-story entrance drop. He had rappelled into it several times and thought it was an interesting cave, and it was only a short distance from the road. I said sure, so after driving another mile or so he pulled over and stopped. We were in a beautiful area with a magnificent view across the desert to the west, toward the distinctive triangular peaks of the Cornudas Mountains. Because it was June, many of the nearby agaves were in full bloom, with multiple clusters of vibrant yellow flowers crowning their stalks, some of which were up to twenty feet tall.

After climbing the rocky embankment on the east side of the road, Chance and I followed Lance into the adjacent forest of juniper and piñon pines. Lance said he wasn't sure about the cave's exact location, but he did know the general direction and the approximate distance we had to walk. I asked where the name "Robbers' Loot" came from, and he said there was a legend that robbers had once hidden their stash of gold at the bottom of the entrance drop. On one of his previous visits, he had even found some old pickaxes at the bottom, which made him think someone might have been searching for the stolen loot—even though digging in or otherwise damaging a cave is both illegal and irresponsible.

I spotted a couple of large holes through the trees that appeared to have been dug by humans and pointed them out to Lance, but he didn't recognize them. Eventually we came to a stop, and after looking around glumly Lance said he might not be able to find the entrance after all; if it was nearby, we should have seen it already. Hiking back to his truck, we decided to try again. This time we spread out and kept some distance between us. After walking in the same direction for about five minutes,

I spotted an unmistakable depression through the trees and realized it had to be the cave entrance.

Shouting to Lance that I had found it, I grasped Chance by the collar and walked him over to take a look. The depression was about twenty-five feet across with steeply sloping sides and what appeared to be a pit at the bottom, partly concealed by a rock outcrop and scruffy vegetation. Just beyond the depression were the large holes I had seen earlier, which meant we had been within sight of the cave during our first search after all. When Lance joined us, he confirmed that the entrance, a small opening with a locked metal gate, was at the bottom of the pit, about ten or twelve feet down. He began making his way cautiously down the slope of loose sand and rock toward the drop-off, while I continued to hold Chance's collar so he wouldn't follow. When Lance reached the pit, he braced himself against the rocks and an old tree stump to gaze over the edge, and I may have asked him what he could see, although I don't remember.

Lance immediately shouted, "*Holy shit!*" and wheeled around as though to scramble up the slope. His eyes were as big as saucers, and he lurched frantically to one side, grasping at the tree stump to pull himself away from the edge. Because he had a phobia about bees, my first thought was that he must have seen one. Then a mountain lion—*a mountain lion!*—bolted out of the pit onto the spot where Lance had been standing and began charging up the slope toward me and Chance. Lance shouted, "Doug! Hold on to Chance!" and I gripped the dog's collar tightly and pulled him against me as the lion *passed within two feet of us*, bounded around the depression, and disappeared into the trees. I could have reached out and touched it.

We stood for a moment in stunned silence, hardly believing what had just happened. Lance was still clutching the tree stump, looking pale and shaken. "Oh, God!" he finally gasped, his voice trembling. "I thought it was jumping up to attack me." He then began stumbling up the slope, holding out one of his hands. "Look how I'm shaking." On reaching me he added, "That had to be *the* biggest adrenaline rush of my entire life." As it slowly sank in that we had just seen a mountain lion up close and in the wild, and as Lance came down from his adrenaline high, we began laughing raucously and slapping one another on the back.

"Hey! That was a mountain lion! We saw a mountain lion!"

Of course we had to compare our impressions of what had just happened. Lance said that when he looked over the edge of the pit, he had seen something moving in the shadows below, and at first he thought it was a raccoon. Then he decided it was a large fox, and then it hit him that he was seeing a mountain lion. That's when he panicked, thinking the lion was going to attack him. But that wasn't all. As the lion jumped onto the slope, he had felt it *brush against his leg*. Lance asked if I had been afraid, and I told him no. When I saw the lion charging past him, I realized it was trying to escape and probably felt more threatened than we did. Beyond that I marveled at its huge size—much larger than Chance's nearly one hundred pounds—along with the incredible power in its haunches and legs, and its truly magnificent tail, which appeared to be at least as long as its body and as thick as some of the nearby tree limbs. As for Chance, because he didn't react to the lion's sudden appearance or try to chase after it, I wondered if he even realized what had happened.

What was the lion doing in the pit? I suggested it might be using the cave entrance as a den, but Lance didn't think so. His guess was that it probably had been in the area during our first search, heard us coming, and decided to use the pit as a hiding place. When we came back the second time and found the depression, it felt cornered and wanted to get away. That sounded reasonable, and I had to agree.

What a stroke of luck. We had seen a mountain lion at close range and were none the worse for it. Despite the intervening years, this incident still amazes me, and it remains the most memorable animal sighting of my life. In *Pilgrim at Tinker Creek*, Annie Dillard concludes that such moments are one reason why we humans feel compelled to seek and discover the most elusive mysteries of the natural world. The news, she says, isn't that wild animals are wary but that they can be seen. I know that's true of mountain lions. And while staring into that lion's eyes didn't unlock the door to any of nature's secrets, it did confirm my belief that the natural world is abundantly mysterious and transcendent. If my wits had been about me as that magnificent tail disappeared into the junipers and piñon pines, I might even have recalled the words of Emily Dickinson:

In the name of the Bee—
And of the Butterfly—
And of the Breeze—Amen!

Mexican Free-Tails

BATS CAPTIVATED EARLY pueblo peoples as much as they amuse modern bat flight audiences. Mimbres ceramic bowls painted hundreds of years ago include whimsical images of bats and batlike creatures, some combining long, snakelike tails or birdlike beaks and feathers with bat wings, heads, and feet. My favorite shows a clearly recognizable bat wearing a raccoonlike mask. All are decorated with stylized geometric designs that give them a strangely modern look, as though they were painted by cubists born many centuries too soon.

Bats also play a relatively minor but entertaining role in pueblo mythology. A tale from Acoma describes the great battle between Miochin, the spirit of summer, and Shakak, the spirit of winter. Miochin places the bat in the forefront of his army of warm-weather animals, and the little creature uses its tough wings to brush aside the snow, sleet, and icicles that winter throws against it. Inspired by the bat's perseverance, the animals of summer rally and defeat the animals of winter.

Of all the creatures I saw at Carlsbad Caverns, bats seemed most like the First People because they were as much at home in the darkness of caves as they were on the earth's surface. That made them the most important living connection between the underworld and the world of our daily experience. Yet they weren't the only winged creatures to fly in and out of the park's largest cave. The mud nests of several thousand cave swallows clung precariously to the walls and ceiling of the twilight zone, and the swallows were constantly swooping back and forth through the Natural Entrance from early spring through early fall. Their antics were an entertaining warm-up to every bat flight, and they amused me as much as they did the visitors. I especially admired their industriousness—they never seemed to rest—and I even came to appreciate their raucous chirping and the eerie way they sometimes followed me, like avian stalkers, as I rode my bike to Whites City and back.

I often noticed that the swallows seemed to do things just for the fun of it. They would dive straight down into the Natural Entrance at tremendous speeds, seemingly intent on crashing, only to change direction at the last moment and glide effortlessly into the twilight zone. They would also gather in large flocks and circle at breakneck speed under the entrance's rock overhang, letting out a thunderous "chirp!" in unison every time they passed the back wall. I often wondered if they were counting their revolutions. When the cave swallows headed south for the winter, the Natural Entrance became a lonely place, and I always looked forward to their return every spring.

Occasionally a few visitors at bat flights mistook the birds for bats, so at the beginning of my programs I explained that they were swallows and that they would probably disappear into the twilight zone just before the bat flight began. If there were any canyon wrens near the amphitheater, I also pointed them out. However endearing the swallows' friendly chirping might be, I much preferred the canyon wrens' plaintive calls before and during my programs, because their beautifully cascading notes seemed to capture the desert's evening serenity better than any other sound.

Bat flights could be quite impressive. When the first bats appeared in the cave entrance, my audiences—as many as nine hundred people on a good night—would become quiet and attentive, gazing in wonder at the unfolding drama. The number of bats would increase gradually at first, until many thousands were swirling out of the cave in a huge, counterclockwise spiral, then taking flight in a long, undulating stream across the desert to the southeast, toward their hunting grounds in the distant agricultural fields along the Black and Pecos Rivers. Sometimes the flights would last for hours. Many visitors had never seen bats and were surprised by their small size and by the barely audible clicking sounds they made. It was quite unfortunate that bat flights drew the odor of guano and cave swallow droppings out of the cave, much to the audiences' chagrin.

Because it was impossible to predict exactly when a flight would begin, the interpretive ranger assigned to give the bat flight program would set the program's time by studying the flight times recorded on previous evenings and then making an educated guess. One afternoon I happened to be in the temporary building when one of the other interpreters came in to announce that the bats were already flying out of the cave, several hours before the program was scheduled to begin.

The Mexican free-tailed bats seen in the flights were one of sixteen bat species that roosted in the park between early spring and early fall. While the other species were less social, living in small groups or roosting individually in trees or rock crevices, the free-tails dearly loved company. Their colony in the Bat Cave numbered almost half a million—double that number during the spring and fall migrations—with as many as 350 individuals snuggling together in each square foot of cave ceiling. Some free-tailed colonies in Texas were known to be even larger than the one at Carlsbad Cavern. The one at Bracken Cave was estimated to contain at least twenty million bats: when the colony emerged from its roost every evening, it was clearly visible on local Doppler radar screens.

Two other bat species, the cave myotis and fringed myotis, also roosted in Carlsbad Cavern, near the cave's deepest known point at the Lake of the Clouds. Visitors often asked why they roosted in a spot that required them to fly almost two miles into the cave when they returned from their nightly foraging. The answer had to do with the small size of their colonies. Theoretically, the huge Mexican free-tailed colony could roost wherever it wanted, because it generated enough collective body heat to keep every bat toasty warm throughout the day, especially the nursing pups. The cave myotis and fringed myotis, on the other hand, had to be selective about where they roosted, because their collective body heat was relatively meager and dissipated easily. The best place in a cave for them to roost was at its warmest spot, which in Carlsbad Cavern happened to be the Lake of the Clouds.

Because the Mexican free-tails had been roosting in the Bat Cave for thousands of years, a tremendous accumulation of guano covered its floor, even after twenty years of guano mining. One January while the bats were at their winter ranges in central Mexico, I took part in an orientation trip into the Bat Cave with several other park staff members, so we would be able to answer visitors' questions about the bats' roosting place. The Bat Cave turned out to be much smaller than I had expected, but the amount of guano was staggering. We made our way cautiously over huge drifts of the stuff, our boots sinking deeply into the uppermost powdery layer and thick clouds of guano dust billowing around us. Even though we wore respirators over our mouths and noses, it was difficult to breathe, and I found it hard to imagine the bats living comfortably in such a place. Yet their lungs were perfectly adapted to the high levels of ammonia in the air. I also couldn't help thinking about the guano miners. Working in the Bat Cave must have been torturous and unhealthy for them. How had they fared?

〜 During the first half of my bat flight programs, I introduced Mexican free-tails to my audiences by describing their primary characteristics. Being mammals, they share a number of traits with human beings, such as having hair, being warm-blooded, giving live birth, and nursing their young with mammary glands. Like most other mammals, they're very small, with an average weight of less than an ounce and a wingspan of only eleven inches. I liked to point out to the children in my audiences that if we could stuff a Mexican free-tailed bat into an envelope, we could mail it anywhere in the United States with just one first-class postage stamp.

Mexican free-tails take their name from the fact that their short tails extend freely beyond the skin membrane stretched between their hind legs. Because they share the same skeletal structure with human beings, the bones in their wings correspond to the bones in the human arm and hand. Compared to other bat species, free-tailed wings are relatively narrow, which makes them highly efficient for long-distance flight. It may also explain why the free-tails fly out of the cave in a counterclockwise spiral: because their narrow wings provide only a moderate degree of lift, they have to gain altitude slowly over a relatively long distance—in this case, by flying in a spiral that fits the shape of the Natural Entrance.

The most amazing aspect of Mexican free-tails, of course, is their ability to echolocate, a trait they share with many other bat species. They navigate and locate their insect prey in complete darkness by emitting ultrasonic sounds through their mouths, then adjusting their direction and speed based on the echoes returning from nearby objects. The sonar technology used in submarines, which detects the echo of sound waves underwater, is very similar, although much slower. Echolocation even allows free-tails to identify the size and type of each insect they pursue. While they prefer moths, they devour other insects greedily, and pregnant or lactating females may consume more than half their weight in insect prey each night.

I once saw three Mexican free-tailed bats at close range during a program given at the park by a woman who was licensed by the state to care for injured bats that were unable to survive in the wild. She wore leather gloves while handling the bats, and when she placed them on her sweater they would scamper over her shoulders, down her arms, and across her back with their useless wings folded along their sides. To feed them, she held live worms and grubs in front of their faces with a small forceps, and the bats would grab them with their teeth and gobble them down so quickly that it seemed instantaneous.

Visitors at bat flights were always curious and asked many questions about the bats' behavior and anatomy. They occasionally wanted to know if the free-tails would fly clockwise rather than counterclockwise if Carlsbad Cavern were in the Southern Hemisphere. I had to explain that they probably wouldn't, because the direction they take seems to depend on the shape of the cave's entrance; if they flew in a clockwise direction, they would run into the cave wall. Visitors also asked "how bats go to the bathroom" when they're hanging upside down by their feet. Simple. They just change positions if they need to, so they're hanging by their thumbs or by one thumb and one foot. Children often wanted to know about bat mothers and the techniques they use to locate their pups when they return from hunting. With thousands of pups to choose from, how are they able to find their own? Studies have shown that every mother just remembers the approximate location where she left her pup on the cave ceiling, and when she returns there she identifies her own offspring by its smell and by the unique sound of its squeak.

My favorite question always came from children: "How do you tell the difference between a girl bat and a boy bat?" (I should mention here that I always repeated a visitor's question to make sure everyone in the audience heard it.)

I would respond, "How do you tell the difference between a girl bat and a boy bat? That's a great question. How old are you?"

"I'm seven."

"Seven years old. And what's your name?"

"Lisa."

"Well, Lisa, I think it's wonderful that you're interested in bats. The answer to your question is very simple. We can tell the difference between a girl bat and a boy bat in the same way we can tell the difference between a girl human being and a boy human being. So if a bat looks like you, it's a girl, and if it doesn't look like you, it's a boy. Does that make sense?"

Lisa and other children having the same question invariably responded with a single word: "Yes."

⌒ In every bat flight program, I stressed how important bats are to human beings. The Mexican free-tailed colony at Carlsbad Cavern consumed many tons of insects nightly, and the huge colony at Bracken Cave many times more. A study of free-tails in the Bat Cave had also shown that over half the insects they devour are agricultural pests known to feed on cotton and alfalfa. Moreover, some bat species in the Southwest are primary pollinators of such important plants as the saguaro cactus and the type of agave used to make tequila. Several plant species even open their flowers only at night, specifically to attract bats. In tropical regions, fruit-eating bats pollinate or spread the seeds of so many different plant species that researchers believe they're responsible for the continued existence of rain forests. The rain forests, in turn, add tremendous amounts of oxygen to our atmosphere and provide numerous products we humans need or desire.

I also emphasized in my programs that, given the importance of bats, we humans need to promote their well-being, because they're in trouble. Worldwide, both the number of bats and the number of their species appear to be declining, apparently due to loss of habitat and other pressures caused by human population growth. Even the free-tailed colony at Carlsbad Cavern may have declined during the twentieth century due to the use of the insecticide DDT in both the United States and Mexico. The bats consumed insects that had ingested the chemical, and bat mothers passed along the detrimental effects to their pups in the milk they produced. The use of DDT was banned in the United States in 1972—although it's still used in regulated amounts in some other countries today—and the size of the bat colony now seems to have stabilized.

I encouraged visitors to help bats by supporting long-term efforts to preserve them and their habitat, and by learning more about them, to help counteract the misconceptions and negative stereotypes that often work against them. Many people think bats routinely attack humans, that they're more prone to spread rabies than other forms of wildlife, and that all bats are vampires. Some people even kill bats whenever they can because they consider them to be evil and antagonistic toward humans. Nothing could be further from the truth.

⌒ Because of the bats' positive role in keeping the earth healthy, I saw every bat flight as a link between the creative impulse of the underworld and the world of the surface. The bats certainly experienced the cave as a place of creation—they gave birth in the Bat Cave and raised their pups there, after all—and I liked to imagine that when they emerged from its darkness, they were bringing that creative spirit with them into the upper world. How? By using their powers as the First People and daughters of Ute'tsiti used theirs, to promote human welfare. It seemed to me that every bat spiraling out of the Natural Entrance was a little creative agent.

The most memorable bat flight of my six years at Carlsbad Caverns illustrated this connection in a remarkable way. Dave and I were off duty that evening, so we decided to walk down the trail from the housing area with Allie, Dave's infant daughter, to evaluate the bat flight. Would it be outstanding, moderate, or disappointing? We stopped near the administration building, which was well above the level of the amphitheater, so we could look down into the Natural Entrance and see the bats spiraling out of the cave. Because thunderstorms had been moving across the region that afternoon, it was extremely windy, and the emerging bats seemed to be having difficulty flying toward the southeast.

The evening was exceptionally beautiful, with towering cloud formations covering much of the sky, and as they began to capture the light of the setting sun, the desert came to life in a profusion of vibrantly glowing colors. The rosy-pink and orange hues above the High Guads became so intense that they illuminated the entire eastern face of the mountains, transforming it from a dark silhouette into a soft-orange version of the peaks and canyons we ordinarily saw under the midday sun. Yet the most striking colors were along the southeastern horizon, where a huge thunderstorm was rapidly becoming a brightly glowing inferno of orange cumulus clouds that towered into the stratosphere. Regardless of what the bat flight looked like, the setting was spectacular.

Then something unusual happened. Like a cat playing with a mouse, the wind began to play with the column of bats as it emerged from the cave, tossing it first in one direction and then another, twisting it erratically, breaking it apart, scattering it over the amphitheater—we could hear the audience "ooh-ing" and "ah-ing" when that happened—stretching it, compressing it, and suddenly throwing it hundreds of feet into the air, where we could see the bats silhouetted against the bright orange clouds, doggedly trying to fly southeast. Eventually the wind blew the column in the direction of the visitor center, where with great effort the bats began veering toward the north and then back to the east, struggling to regain their southeastern momentum. Like a huge, transparent snake, the column slowly began to move in our direction.

Soon the bats were flying directly above our heads, dipping so low we could have reached up and tickled their furry bellies. Despite their quick movements, we could distinguish them individually and quite clearly, their little wings pumping furiously against the wind. We could almost feel their tiny hearts beating. Then the clouds shifted, and the column exploded into a firestorm of pink and orange flames as a ray of sunlight caught the bats from behind, illuminating their wing membranes and turning them into a glittering parade of stately monarch butterflies. I had never seen a more stunning transformation.

Then it ended, as suddenly as it had begun. The clouds continued to shift, and the column of bats became a transparent snake again, curling away from us and drifting slowly across the evening sky toward the southeastern horizon. Throughout the night, each little creative agent would bless the local farmers by gorging on insects, and before morning each would return individually to the Bat Cave for a well-earned rest. We watched the column until it finally disappeared in the bright orange clouds, linking the darkness of the underworld with the radiant light of heaven.

Climbing High

LIKE THE DESERT, caves have always been places of exploration and discovery. Yet they changed dramatically with the advent of nylon ropes and technical equipment, becoming far more accessible and much safer. Jim White and Robert Nymeyer could only gaze up at the Spirit World in Carlsbad Cavern and wonder what was there, while today the area has been fully explored and surveyed. Nymeyer's rescue from Hell Below was an unprecedented and dangerous undertaking, yet today's vertical cave rescues are relatively safe and efficient. In my own case, nylon ropes and technical equipment allowed me to experience three of the high points of my climbing career at Carlsbad Caverns: serving as a member of the park's technical rescue team, taking part in an orientation trip to an area of Carlsbad Cavern known as Chocolate High, and making a fifty-story rappel in Ellison's Cave in northwestern Georgia.

My work on the rescue team was especially rewarding because I was using my rope skills in a way that might help visitors who were caving in the park or in the nearby national forest. While I was never needed for a rescue operation, I benefited from the training I attended and thoroughly enjoyed the experience. It definitely improved my rope skills.

I became interested in technical rescue after Lance told me about an occurrence in Ogle Cave. He and several other members of the rescue team had been called out when word reached the visitor center that a woman had become exhausted during the long climb out of Ogle. Despite patient coaxing from the other members of her party, she couldn't make it to the surface. When the rescue team arrived at the cave, she had been hanging on rope for almost three hours.

The operation was fairly straightforward, but challenging nonetheless. The team decided to anchor a second rope next to the woman's, then drop the running end down to a broad ledge a short distance below her. Waiting on the ledge was Collin, a member of the cave-resources staff who had been leading the woman's group. Lance then rappelled down the second rope to the woman, pulled up the running end of her rope, and used it with her descender to rig a simple lowering system, after which he lowered her down to Collin. He then rappelled to the ledge, where he and Collin rigged a haul system for raising the woman to the surface. When everything was ready, the team members who remained on the surface—including Harry, the park's science technician; Jake the seasonal; and Paul, a volunteer with an extremely droll sense of humor—pulled the woman to safety. The rescue went smoothly because everyone knew what to do and worked together to achieve a successful outcome. That appealed to me.

Lance also told me about the largest and most difficult cave rescue in the park's history, which had taken place in Lechuguilla Cave in March 1991. One of the cave's most experienced explorers and surveyors, Emily Davis Mobley, broke her leg in an accident near the Western Borehole, over a mile inside the entrance and about one hundred stories below the surface. Her rescue involved more than 150 cavers and support personnel, required eight thousand feet of rope and hundreds of carabiners, and lasted almost four days.

I became a member of the technical rescue team during my second year at the park, then attended numerous training courses sponsored by the cave-resources staff over the next four years. Scores of simulated rescues allowed me to work all of the team positions. I was amazed by how the haul system made it easy to raise and lower a litter and litter attendant safely, despite the complexity of its pulleys and braking devices. It was especially rewarding to serve as an "edge-tender" because this involved coordinating the actions of the other team members as well as moving the litter safely over the edge of a drop-off. I also favored pulling on the haul team because it required both teamwork and physical stamina.

⌒ The only drawback to technical training was that it didn't include any long climbs or rappels. The longest drop I made during our simulated rescues was only eight stories. That didn't even begin to approach my twenty-six-story drop in Cave of the Madonna. Having learned to manage my fear of heights, I wanted to tackle some of the truly breathtaking climbs I had heard about, like the thirty-story climb into an area of Carlsbad Cavern known as Chocolate High. Regrettably, it wasn't likely that would happen, because areas of the cave that weren't accessible on the paved trails or on our caving tours were usually closed to visitors and staff members alike. Occasionally the Cave Resources Office issued special permits for small groups of staff members to visit restricted areas so we could talk more knowledgeably about the cave with park visitors. But because I wasn't aware that anyone had ever been given a permit for Chocolate High, I put it out of my mind.

I did go on several other orientation trips, however, including one to the Lake of the Clouds. Located almost 104 stories below the surface, it was one of the loveliest bodies of water I had ever seen: a crystal-clear drip pool about sixty feet across and twelve feet deep with emerald-green water. Its name derives from the cloudlike accretions of white calcite that cover the ceiling directly overhead.

I also went on an after-hours orientation trip into the Bottomless Pit with a dozen other staff members, to pick up trash that visitors had thrown from the Big Room Trail. While I was waiting along the trail for my turn on rope, I could see the head lamps of my coworkers as they walked around the pit, and I realized for the first time that it's possible to see the bottom from the trail. It's so dark down there that it really had looked bottomless. We spent about an hour picking up trash and putting it into plastic garbage bags, and we collected everything from coins to candy wrappers, park brochures, safety pins, baby pacifiers, earrings, banana peels, apple cores, and—this is the absolute truth—a man's white cotton briefs and a woman's nylon panties.

During another trip, I served on a four-person team that was helping to resurvey Carlsbad Cavern. The Cave Resources Office had been engaged in this project for several years and was computerizing the new data. When I took part, it looked as though the original survey of 30.9 miles had fallen significantly short of the cave's actual length. Our team surveyed 150 feet of tight passages near the entrance to the New Section, about forty stories below the surface. This was both tedious and time-consuming. Because we had to slither along on our bellies most of the time, it took almost five hours. We took turns measuring distances with a tape measure, determining the azimuth or direction of each passage with a compass, and computing the degree of slope using a piece of equipment called a clinometer. It was a good experience, and it was satisfying to realize that my effort had contributed in a small way to our knowledge of Carlsbad Cavern.

⟜ Even though I didn't expect to visit Chocolate High, I still wanted to learn more about it. Lance said it had been discovered just a few years earlier when Don Doucette, Harvey Miller, Brian Becker, and Phil Hurst—a team representing several caving organizations and working in cooperation with the park—climbed a previously unexplored crevice in a wall of the New Mexico Room, which was located near the four scenic chambers. The crevice originated behind a deep-brown stalagmite known as the Chocolate Drop, ascended to a wide vertical joint in the ceiling, then continued straight up the wall of the joint for an incredible thirty stories, to a maze of previously unknown and exceptionally beautiful passages. By any standard, the men's slow and extremely dangerous climb was an amazing achievement. They named the new area Chocolate High. Its exploration eventually added more than a mile to the known length of Carlsbad Cavern—the most significant addition since the discovery of the New Section almost thirty years earlier.

To return to the New Mexico Room, the men anchored a three-hundred-foot rope in Chocolate High and used it to descend back through the crevice. Shortly after their discovery, the Cave Resources Office decided to anchor the rope permanently, so Lance and Harry, the park's science technician, made the thirty-story climb to install anchor bolts. They began by pulling the rope out of the crevice in the wall and bringing it forward, so it would hang in front of the Chocolate Drop and go straight up the joint in the ceiling. Then they climbed the rope and placed four bolts along the joint at appropriate intervals, using a battery-powered drill and tying the rope securely to each bolt. They located the first bolt about eleven stories above the floor of the New Mexico Room, the second about nine stories above that, and the third and fourth on the opposite side of the joint, along a nearly vertical slope that led to the final anchor at the top of the climb. Lance's description of this feat amazed me so completely that I had trouble imagining what it must have been like. *Thirty stories* on one rope.

⌒ One afternoon as I was working at the visitor center information desk, Pete came over and told me that he and Lance had obtained a permit for an orientation trip to Chocolate High. They had invited Beth, the volunteer from England, to go with them, and they wanted to know if I would like to go as well. I was almost beside myself with excitement. Pete said that before going on the trip, we would have to learn a climbing maneuver called a "rebelay," which we would use at each of the four anchor bolts to transfer our climbing equipment from one segment of the rope to the next.

That evening I met my friends at the climbing area in the visitor center lobby to watch Lance demonstrate the technique. We spent the entire evening practicing, then met several times over the following weeks to practice again. A few days before the trip, Lance had each of us complete a rebelay to his satisfaction, and I have to admit that I felt apprehensive about clipping onto the rope, thinking I might suddenly forget everything I had learned. That didn't happen, though, and I performed a flawless rebelay. When Pete and Beth did the same, Lance said we were ready.

On the night of the trip, we went down in one of the elevators and followed Lance along the paved trail to the bottom of the Main Corridor. There we scrambled through a small opening that I hadn't even realized was there. Moments later we were walking across the uneven floor of the New Mexico Room toward the rope that would take us to Chocolate High. We found it just as Lance had described it, hanging in front of the Chocolate Drop, a large stalagmite shaped like a foil-wrapped chocolate kiss.

My excitement grew as we took off our packs and started putting on our harnesses. This was the climb I had been waiting for. Because we would be passing fragile drapery formations along the way, each of us had brought along a short tether so we could tie our packs to our harnesses and let them hang below us. That would keep them from bumping against the formations and possibly breaking them. After locking my D-ring, I stood for a moment looking up at the ceiling, where the rope disappeared into the darkness of the joint. It was hard to believe we'd soon be climbing thirty stories straight up and that when we reached Chocolate High we'd have to climb an additional ten stories to reach our goal, a forest of impressive helictites. When we finished climbing, we'd be more than halfway to the surface.

Lance clipped onto the rope first and began his characteristically methodical ascent. When he entered the joint, the glow of his helmet lamp grew dimmer until it finally vanished. After several minutes we heard his faint cry of "Off rope!," indicating that he had passed the first bolt. Pete and then Beth followed, leaving me to gaze at the ceiling, wondering if Lance had yet reached the top of the climb.

When Beth shouted "Off rope!," I clipped on and started up, moving at a steady pace until I reached the ceiling, where I paused to look down. Darkness. Refocusing on the rope, I continued into the joint, which I guessed was about six feet wide. At the first bolt it narrowed to four feet, which made me feel a little cramped, but I clipped onto the bolt's circular rung with my "cow's tail" safety tether, stood up in my foot loop, and began the tedious process of clipping onto the next segment of the rope. This was always the most difficult part of a rebelay for me. For some reason, I ordinarily couldn't reach that next segment without a struggle. In this case, however, I made it easily. After completing my transfer, the first bolt was behind me.

I now came to the fragile drapery formations—broad sheets of beautifully crenelated limestone that cascaded down the walls in multiple tiers, like frozen waterfalls. They were much larger and far more impressive than I had expected, and so close to the rope that I could easily see why it had been necessary to tether our packs. Even though mine was hanging safely below me, it occasionally brushed lightly against a drapery, causing the formation to hum in a low and beautifully resonant tone. It sounded as though I were climbing inside a magnificent Baroque organ filled with lingering echoes of Buxtehude or Bach.

I found the second bolt on the forward edge of a broad overhang at the widest part of the joint, where it was perhaps fifteen to twenty feet across. Beyond the bolt, the rope crossed the joint loosely and continued up the nearly vertical incline. After completing the rebelay, I had to swing from one side of the joint to the other, suspended twenty stories above the floor of the New Mexico Room. It was an invigorating sensation and without question the best part of the climb. Of course I looked down, but there was nothing to see except two hundred feet of pitch-black darkness.

Because the draperies were now behind me, I could push myself away from the wall with my feet, and I walked up the steep incline to the anchor in Chocolate High, completing the last two rebelays without any problem. I found my friends waiting just beyond the anchor, eager to tackle the ten-story climb to our final destination. We now made our way through a majestic chamber called the Chenille Basin, crossing the floor of a dry pool that reminded me of the one we had seen in Cave of the Madonna. However, the ledges of shelfstone that marked the old waterline were far above our heads and covered with glittering aragonite crystals.

After making the final climb, we found the helictite forest in a low passage, covering most of the floor. Without a doubt, it was the most amazing I had ever seen. The largest helictite was half an inch thick and twisted upward in an erratic corkscrew for about three feet. I wouldn't have believed it if I hadn't seen it with my own eyes.

⌒ An unfortunate incident occurred during the final, ten-story climb in Chocolate High. The rope went up a rugged wall at the far end of the Chenille Basin. My friends had already completed the climb and were waiting at the top. I was on rope and had climbed what I thought was about ten stories when I came to a moderately sized opening in the wall. The rope continued straight up, but I noticed that a second rope had been anchored around a large stalagmite in the center of the opening and that it trailed away into a passage on the opening's far side. For some reason, I assumed my friends were waiting in that passage. Without giving it a second thought, I pulled myself into the opening, clipped off, and shouted "Off rope!" A brief moment of silence was followed by the muffled sound of Lance's voice calling from somewhere far above me.

"Where are you?"

"I'm right here," I called back. "Where are you?"

"Are you off rope?"

"Yes. Where are you?"

"I'm up here at the top of the climb."

"Oh." I was puzzled. "I'm standing next to a rope anchored around a stalagmite."

"You weren't supposed to clip off there. The climb ends up here, where we are."

That's when the truth hit me. Instead of pulling myself into the opening, I should have continued up the wall. And there was a problem: the rope I had been climbing was now hanging several feet away from the wall, just beyond my reach. There was no way I could retrieve it safely. How could I have been so stupid? Again I heard Lance's voice.

"Stay right where you are and don't move. I'm coming down."

A few moments later, Lance pulled himself into the opening and handed me the running end of the rope with a terse "Don't let go of that." As he began a changeover, the gravity of what I had done continued to sink in. I had made the same mistake as the climber who was killed in Vanishing River Cave: I had clipped off the rope too soon, in a location where my safety was compromised. Before clipping off, I should have realized that I wouldn't be able to retrieve the rope once I had released it. It was a serious error, and one I vowed never to repeat.

When Lance finished his changeover and was about to start back up the rope, he turned and looked me in the eye. "Don't ever do that again," he stated flatly.

"Don't worry," I replied. "I won't."

And I meant it.

Ellison's Cave

MY TRIP INTO Ellison's Cave actually began with Lance's 109-story descent into Sotano de las Golondrinas in Mexico. After returning from his trip, Lance showed us the photos he had taken, including one of himself and his friend Bob, a member of the cave-resources staff, standing beside huge coils of rope near the edge of the drop. Lance was grinning broadly under a white cowboy hat while Bob looked serious, almost grim. Once they reached the bottom of the pit, there would be a grueling two-hour climb back to the surface. Photos taken at the bottom showed small trees and a carpet of lush vegetation covering the rubble-strewn floor in near-twilight conditions, with the rope trailing away into a remote circle of daylight high overhead.

After seeing the photos, Dave and I, along with our friend Iffy, naturally wanted to make the drop as well, and we often talked with Lance about making another Golondrinas trip together. The problem was that we couldn't find a time when all of us were free, so we eventually decided on a lesser goal: Fantastic Pit, one of the deepest underground free-fall drops in the United States, located in Ellison's Cave in northwestern Georgia. At fifty-nine stories, it was only half as deep as Golondrinas, but it was easier to reach and would require less travel time. Because we didn't know how to arrange a trip, we contacted an Atlanta chapter—called a "grotto"—of the National Speleological Society. One of its members, a man named Brad, volunteered to get the necessary permit. Another member named Andy, who had been into Ellison's Cave many times, would be the trip leader. Because Lance was scheduled to attend a training course in Glynco, Georgia, at the time, we decided that Dave and I would drive to northwestern Georgia and meet him that weekend at Pigeon Mountain, where Ellison's Cave was located. Regrettably, Iffy had other commitments and couldn't make it.

⌒ Dave and I arrived at the base of the mountain on Friday evening and found Andy and Brad waiting for us along with Jonathan, a college student from Atlanta, who also was making the trip. Lance arrived a short time later. We were in a beautiful rural area with thick hardwood forests covering the mountains, and small farms and a few crossroads settlements checkering the valleys. We camped next to Ellison's "resurgence," the spot where water seeped out of the mountainside after flowing through the cave. It consisted of a large pool of blue-tinted water known as the Blue Hole, which fed a shallow stream on the eastern side of the mountain. Because we were planning to get an early start the next morning, we bedded down shortly after our arrival, with Lance sleeping in the back of his pickup and Dave and I sharing my two-person tent.

The murmuring of the stream soon lulled Dave to sleep, but I lay awake thinking about the next day's rappel. Because I was recovering from a miserable cold, I lacked the enthusiasm I had felt during our climb into Chocolate High and was disheartened that my attitude could fluctuate so dramatically from one caving trip to the next. While I usually felt highly motivated, this time I was having doubts and feeling troubled. Was I attempting too much? The drop into Fantastic Pit would be twice as long as the climb to Chocolate High, and I still felt weak from my cold. Also, Dave and I would be using "racks" for the first time instead of our usual "simples," which were useless for such a long rappel. I recalled that Becky had been using a rack when she fell more than six stories during our climbing demonstration at the Natural Entrance. If I lost control of my own rack, I could plunge almost *sixty* stories to the bottom of Fantastic Pit. Maybe I shouldn't attempt it. Sometime after midnight, I finally drifted off to sleep.

We were up before sunrise and ate a quick breakfast, then started up the mile-long trail to the cave. It felt good to be hiking through a hardwood forest again, and as the sun rose over the eastern mountains, the promise of a wonderful spring day made me feel a little better, despite the early morning chill. About halfway up the mountainside, we arrived at the cave entrance, a small hole about two feet wide in the side of a rocky depression. Then: *disappointment.* A stream of ice-cold water was flowing into the entrance, something Andy and Brad had never seen before. The spring rains had apparently been very heavy in the area, causing excessive runoff.

Andy said the stream was a major setback because it would be dropping into Fantastic Pit as a waterfall. Because we hadn't brought any clothing to protect us from the danger of hypothermia, rappelling into Fantastic was now out of the question. This is because climbing or rappelling through a cold waterfall without protective clothing can lower a climber's body temperature to the point where it can't recover, resulting in death. The only safeguard is to wear waterproof or water-repellant clothing. When Lance rappelled through waterfalls in Sistema Cheve in Mexico, he wore underclothing made of polypropylene and an outer layer of water-repellant polyvinyl chloride, commonly known as PVC.

To say we were crestfallen would be an understatement. We had been planning our trip for months and had traveled many miles to reach Pigeon Mountain. Now what were we to do? Andy said there might be an alternative. Ellison's Cave had two other deep pits, known as Smokey One and Smokey Two, and they would probably be dry. He suggested we descend into Smokey One, which at 500 feet, or fifty stories, would still be a challenging drop. We agreed.

We crawled into the entrance one at a time and followed the stream along a narrow passage, crouching awkwardly beneath the low ceiling and wading ankle-deep through the cold water. After several hundred yards, the stream surged over a sheer drop-off and thundered into the darkness of a huge pit on the left side of the passage. Andy said we had reached the Warm-Up Pit and that it was about thirteen stories deep. It would be our first rappel. We anchored our rope on a dry ledge nearby, a location that would keep us out of the waterfall. The constant thundering made it difficult to hear one another. Just before Dave clipped onto the rope, he asked Lance to check his equipment for safety, and Lance found that he had neglected to lock the carabiner connecting his rack to his seat harness. Dave would tell me later that this discovery shook his confidence.

The drop that followed was my first experience with an underground waterfall, and it was absolutely fantastic. The water fell onto a sloping ledge about halfway down the pit, splashing clouds of misty spray into the air as it spilled over the edge and cascaded onto the rocks far below. I was within a few feet of the water as I descended, and as I entered the spray the beam of my helmet lamp began to reveal faint traces of a rainbow. It was more thrilling than anything I had ever done on rope. I was reluctant to touch down at the bottom of the drop.

About ten years after leaving Carlsbad Caverns, I would learn that two college students had just died in Ellison's Cave when they tried to retrieve a pack one of their party had accidentally dropped into the Warm-Up Pit. Instead of anchoring one of their ropes at the standard rigging point on the dry ledge, the first man evidently anchored it at the spot where the stream dropped into the pit and then descended through the waterfall without protective clothing. When he appeared to need help, the second man went down. Neither returned. The other members of their party called for help, and rescuers later found both men hanging in the waterfall about four stories above the floor of the pit, apparent victims of hypothermia.

Two passages continued out of the Warm-Up Pit, with the stream coursing down the one on our right, toward Fantastic Pit. We took the other passage, and after completing two short climbs on permanently anchored ropes and another rappel of about seven stories, we finally arrived at the edge of Smokey One. There my apprehension returned. I still felt wretched from my cold, and the climb up the mountain, coupled with our drop into the Warm-Up Pit, had just about worn me out. Maybe I shouldn't push myself. I certainly didn't want to discover at the bottom of Smokey One that I didn't have enough energy to climb back out.

Andy anchored our rope in a small alcove beside the drop-off, using two bolts on the underside of an overhanging ledge so the rope would hang about a foot away from the wall of the pit. He trailed the remainder of the working end to a backup bolt on the far side of the alcove. When everything was ready, Andy attached his descender and started down, leaving us hushed and expectant until we heard his faint cry of "Off-rope!" That's when the reality of the situation hit me. I told Lance and Dave that I was having second thoughts about making the drop. They advised me not to try it if I wasn't sure, so I thought about it long and hard as Brad and then Lance went down. By the time Dave started threading the rope into his rack, I had decided not to go. Better safe than sorry.

Then Dave went over the edge and began his descent, and I realized that if I didn't make the drop I'd probably never have the chance again, and I would regret it. *I had to go.* At Dave's barely audible cry that he was off rope, I resolutely clipped onto the working end with my safety. The running end was *incredibly* heavy—Jonathan helped me lift it—and when I finally eased over the lip, I found to my amazement that the extreme friction it created on my rack actually prevented me from sliding down the rope. I had to lift the running end with both hands so the resulting slack would let me slip down a few inches. Then I had to lift it again . . . and again . . . and again. It would be impossible to lose control of my rack, and I faced the prospect of having to *pull* myself down the rope. I had worried over nothing. After descending about ten feet, I noticed a small bat roosting in a crevice directly in front of me, apparently hibernating and unaware of my presence. I couldn't tell what species it was, but its dark-brown fur was covered with tiny dewdrops. Wow.

The circular pit measured about ten to fifteen yards across and went straight down like a rifle barrel into the most sinister-looking darkness I had ever seen. *Fifty stories.* As I continued downward, the wall gradually receded until I was hanging about halfway into the center of the pit. While Andy had been correct in predicting there would be no waterfall, the walls glistened with seeping water, and constant dripping had etched long vertical flutes and other fantastic shapes into the rock. Even the air was saturated with water vapor, which moved slowly upward from passages far below. Every time I moved my head, the beam of my helmet lamp sliced through the thin fog swirling around me, like a lightsaber.

With nothing to do except keep pulling myself down the rope, the rappel soon became monotonous and exhausting, and I began to imagine it might never end. Occasionally I would look up to see the rope disappearing into the darkness overhead, and from time to time a gleaming drop of water would fall through my light beam, like a tiny meteorite rocketing down to earth. When I looked down, I again saw the rope disappear, but sometimes I could see a small and very faint gleam of light far below. While it was impossible to tell how high I was, several pinpoints of light eventually appeared in the gleam, and then I could make out tiny human figures. Because the rope was becoming lighter as I descended, I now had to use my rack to regulate my speed. As the figures grew larger I began to hear faint voices. I was extremely happy when I finally landed on the floor of the pit and realized the fifty-story drop was behind me. Now all I had to do was climb back out.

When everyone was down, we spent about four hours exploring the cave around the bottom of Smokey One, even crawling on our hands and knees through flowing water in extremely low passages. We found gypsum in several areas, lying in sparkling crusts that had broken away from the walls, or growing as long, twisted flowers. (Because gypsum is a common mineral that dissolves easily in water, small to moderate amounts can be found in caves that haven't been created primarily by sulfuric acid.) As we started retracing our steps back to Smokey One, we began to notice a few bats roosting on the walls and ceiling, and occasionally we even heard the flutter of wings going by in the semidarkness. Andy said we had traveled about two-thirds of the way through the mountain, toward the cave's second entrance on its western slope.

At the bottom of Smokey One, we had to decide whether we would climb the rope simultaneously or one at a time (due to the nature of technical equipment, it's possible to have more than one person on rope when climbing, but not when descending). Lance said having more than one climber would increase the bounce. Because that didn't appeal to Dave—or to me, for that matter—Dave and I went up one at a time. The downside of our decision was that it made our wait at the bottom long and miserable. Because my clothing was damp, I had to keep moving around to stay warm, and I was thankful I wouldn't be the last person up the rope; that honor had been given to Jonathan. Before starting up, we noticed the muffled sound of a waterfall coming from Fantastic Pit, which meant Andy's prediction had been correct. The others went over to the bottom of Fantastic to take a look, but I decided to stay where I was and conserve my energy for the long climb.

When everyone returned, Andy attached himself to the rope and went up first, followed by Brad, Lance, and Dave. Because I knew the rope was going to stretch considerably—Dave's effort to become airborne had been truly comical—I sat down on the cave floor when it was my turn and kept pulling it through my croll until I finally lifted off. Then I began swinging slowly back and forth like a pendulum while bouncing gently up and down by three or four feet. The bounces continued but gradually diminished as I ascended the rope. (Dave told me later that the constant bobbing almost made him sick.) I was so exhausted that I had to climb slowly and rest for about ten seconds each time I stood up in my foot loop, and it didn't take long for the repetition to become sheer drudgery. Yet repetition was the only thing that would get me out of Smokey One, so I kept at it. Because Lance had told me that "slow and steady" would get me to the top, I kept repeating those words to myself as I moved upward, along with "relax" and "trust the rope." I must have said those words more than a hundred times before I finally reached the top.

It's impossible to describe the feeling of relief and satisfaction that surged through me as I stood next to Lance and Andy and shouted "Off rope!" to Jonathan. It had taken me a full hour to reach the top of the climb, compared to about forty-five minutes for Dave, forty minutes each for Brad and Jonathan, and an amazing twenty-five minutes each for Lance and Andy. Despite my slow time, I was pleased with my accomplishment. I had done my best and was proud to have made the rappel—truly a high point of my climbing career.

We crawled out of the cave entrance about thirteen hours after we entered and hiked down the trail to the Blue Hole under a full moon. Because Jonathan was the junior member of our group, he carried the rope slung across his shoulder. I felt much better now that we had completed the drop, and I even began to suspect that my stress and exhaustion had resulted from my apprehension about rappelling fifty stories, rather than from my cold. Several months later, when I mentioned to Lance and Dave that I had come very close to backing out of the drop into Smokey One, Lance's reply made me glad I had gone through with it. "Doug," he said, "if you hadn't gone down, we would have respected you only a little bit less."

The Joys of Friendship

MY LIBRARY RESEARCH had shown that mythology can help humans interpret the world around them, and myths had already informed me about the darkness of caves, the bounty and imperfections of the desert, and the influence animals have on our imaginations. Now I would discover that myths can characterize human relationships, particularly friendships. While I was involved in many wonderful friendships at Carlsbad Caverns, one of them unfolded in such a remarkable way that it became an essential part of my story. It shaped my adventures underground and in the desert, sustained me through difficult times, taught me a great deal about myself, and gave me immeasurable pleasure. I'm referring to the friendship I shared with Lance, Dave, and Iffy.

I met Iffy just before he joined the park staff, when he arrived at Carlsbad Caverns as a visitor and went on my caving tour to the Hall of the White Giant. He stayed close to me throughout the tour and plied me with questions about what it was like to be a park ranger and how he could get a job with the National Park Service. I told him that becoming a volunteer or seasonal ranger was a good way to start, and when we got back to the visitor center I took him to the information desk to get a volunteer application. He said that he lived in South Carolina and was traveling through the western states on an extended road trip, visiting national parks and other points of interest. The size of the cave and the excitement of the caving tour had impressed him so much that he now wanted to become a park ranger and work at Carlsbad Caverns. I liked his attitude and wished him luck.

About two months later, Iffy returned to the park as a volunteer—eventually he would become a seasonal interpreter—and moved into the seasonal dorm in the housing area, where in extended late-night conversations I found that he loved to talk, that he was always straightforward and direct, and that he had an infectious laugh. He had been born in Pakistan and had immigrated to the United States with his family at the age of twelve. "Iffy" was short for his full name, Iftikhar. His English was impeccably American, but he also spoke fluent Urdu, the predominant language of Pakistan, and passable Mandarin Chinese, because he had spent an entire year traveling in China. He also liked to cook meals with plenty of rice, chicken, lentils, spinach, and hot curry.

Iffy was an intelligent person, and I often thought his wire-rimmed glasses gave him an air of studiousness. But studious he wasn't. He hated to read and avoided books because, he told me, they didn't offer any immediate, practical benefit. His idea of an enjoyable evening was to play darts, drink beer, and talk about hunting, four-wheeling, or car engines with anyone who happened to be around. He didn't like to hike, either. He would walk long distances if it involved hunting quail or rabbits, but he never walked for pleasure, and it was impossible to persuade him to go on a day hike along the escarpment or into the High Guads, except as part of a caving trip. He spent much of his off-duty time working on his white Jeep Cherokee, which he prized above all else, or trying to figure out how he could store both his spare tire and his meager possessions in its cramped cargo space. He definitely had a knack for packing, because he liked being on the road and had taken a number of long road trips over the preceding years, like the one that brought him to Carlsbad Caverns. I often suspected he was a vagabond by nature, and while I thought of Dave as "the Hunter," I gradually came to think of Iffy as "the Wanderer."

The most intriguing thing about Iffy, however, was his Spartan outlook. He kept his life simple and his belongings pared to the bare-bones minimum—he almost rivaled Gandhi in that respect—and he never seemed to be concerned about where he might go or what he might do next. I wouldn't have called him lackadaisical, but he lived in the moment more than any other person I had ever known and was completely satisfied with his life just as it was. He also relished intentional inactivity, often sitting on the dorm couch for long periods without saying or doing anything at all, which prompted me to wonder what he might be thinking—if indeed he was thinking. He reminded me of a cartoon I had seen years earlier that showed an old bullfrog sitting on a log in a swamp; the caption underneath read, "Sometimes I just sits and thinks . . . and sometimes I just sits." Iffy was fascinating to the point of being inscrutable, and I liked him for that reason.

⌒ If I were to choose one mythical character to represent my friendship with Lance, Dave, and Iffy, it would have to be Old Man Coyote. My three friends definitely had a free-and-easy approach to things, like Coyote when he scattered the stars haphazardly across the sky, while I was endlessly fastidious, like the War Twins trying to create those perfect constellations. My friends were into cars, motorcycles, tools, guns, sports equipment, and other physical objects that were either mechanical or practical, while I loved books, abstractions, and philosophical questions. They saw life in a straightforward way and approached it directly, while I saw it as a problem to be studied and analyzed, in the misguided hope of understanding it. They went with the flow and tried to keep things simple, while I had a knack for making things complicated and difficult. They also took chances, easily accomplishing things I had never even considered doing, while I was cautious and often held back. I was the silk purse to their sow's ear, and I sometimes wondered how such an improbable friendship was possible.

Yet we thoroughly enjoyed one another's company and did everything together. I even liked our differences because they allowed me to learn new things while being physically active at the same time—two things that I enjoyed and that our friendship required. My friends definitely helped me achieve the goals I had set for myself, especially becoming an experienced caver and exploring the Chihuahuan Desert, by showing me how to do things and motivating me when I felt discouraged. Just as Coyote was a benefactor who taught humans their cultural roles and showed them how to plant crops and use fire, my friends taught me skills I wouldn't have developed otherwise.

They did this without resorting to thievery, as Coyote often did. In a story called "Coyote Steals Fire," the mythical canine travels upriver to the land where the prehuman keepers of fire jealously guard their trust. Upon arriving he finds only the children at home, because the adults have gone hunting. Coyote offers to paint the children's faces to make them beautiful, but they suspect trickery. Eventually they relent, and Coyote paints them with intricate designs. Then, while the children admire their reflections in a basin of water, Coyote places fir bark between his toes, brings it close to the fire, and creates a smoldering ember. He then runs away and carries the ember back down the river, reaching home just before human beings are created. As it turns out, Coyote's thievery ultimately benefits people.

⌒ Four-wheeling is a good example of my friends' mentoring abilities. Shortly after visiting Cave of the Madonna, I decided to trade in my Volkswagen Jetta for a high-clearance Jeep so I wouldn't have to rely on Lance or Pete when I wanted to go caving or hiking in the High Guads. Following Lance's advice, I had the dealership install skid plates to protect the oil pan and gas tank, and when I got home he came over to take a look. His verdict was that I now had enough clearance to tackle the roughest dirt roads in the area. Several days later, we drove my Jeep to the mouth of Big Canyon with Tammy, one of the seasonal interpreters, for our first overnight hike together.

Over the following months, I made several four-wheeling trips with Dave along the rugged dirt roads on the northwest side of the High Guads. Our primary purpose was to scout the canyons where Dave, his dad, and Lance were planning to go deer hunting that fall, but I also wanted to test my skills at four-wheeling. The most challenging road was a barely visible trace that descended a series of limestone steps to the bottom of Turkey Canyon. The steps varied in height from a few inches to almost a foot, and Dave gave me a continuous stream of suggestions about how to navigate each one. At an especially difficult spot, he even got out to scout ahead and find the least treacherous route. My skid plates definitely got a workout that day.

Because Iffy was an experienced four-wheeler, he gave me plenty of valuable advice. Once when we were quail hunting with Dave on the arid plains east of Carlsbad, he conducted an impromptu lesson in which he pointed out things I had been doing wrong while shifting gears. And when we were exploring some of the dirt roads near Dark Canyon, he taught me how to climb steep hills without losing traction. It was great fun, but it also proved I had a lot to learn.

It wasn't long before I decided to replace my Jeep's original tires with new all-terrain models, which were better for four-wheeling, and I asked Iffy to help me select them at the Sears store in Roswell. He made sure I got the correct size—four 235-75 tires for fifteen-inch rims—and even suggested I check with another tire dealership on the way home to see if they would give me a used 235-75 tire as a spare, in exchange for the unused spare that went with my original tires. The second dealership agreed to do it, and they mounted the used spare on my rim and balanced it for free. I wouldn't have thought about doing something like that, and I began to appreciate Iffy's practical way of thinking.

⌐ Four-wheeling exposed me to the Chihuahuan Desert in a new way, and the same was true of another activity my friends introduced me to: quail hunting. Although Coyote never hunted quail—at least to my knowledge—he frequently hunted ducks with Badger, and he hunted rabbits by making himself small and chasing them into their holes, where he killed them. In a story called "Old Man Coyote and the Buffalo," he even hunts by using trickery instead of a bow and arrows. Because he's very hungry and wants to eat buffalo meat, he challenges a herd of buffalo to a race across the prairie, knowing there's a deep ravine in their path. He places his robe over the ravine and tells the buffalo they should make the race more exciting by closing their eyes when they reach the robe. The buffalo accept this extra challenge, fall into the ravine, and are killed. Coyote then has a great feast of buffalo meat.

Like Coyote, my friends were dedicated hunters, and as quail season approached they became so excited by the prospect of hunting together that they talked about little else. After listening to their discussions of guns, ammunition, and the proper way to flush quail, and realizing I didn't share their enthusiasm, I decided they must have the proverbial hunting instinct, while I didn't. Yet I still wanted to go with them on their hunt, even though I didn't own a gun, just to see what it was like and to help them flush quail. They agreed to take me along.

The day of our first hunt finally arrived. It was a beautifully clear morning as we drove into the wide-open spaces below the escarpment and found a good spot with plenty of thick brush where quail might be hiding. Our plan was to spread out in a reasonably straight line and walk across the area, flushing quail as we went. We covered about five miles that day, but the only things we flushed were a jackrabbit and an owl. Not a very successful hunt, but at least I had taken part and learned how to flush small game.

We went on many additional quail hunts over the following years, walking between five and ten miles each time, and I looked forward to every one of them. In time I could recognize each of my friends at a distance by the way they walked and fired their guns. I could easily tell when Dave had made a kill, because he would run over and grab the fallen quail by its head, twirl it around to break its neck, and put it into the cloth bag on his belt. I also learned to tell the difference between the sound of quail taking flight and the sound of doves. Dave could perfectly imitate the sound of quail by fluttering his tongue while blowing through his pursed lips, but as often as I tried, I could never do it. At the end of one hunt, I even helped my friends clean the dozen or so quail they had bagged. Dave showed me how to peel back the skin, break off the legs and wings, and pull out the intestines and organs with my fingers—an entirely new experience for me.

⌇ Of course we also went caving together, and our trips often brought to mind a humorous story from Laguna Pueblo. While it doesn't mention caves, it's about as close as Coyote comes to being on rope. It seems that Coyote and his many cousins were watching a nearby ceremony from the top of a sheer cliff. At its conclusion, the dancers planned to enjoy a feast, which was spread out at the base of the precipice. Coyote convinced his cousins that they should form a living chain by holding one another's tails between their teeth, then lower themselves down to steal some food. They formed the chain with Coyote near the top, but as they dangled over the cliff one of them broke wind—and Coyote opened his mouth to ask, "What stinks?"

While nothing quite this tragic happened on caving trips with my three friends, they were memorable for other reasons. One trip was to Gunsight Cave, located in the rugged cliffs above Black Canyon. Because the huge entrance was about ten stories high and equally as wide, we could have walked into it, but we wanted to rappel down from the top of the overhanging cliff, a drop of about fifteen stories.

We drove into the High Guads the day before and camped near Guadalupe Ridge, intending to get an early start the next morning. Lance called our campsite "Dead Cow Camp" because the remains of a dead cow had been lying nearby when he had camped there previously with some of his other friends. The site was beautifully situated in a small grove of ponderosas near the head of Black Canyon. We had a good time trying to rig a climbing rope in one of the trees, hoping to do some practice climbing, but we had to retreat when a thunderstorm moved in from the southwest with lightning and a strong wind that began whipping the ponderosas violently back and forth. Lance stayed in our tree long enough to de-rig the rope, and when the storm finally hit we were safely inside the camper shell of Lance's pickup.

We cooked steaks for dinner that night and had a campfire under the stars, after which Lance and I crawled into our sleeping bags. Dave and Iffy stayed up until well after midnight, talking and laughing as they drank most of our beer. I suspected they would regret it the next morning. When the sun finally rose and we gathered around the tailgate of Lance's pickup for breakfast, Dave and Iffy were quiet and subdued, but they packed their gear and were ready for the hike to Gunsight Cave by the time we started down the trail. We followed the ridge above Black Canyon for almost two miles, then left the trail and hiked obliquely down the side of the canyon until we reached the top of the cliff directly above the cave.

The ensuing drop was unique because the cave was poised above a thirty-five-story slope that extended to the dry wash in the canyon bottom. Of all the rappels I made at Carlsbad Caverns, this was the most dramatic, and I felt immensely gratified and happy to be there. I was with my best friends, doing something I thoroughly enjoyed, surrounded by the incomparable beauty of the Guadalupe Mountains. How could I have asked for more?

⌒ My adventures with Lance, Dave, and Iffy showed how closely the desert and its caves are linked as places of exploration and discovery. While we approached them differently—caves required specialized skills and equipment, while the desert called only for a daypack and plenty of water—our camaraderie and sense of adventure were always the same. Also, many caving trips involved hiking several miles through the desert to reach a cave entrance. In a single trip, we might experience bright sunlight and absolute darkness, temperature fluctuations of up to fifty degrees, desolate canyons, shimmering cave pools, delicate yucca blossoms, and squiggly helictites. Our friendship was built around whatever adventures were at hand, both below and above the earth's surface.

In this we were like Old Man Coyote, who lived the ultimate life of adventure. Who else had climbed into the night sky with the War Twins, traveled to the land of the fire-keepers, and raced a herd of buffalo? In his greatest adventure, Coyote even rides a comet. Thinking himself powerful enough to withstand the comet's tremendous speed, he grabs hold and goes hurtling through space. However, parts of him begin to break off and plummet back to earth: his right leg, his left foot, his left forearm, his tail, and so on. Finally, only his right hand is still holding onto the comet, while on earth his other body parts search for one another and eventually reassemble. Coyote then admits to the Great Mystery that he was wrong to think himself powerful enough to do whatever he wanted and asks for his right hand back. I'm happy to say that none of the adventures I shared with my friends ended as unfortunately as this one: the Great Mystery says Coyote must wait until the comet returns after one hundred lifetimes.

Sharing One Soul

I OFTEN CAUGHT glimpses of Old Man Coyote in my three friends' personalities, especially his love of trickery and one-upmanship. In a particularly amusing tale, Coyote convinces Badger that they should exchange an unmentionable body part, although the trick backfires and Coyote comes up short, so to speak. Always the lecher, he schemes in another story to seduce his own daughter by making her think he's someone else. In a third, he steals water from the frog people, who have impounded all the world's water behind an earthen dam. Coyote convinces the frogs that a deer bone is actually a valuable shell and gives it to them in exchange for a drink of water. He then says that he's so thirsty he'll have to submerge the entire upper half of his body while drinking, but once he's underwater he digs a hole through the dam. The water rushes out to become the world's lakes, rivers, and streams, while Coyote delights in having tricked the frogs.

Like Coyote, my friends and I were addicted to the pleasures of one-upmanship—I'm convinced it's an inborn character trait—and we spent countless hours bantering back and forth to learn one another's weaknesses and discover new techniques of mutual harassment. We followed only two rules: (1) anything goes and (2) show no mercy. I can't overstate the importance of the resulting game in our friendship.

Because Lance always kept up his guard, it was difficult for me to give him a hard time. When an opportunity did come along, I often let it pass because I knew his revenge would be swift and brutal. I had more weaknesses than he did, and he invariably took advantage of them. When we went hiking, he sometimes gathered his shoulder-length hair into a topknot and slipped a rubber band around it to keep it from blowing into his face. It looked silly flopping around on top of his head, but I never razzed him about it; he might come back at me with the fact that I was clumsy and often stumbled when we went hiking or caving, or he might even remind me that I had fallen flat on my face the first time we hiked the trail to Lechuguilla Cave. No, it was just too risky.

While Iffy was fairly good at dodging verbal attacks, Dave was an easy target. He was notorious for wearing his lucky ball cap and the same dirty shirt every time he went hiking, hunting, or caving—his wife, Kelly, was always telling him to wash them or wear something else—so we gave him a hard time about it. And when he asked during one of his guided-tour blackouts if the visitors had any questions, a female voice had replied, "Are you available?" We gave him a hard time about that, too. Then there was the time when Marie, a motherly and very likable woman who was one of the park's cashiers, told Dave he had beautiful blue eyes. That was my personal favorite.

My own vulnerabilities, especially my frequent mental lapses, were so glaring that my friends easily exploited them. Shortly after our first trip into Lechuguilla Cave, I asked Lance to proofread the trip report I had written. When he returned it to me the next day he asked, "Why did you say we had to use a hand line when we entered the Rift? There's no hand line there."

"Yes there is. We crawled into a low passage with a rope anchored along one wall, and we used it as a hand line because there was a drop-off at the end of the passage."

"You're crazy," Lance insisted. "There's no rope at the beginning of the Rift. Take my word for it."

"Lance, I'm sure there was a rope, and we used it as a hand line. I remember it."

"Look, I've been into Lech many, many times, and I can tell you there's no rope at the beginning of the Rift. Trust me."

"Well, I'm sure there was a rope."

Over the next few days, I tried to reassure myself that there was a rope at the beginning of the Rift, but gradually I came to realize I had been thinking about Carlsbad Cavern, at the beginning of a large tunnel called Talcum Passage. *That's* where we had used the rope as a hand line. With great trepidation, I admitted my error to Lance, and for months afterward I kept hearing, "Hey, Doug, is there a rope in the Rift? Is there, Doug? Is there a rope in the Rift?"

In spite of my perpetual losing streak, I never dismissed our game as being trivial because I knew it served an important purpose. Lance had hinted at it in the underground lunchroom during my first year at the park, when he harassed me by saying, "croll, croll, croll," and later admitted he wouldn't do it if he didn't like me. As in many other friendships, the game was our way of telling one another we were friends.

⌐ I saw other traces of Old Man Coyote in my friends' personalities, including his inconsistency, practicality, and lack of concern for protocol. Lance, for instance—the most inconsistent person I had ever known—helped me appreciate life's contradictions. Whenever he put on his climbing gear or started caving, he became methodical and orderly, with every one of his movements having an obvious purpose and clearly being necessary. This enabled him to slither through tight squeezes like a reptile and move up or down ropes like a well-oiled machine. He also managed his equipment impeccably by following the very rational principle of having a place for everything and keeping everything in its place.

But did this orderly approach spill over into other areas of his life? Not by a long shot. His apartment was a disaster area, with furniture out of place, clothes lying around on the floor, books and papers cluttering every surface, and a thick layer of dust and grime covering everything. Once I even heard him tell another member of the park staff, "I could live in a rat's nest." When he came over to my apartment for movie nights, he invariably complained that it was too neat, and he often went into the kitchen to scatter the perfectly arranged magnets on my refrigerator. Sometimes he even tossed the sofa pillows onto the living room floor.

He was also a sloppy planner. I could never pin him down on a day or time for our next hike or caving trip. It was always, "Well, I don't know.

Maybe. We'll have to wait and see." He simply couldn't make a firm commitment. Beyond that he was always telling me I was in a rut and never did anything out of the ordinary, and that I needed to be more spontaneous. Whenever we took a trip in my Jeep and he sat next to me in the front passenger seat, he'd start fiddling with the dashboard controls as I backed down the driveway, turning the radio and windshield wipers on and off, opening and closing the glove compartment, flipping the turn signal lever up and down, drumming his fingers against the dashboard. Why? Because he thought I needed a little chaos in my life.

When I first met Lance, it was hard for me to appreciate his contradictions. If he was a methodical and orderly caver, why wasn't he the same kind of housekeeper and planner? It didn't make sense. Yet when I started reading stories about Old Man Coyote, I immediately realized that Lance and Coyote were kindred spirits who shared a penchant for disorder and inconsistency. Because there was no accounting for Old Man Coyote, there also was no accounting for Lance. Maybe he was unknowable, like the bats when they retreated into the dark recesses of the Bat Cave, where they didn't have to contend with the prying eyes of human beings: "We need to witness our own limits transgressed, and some life pasturing freely where we never wander." Maybe Thoreau was right.

Besides, the desert landscape was full of contradictions. One afternoon as I was hiking below El Capitán in Guadalupe Mountains National Park, I left the trail and headed cross-country toward one of my favorite dry washes. Because it hadn't rained for several months, the desert vegetation was uniformly drab and colorless—which would have been depressing if the rainy season hadn't been just around the corner. On a broad ridge above the wash, I came to a small barrel cactus, perhaps six inches tall, and stopped. Before me was one of the loveliest flowers I had ever seen, its delicate petals only partially opened to create a small goblet filled with the most exquisite pastel shades of pink, orange, and yellow. A tiny bee was bathing in the bright-yellow pollen at the flower's center, oblivious to everything except the incredible treasure it had just discovered. *Beauty and bounty in the midst of desolation.*

On another hike along the same trail, just before I reached the base of El Capitán, I passed through an area of thick brush, where something extraordinary happened. Scores of grasshoppers began popping out of the vegetation, bouncing off my legs and zinging past my shoulders in a flurry of bright-red and orange wings, like autumn leaves in the wind. Again I stopped. A praying mantis lounged in the grass beside the trail, eating the remains of a dead grasshopper. It held a detached leg like a drumstick, bringing it up to its triangular face each time it took another bite, its miniature bowling-ball eyes staring up at me as though I had interrupted both its dinner and the grasshopper's funeral. *Death in the midst of life.*

If the desert could host such profound contradictions, surely there was room in the world for a person like Lance. He was an exact copy of life itself: messy, inconsistent, and unpredictable. Much later it would even occur to me that his inconsistencies followed their own simple logic: he was methodical and orderly when he went caving because it helped him accomplish his goal of exploring caves safely. Because keeping his apartment clean and orderly didn't serve any comparable purpose, it wasn't important. That actually made sense.

⌒ Dave and Iffy showed me what it was like to approach life's challenges with Old Man Coyote's straightforwardness, although I have to admit that I often found it hard to apply what I learned to my own way of doing things. One evening when Lance was giving the bat flight program, Dave, Iffy, and I drove into the town of Carlsbad to play pool at one of the local bars. Because it was crowded, we had to wait for a pool table, and when we finally got one it was difficult to take some of our shots because the customer tables were crowded so closely around it. A man in his late twenties or early thirties was sitting at a table near one of the corner pockets, and he seemed especially irritated when we invaded his personal space. This was Barney. (I call him that because we never learned his real name.)

Because Barney wore a cowboy hat and boots, he may have been a local cowboy, and I had the feeling that he was trying to impress the women at his table. When I inadvertently bumped against him while taking a shot, he muttered a lewd and insulting remark, loudly enough for the women to hear. My usual reaction in such cases is to ignore the comment and go on about my business, and that's what I did. A short time later, when I was on the other side of the pool table, Dave asked me what Barney had said. When I told him, he glared menacingly in Barney's direction, then moved casually toward the corner of the table to take his shot.

Within seconds I had a firm grip on Barney's boot and was tugging on his leg. That's when I realized Dave and Barney were rolling around on the floor, flailing away at one another, while people around us were scrambling and knocking over chairs to get out of the way. I still have no recollection of running over to help Dave, or of grabbing Barney's ankle. Iffy was on top of Dave, trying to pull him off Barney, while the bouncer, a burly man who had been sitting at the bar, came running over, shouting, "All right, knock it off!" He and Iffy quickly pulled Dave and Barney apart.

Iffy immediately took control of the situation by announcing in a loud voice, "Okay, it's all over! We're leaving!" The bouncer glared at Dave and seemed ready to say something, but Iffy cut him off: "Hey, everything's cool. We're out of here." Then he started urging Dave toward the door. We left Barney sitting on a nearby chair, nursing his wounds. I wondered what the women at his table thought about him now. Dave looked glum as we walked across the parking lot, so Iffy told him, "Forget it, Dave. We don't need to play any more pool tonight." Then we were in Iffy's Jeep, driving away.

Dave was remorseful on the way home, lamenting that he shouldn't have gotten into a fight, because he had a family and needed to act responsibly. Iffy simply reiterated that he should forget it: it was over and done with. For my part, I was seeing Dave in an entirely new light. He had approached the situation head on by standing up to Barney, while I had backed away. He had acted on his conviction that we shouldn't give in to someone who was clearly out of line—Dave told me later that Barney had made another nasty comment—and when things got rough he had given Barney something to think about. I realized I could never do what Dave had done, but I respected him immensely for having done it. I felt the same way about Iffy. He had known exactly what to do and defused an incident that could easily have become much worse. At a critical moment, his quick thinking and decisiveness had gotten us out of the bar safely.

⌒ I respected Iffy for advising Dave to put the Barney incident behind him. I had already noticed that Iffy never let things get him down. Whenever he realized a problem had no solution, he would let go of it—just as Coyote had let go of trying to make the night sky perfect. In marked contrast, I usually took things too seriously and became upset over situations I couldn't control. This became evident late one night when Dave, Iffy, and I were driving back to the park after visiting Midland, Texas. It had been a long trip, and because I was driving I had removed my contact lenses to give my eyes a rest. This probably wasn't a good idea, because there was no moon and it was exceptionally dark. We were driving through the sand hills west of Orla, rapidly approaching a low rise, when a small herd of feral pigs suddenly appeared out of the darkness directly in front of us. I immediately hit the brakes and swerved to avoid hitting them, but I didn't react quickly enough. A couple of sickening thuds announced I had run over at least two pigs.

As we removed the carcasses from the road, I felt remorse and blamed myself for not being more alert. How could I have been so careless? For the rest of the trip, I was sullen and introspective. But not Dave and Iffy. They joked and laughed continually about what had happened, telling one another that the dead pigs had been minding their own business when a crazed human being with a blood lust had come barreling out of the darkness to brutally wipe them out. Their loud guffaws and taking the incident lightly made me feel even worse. How could they be so callous?

I did a great deal of thinking over the next few days about my friends' reaction and my own inability to let go of my feelings. Dave and Iffy could joke about what had happened because they immediately realized we couldn't do anything about it. Feeling regret or remorse was a waste of time because the damage was already done; it was better to treat the incident lightly and get over it. Yet I couldn't do that, and I thought of the truism that "life is a tragedy to those who feel and a comedy to those who think." Still, I could see the advantage in Dave and Iffy's way of thinking. While I certainly didn't want to become immune to my feelings, I did resolve to be more mindful of the times when they were clearly working against me.

The feral-pig incident also emphasized that my friends were better attuned to life's inevitable harshness, especially the prevalence of suffering and death. I had noticed this every time we went quail hunting, whenever Dave picked up a fallen quail and twirled it around to break its neck—something I had never done. He and Iffy approached both life and death in a matter-of-fact way that I found hard to emulate, and they accepted the inevitability of things I often struggled against. Once more I thought of Old Man Coyote, with his own practical approach to life and death. My three friends were like him in so many ways, and I think that's one reason why I liked them so much. They were the part of me that had been missing.

⌒ My friendship with Lance, Dave, and Iffy ultimately taught me that Aristotle was right when he defined friendship as "one soul in two or more bodies." (He actually defined it as one soul in two bodies, but I've altered his words to include all three of my friends.) One afternoon as I was browsing in the park library, I came upon a magazine with an article about a young woman who had been killed in a caving accident. She was the last person in her group to make the long climb out of a deep cave in the eastern United States, and while she was on rope a part of the cave wall had collapsed, taking her with it. When her friends realized what had happened, they went for help, but the woman was already dead by the time rescuers arrived. A photo with the article showed a young woman in her early twenties with radiant blonde hair and a lovely smile.

Later that afternoon, I mentioned the article to Dave and related the story of the accident. He immediately asked why the woman's friends hadn't rappelled down to see if they could help her. I had wondered about that myself, but the article didn't give a reason. I suggested they might not have had another rope, or perhaps they had decided it was too risky. Without hesitating Dave replied, "If it had been you or Lance or Iffy, I would have found a way. I would have gone down to help you." Even before he finished speaking, I realized that Lance, Iffy, and I would have done the same thing. That's friendship: one soul in two or more bodies.

CHAPTER NINETEEN

Lechuguilla Cave

IT WAS ALWAYS edifying to trail Lance's guided tours because he communicated his intense love of caves so effectively. Often when conducting a blackout, he would describe one of his caving adventures in Mexico or the deep caves of the Guadalupe Mountains, speaking quietly into the darkness about the magnificent or unusual things he had seen, while the visitors and I listened with rapt attention. He never failed to include a strong preservation message.

"I see caves as the ultimate form of wilderness, and not just because they tend to be relatively well-preserved compared to some places on the earth's surface. They offer a kind of solitude that's hard to find aboveground, a real alternative to the hectic pace of our day-to-day lives. That's why we have to do everything we can to keep them in a basically unspoiled condition. Limiting our impact will help maintain that wilderness character."

One of the caves Lance talked about in his blackouts had been discovered in the backcountry of Carlsbad Caverns National Park just a few years earlier and was so spectacular and unique that the National Geographic Society had already featured it in several magazine articles and a television documentary. Thought at the time to be at least 92 miles long and almost 157 stories deep—it's now known to be 138.3 miles long and more than 160 stories deep—it contained an amazing number of unique gypsum formations and other imposing features that staggered the imagination and rivaled or surpassed those of most other caves. It had already become legendary in the international caving community, and most cavers would have given anything to take part in its continuing exploration. Lance had been into it several times and knew from experience that it lived up to its reputation. He mentioned it during his tours because it perfectly illustrated his idea of underground wilderness. It was even administered as wilderness, because its entrance was located in the park's designated wilderness area. What cave was it? *Lechuguilla!*

People in the surrounding area had known about the entrance to Lechuguilla Cave since at least the first decades of the twentieth century, when it was thought to be nothing more than a ninety-foot pit in the side of a rocky, arid canyon. Beginning in 1914, miners dug bat guano from its floor and hauled it away for shipment to the citrus groves of Southern California. In 1953 a team of cavers who were surveying the pit in cooperation with the park noticed that a strong wind sometimes blew upward through rubble on the floor, indicating that another passage must lie below. In 1976 the Cave Research Foundation, again working in cooperation with the park, began a series of digs to locate the source of the wind. Ten years later, a team of dedicated cavers—Rick Bridges, Dave Allured, and Neil Backstrom—finally broke through the rubble to uncover what has become one of the greatest caves of the world, more spectacular in many ways than Carlsbad Cavern itself.

Entry into Lechuguilla Cave was limited to authorized park staff members for management purposes only, and to volunteers and scientists engaged in surveying or research projects. Visitors sometimes asked why that was the case, and I had to explain that opening Lechuguilla to the public simply wasn't feasible. For one thing, the cave's most significant features were widely scattered throughout its ninety-two miles of passages, making a trail like the one in Carlsbad Cavern impossible. Also, exposing the extremely fragile gypsum formations and other delicate features to public visitation would inevitably lead to their deterioration and, in some cases, their eventual destruction. In view of this, the park had decided to interpret Lechuguilla Cave through the hundreds of amazing color photographs that had been taken throughout its exploration.

I had seen many of the photos and agreed that they were an appropriate way to convey the beauty and grandeur of such a remarkable cave. And like everyone else, I assumed I would never experience Lechuguilla in any other way.

⌒ One morning Pete came up to me while I was eating lunch in the temporary building and asked if I was interested in going on a one-day orientation trip into Lechuguilla Cave. *Was I? Absolutely!* He felt it was important for qualified park interpreters to make the trip, because it would allow us to talk more knowledgeably with visitors about one of the park's most important resources while also broadening our perspective on caves and caving. He had already asked the park's Cave Resources Office to approve an orientation trip to a chamber called the Chandelier Ballroom, which contained Lechuguilla's most spectacular and famous gypsum formations.

I could hardly believe my good fortune, or conceal my excitement for the rest of the day. Later that week, Lance came up to me in the visitor center basement as I was storing gear in my locker.

"Hey, the trip's been approved. We're going into Lech two weeks from tomorrow."

"Are you kidding? That's great!"

"Pete's going to be the trip leader, and I'll be checking him out. Tammy and Laura are going along, too." Tammy was a seasonal interpreter with a natural inclination for gutsy caving, while Laura was a no-nonsense protection ranger with caving experience. There would be five of us making the trip.

"We'll be doing some practice climbing in the lobby tonight," Lance informed me. "You might want to be there."

"Absolutely. Wow, this is hard to believe. Lechuguilla!"

"Don't get so excited. It'll be a hard trip."

By now I considered myself to be a fairly competent caver and climber. Although I still had a lot to learn and needed more experience, I had completed drops that were much longer than Boulder Falls, the fifteen-story rappel we would make in Lechuguilla. I had also developed a rudimentary knowledge of caves through my library research—I had read all of Carol Hill, Harvey DuChene, and Robert Nymeyer—and my caving trips in the High Guads and elsewhere. The wonders I had seen underground had captured my imagination, but I knew they would pale when compared to the things we were going to see in Lechuguilla. It was a world-class cave—the first I would visit after Carlsbad Cavern—and it would undoubtedly be the high point of my caving career.

The night before the trip, I was so excited that I didn't get much sleep, and when I woke up the next morning, my first thought was *Lechuguilla Cave!* We gathered early at Lance's apartment and loaded our equipment and rope into Pete and Lance's pickup trucks. We would use the rope only for the initial drop into the cave entrance; after that we would use ropes that were anchored permanently in the cave. From the housing area, we drove to a small dirt parking lot in a lonely canyon near the park's boundary. It was a clear, hot morning, and everyone seemed eager to get started. However, as we unloaded our packs from the trucks, Laura said something to Lance that caught my attention.

"You know, I've never used frog equipment outside of training. I hope it won't give me any problems."

"Don't worry about it. You'll do fine."

"I'm still not that used to it, and I'm thinking about that long climb out at Boulder Falls."

"Hey, once you get started, it'll be okay. Trust me."

"Well, I hope you're right."

Although I didn't mention it, I was starting to feel a little concerned myself, but for a different reason. The trip was going to take at least twelve hours, and I wondered if I would have enough energy to make it all the way to the Chandelier Ballroom and back again after getting only a few hours of sleep the previous night. Lance had said we would be descending about ninety-eight stories, and I had no idea how many miles we were going to cover.

From the parking area, we hiked about a mile along a rocky trail that went up the canyon and over the ridge to the east, then down into a broad dry wash and up the other side to Lechuguilla Cave. The entrance was a wide pit surrounded by bushes about halfway up the side of the canyon. It was so stark and understated that it reminded me of the lechuguilla plant itself, with its spiky leaves and nothing to make it look appealing. We began putting on our equipment, and when everyone was ready to get started, Pete took a group photo to mark the occasion.

While I definitely felt excited, I was apprehensive as well, just as I had experienced a sense of excitement mingled with dread before my first long drops into Ogle Cave and Cave of the Madonna. I supposed it was just my fear of the unknown, because each cave was entirely new to me, but that didn't stop me from wondering if Lechuguilla's entrance drop would take us into John Milton's underworld. I was fairly confident I wouldn't freak out, as I had in Hell Below, but the "Dies Irae" chorus from Mozart's *Requiem* nonetheless kept running through my mind:

On that day of wrath
Everything will dissolve in ashes . . .
Dread will flourish
As the Judge arrives
To weigh all things strictly!

Predictably, Lance showed no apprehension at all and was even singing part of a John Prine song that he would continue to sing throughout the trip, something about filling his mouth with marbles and trying to kiss Greta Garbo. Go figure.

Because Pete was leading the trip, he clipped onto the rope first and backed carefully down the narrow crevice that would take him to the edge of the pit. A few moments later, we heard his muffled shout of "Off rope!" and I followed him down. The six-story drop was fairly simple and straightforward, so it renewed my self-confidence. There wasn't much at the bottom of the pit other than musty guano and part of an old wooden ladder left behind by the miners.

Tammy and Laura came down the rope next, followed by Lance with an echoing shout of "*Yee-hah!*" At last we were on our way. We then dropped an additional twelve feet down the first permanently installed rope into a smaller chamber, where we confronted the infamous culvert I had heard so much about, with its heavy metal door. This was where the diggers had broken through the floor back in 1986. The culvert permitted one person at a time to pass through the rubble and enter the passage beyond, while the door prevented air from entering or leaving the cave. This was very important, because otherwise the cave might begin to dry out. That's what had happened in Carlsbad Cavern shortly after the construction of the first elevator shaft in 1931, when active areas and pools in the Big Room began to dry up and disappear. The situation reversed only when the park installed airtight revolving doors at the entrances to the elevator lobby in the underground lunchroom. Several years after our visit to Lechuguilla Cave, the culvert would be replaced by a sophisticated air lock.

As we pulled back the metal door, the air around us suddenly rushed into the culvert, like water into a drain when the plug is pulled. I had expected that to happen, but feeling it brought home the realization that we were entering Lechuguilla Cave. Sometimes the air could whistle through the culvert at fifty miles per hour. Climbing down the ladder through the narrow metal chute wasn't as intimidating as I had expected, but it still seemed a little unnerving. What a way to enter the underworld.

⟋⟍ Beyond the culvert, we found orange plastic tape for the first time, marking both sides of a narrow trail that disappeared into a low passage. A short walk brought us to a steep slope of wet flowstone, which we descended by using the installed hand line. We then continued down the passage until it abruptly sloped away to a sheer drop-off with a seemingly endless void below. Three metal bolts spaced widely apart on the wall anchored a rope that trailed down the slope and disappeared over the edge. This was the fifteen-story drop at Boulder Falls, and the void below was the Colorado Room, the first large chamber in the cave.

There would be two lips to cross in the descent, the first at the bottom of the slope and the second about four stories directly below that, at the bottom of a sheer cliff. From there it was a free drop of about eleven stories to the floor. Pete went down first and I followed, repeating my usual mantra as I backed cautiously to the first lip and eased over.

"Just relax. . . . Trust the rope."

I could see Pete's head lamp as a pinpoint of light far below, and I could even hear his muffled voice calling up to me, although I couldn't understand what he was saying. The feeling of hanging freely at the top of a long drop was exhilarating. I descended at a conservative speed, watching Pete's little circle of light grow larger until I could make him out distinctly. He was holding the end of the rope near the cave wall, offering advice about where to place my feet when I touched the floor.

Pete directed me to a large boulder where we would gather, and I made my way over and sat down to rest while the others came down the rope. It was quite impressive to see each head lamp descending slowly through the darkness overhead, casting a pale glow against the nearby wall. When everyone was down, we took a short break on the boulder, then shouldered our packs and moved on.

The orange tape now led us into another enormous chamber called Glacier Bay, which I recognized from the descriptions I had read. Massive gypsum blocks filled this room like beached icebergs, and the trail followed a difficult route over, around, and through them. As impressive as they were, I knew the blocks were merely guardians of the incredible wonders that lay ahead. After all, I had seen the photographs.

From Glacier Bay, we descended a narrow passage that took us ever deeper into the earth and eventually brought us to the Rift, a wide fissure that stretched far to our right and left. It looked as though a great wedge had split the limestone apart. We turned right, heading toward an intersection of major passages called EF Junction—so named because the E-survey and F-survey came together there—which formed the hub of the cave. We now had to make our way along the edges of four deep and extremely treacherous pits by attaching ourselves to traverse lines with "cow's tail" safety tethers that extended from our seat harnesses. The pits had been dangerous obstacles for early explorers before the traverse lines were tied in place.

The lines began several yards before each drop-off so we could attach our cow's tails in safety before starting across. The most intimidating pit was about twenty yards long—a very narrow fissure dropping straight down—and when I asked Lance how deep it was, he said about ten stories. I began to appreciate my cow's tail as I watched Pete make his way along the traverse line, hugging the cave wall tightly at the very edge of the pit, pushing his cow's tail along the rope, and obviously choosing each foothold carefully. When he was safely across, I attached myself to the line and followed him over, clenching my teeth and not looking down.

Once the pits were behind us, a short walk brought us to a fork in the trail. This was EF Junction, where we gratefully took off our packs and sprawled out on the trail to rest. Lance said we were about halfway to the Chandelier Ballroom, and I was pleased that I had been able to keep up with the rest of the group. However, he added, the most difficult part of the trip lay ahead of us. We now would move southwest and away from the Rift along a series of narrow passages and fissures that formed one of the three great arms of the cave. Our journey would take us into one of Lechuguilla's most imposing areas.

⌒ As we moved out from EF Junction, we began to notice gypsum everywhere, covering the floor of the passage we were following and encrusting the walls and ceiling. I had never seen this much gypsum before, and it was amazingly white, like snow or sugar. Lance said we had entered Snow White's Passage. In some places thick crusts of gypsum had pulled away from the walls or ceiling to reveal sparkling crystals underneath, or delicate spikes of pure-white aragonite, or cave popcorn. It seemed as though we were inside one of those hollow sugar Easter eggs, walking through a world of sugar crystals and icing.

The gypsum passage went on and on, seemingly without end. Pete showed us large areas where corrosion, caused by the condensation of acidic water, had polished the gypsum or white calcite of the walls and ceiling into smooth, shiny surfaces that looked like white marble. In some areas, crystals of dogtooth spar had corroded away until their polished bases, flush with the surrounding surfaces, had created mosaics of fantastic geometric shapes, some larger than silver dollars. I reminded myself that condensation also occurs on the earth's surface, where it contributes to the beauty of cloud formations, thunderstorms, and dewdrops. Even though we were moving through a world that was radically different from everything we knew aboveground, the connections were there: the same natural processes, the same degree of creativity, the same capacity to inspire wonder.

Farther along the passage, we came upon flowstone cascades and small columns that were among the most elegant I had ever seen, oozing out of the wall and ceiling in streams of vivid color: rusty red, chocolate, caramel, even pale yellow. It seemed as though the colors had bubbled up from nowhere. As we discovered ever more wonders, I began to realize that Lechuguilla Cave wasn't like John Milton's underworld at all; rather than being a place of wrath and judgment, it was a place of creation and inconceivable beauty.

The gypsum passage eventually brought us to a low, narrow "tube" passage, just large enough for one person to enter and sloping away from us at about a thirty-degree angle. We had arrived at the Poop Chute, which Lance had warned us about. We would have to lower ourselves into it one at a time, along a rope that had been anchored to the rock. After descending about fifty feet—five stories if it had been straight down—we would come to a narrow vertical crevice called the Little White Bastard, which we would descend on a second rope for an additional five stories.

When it was my turn to enter the chute, I followed Pete's lead by going in feet first on my back, then began lowering myself along the rope with both hands. I used my feet, knees, and elbows against the walls to keep myself from sliding too fast. The chute was tighter than most of the passages on my caving tours, which made for an awkward descent, and I was beginning to feel a little tired. I wondered how far we had come, but my sense of time and distance had deserted me after the drop at Boulder Falls, and I didn't bother looking at my watch. My only thoughts were "We'll get there when we get there" and "It's gonna be hard as hell climbing this passage on the way out."

At the bottom of the Poop Chute, I scooted laterally about ten feet under a very low ceiling to the top of the second rope. It was tied to the wall and extended about twelve feet down a broad balcony to a rounded lip, where it slipped over the edge. Attaching my descender, I eased myself down the rope and peered over the lip into the Little White Bastard. My head lamp illuminated a crevice that narrowed to a width of less than two feet before disappearing into pitch-black darkness. Crawling over the edge, I struggled awkwardly to get myself down the narrow squeeze without losing my pack. It was slow and painful all the way.

At the bottom, I found Pete and Tammy waiting in a high, narrow passage covered with pure-white, very delicate cave popcorn. I studied the walls carefully as we waited for Lance and Laura, and I happened to notice a small laminated sign beside the trail. It was a warning to those who might be tempted to neglect their pee bottles: "Don't Pee Here. Lake Lebarge is Just Below." Lake Lebarge was one of the cave's most impressive pools.

When everyone was down, Pete led us a short distance to a traverse line that went around a sharp bend in the passage above another sheer drop-off.

Tammy and Laura followed him, and Lance and I now brought up the rear. Pete and Lance told us to look down as we dangled from the rope. When it was my turn, I did so and discovered that I was poised hazardously over a very deep pit, its irregular walls lined with intricate clusters of white cave popcorn and aragonite crystals. Then I saw it gazing up at me: a shimmering circle of blue light, an exquisite pool of clear water as deep and blue as the sky itself. Lance said it was called the Gulf of California.

I had seen many cave pools before, including the Lake of the Clouds in Carlsbad Cavern, but never one like this. The only things in my experience to match its clarity and color were the waters I had seen along the coral reefs of the Bahamas. Yet the color there had come from the sky and sun, while this pool glimmered in the darkness of a cave. The effect was hypnotic, and I couldn't pull my gaze away as I used the traverse line to move around the dangerous bend and over a narrow ledge to safety.

⌒ Down we went again, lowering ourselves by hand line to the top of a majestic flowstone waterfall. The vertical drop along its face then brought us to Lake Lebarge. The transparent, perfectly smooth pool extended perhaps fifty feet into the darkness of its chamber. The beams of our head lamps reflected from the water onto the ceiling and walls as great circles of light that bobbed around as we moved, bringing the chamber to life. Lance said the three explorers who discovered Lake Lebarge—Steve Reames, Dave Logan, and Stan Allison—had chosen to name it after the Canadian lake that Robert W. Service made famous in his poem "The Cremation of Sam McGee." To match the poem's context and rhyme, Service had changed the lake's name from "Leberge" to "Lebarge."

Because we wouldn't need our climbing gear again before starting out of the cave, we took off our harnesses and left them on the trail. We then crossed an arm of the pool on stepping-stones and moved along the far wall to discover that the trail now entered a dense forest of delicate aragonite formations. They grew all around us and even overhead in such an amazing array of branches and fantastically clustered spikes that it seemed we had entered a glistening thicket of white bramble bushes, or perhaps a miniature winter landscape in which small trees had been frosted white by an ice storm. We crawled through the spectacular maze very slowly, crouching low to avoid breaking the delicate formations.

As we emerged on the far side of this wonder, standing up as carefully as we could, we encountered the most incredible thing we had seen thus far. Growing within three feet of the trail stood an almost perfectly formed Christmas tree—*yes, a Christmas tree*—made out of sparkling-white aragonite crystals and standing about as high as my shoulder. Perhaps the story of a pine tree growing up from the underworld in the beginning wasn't a myth after all. Smaller Christmas trees grew around it, interweaving their glittering branches and needles in a hopeless tangle. I could hardly believe my eyes or pull myself away from the fantastic sight.

The trail now entered the far side of the chamber, taking us a short distance across wet, slippery flowstone to Lake Chandalar—also named after a lake in Canada—the most dazzling pool we had yet seen. Its glowing blue-green color reflected off the walls and ceiling as the light of our head lamps penetrated all the way to its bottom—an amazing two stories. After removing our muddy boots, we walked carefully over a thick ledge of caramel-colored shelfstone that circled the edge of the pool in graceful crescents. Smaller lily pads of shelfstone seemed to float around the glimmering water. I couldn't imagine a more impressive sight.

We lingered beside Lake Chandalar until Lance began coaxing us away. Time was passing quickly, and we still had a long way to go. Reluctantly putting on our boots, we continued down the trail into yet another gypsum passage called the Lebarge Borehole. It was much larger than Snow White's Passage and had even more spectacular drifts of gypsum on both sides of the trail, as well as thick crusts on the walls. After a short distance we stopped and moved carefully into a small side alcove that contained a fantastic array of gypsum flowers growing from the walls and ceiling. There were scores of them: long, delicate strings of translucent gypsum that curled down from the ceiling or perched on narrow ledges above a shallow pool of water. They looked like small party streamers made of frosted glass, and they continued all the way to the far end of the alcove.

The gypsum flowers confirmed yet another link between caves and the desert that I had begun to recognize in the High Guads: when nature expresses itself underground, it uses the interactions between water, air, and rock—gypsum in this case—to re-create the same forms and patterns we see every day on the earth's surface. We had already discovered the shapes of pine trees and bramble bushes in the aragonite forest, and now the gypsum flowers mimicked party streamers. I had often noticed that helictites repeat the sinuous forms of pigs' tails, snakes, and worms, while cave popcorn duplicates the pebbly appearance of gravel in a dry wash. Flowstone often reproduces the graceful arc of a stream's trickling waterfall, and cave pearls remind us of the nearly perfect spheres we observe in the setting sun and full moon. When nature goes underground, it enjoys repeating itself in ways that are at once familiar and entirely unexpected.

Back in the main passage, we began joking that the endless beauty was starting to dull our senses: "Oh, no! Not another beautiful sight!" Lance didn't react much to this, saying only that we should wait until we saw a place called Tinseltown. For my part, the angry and judgmental sound of Mozart's "Dies Irae" was no longer running through my mind. Now I was hearing the joyful sound of the "Sanctus" from Bach's magnificent *Mass in B Minor*: "Holy! Holy! Holy!"

As the passage gradually became smaller, we crouched down and began crawling into a narrow, mazelike area that glittered with an unbelievable array of gypsum crystals, unlike anything we had seen before. *Tinseltown!* The crystals were transparent planes no larger than pinheads, and they covered every surface, filling the passage with thousands of sparkling lights that floated and undulated in midair, each sparkle more precise and clearer than any star on the coldest winter night. The effect was so striking that it seemed our descent into the underworld had actually carried us into the starry heavens. Twinkling constellations formed, shifted, and dissolved around us as we moved; shining galaxies whirled, pivoted, and fell away; comets and solar systems blinked at us through the darkness, while the Milky Way went streaming before us, jumping from wall to wall and from floor to ceiling along that glittering gypsum passage. It was so incredible that I could hardly form a thought or say a word, so I just floated into the sparkling lights, listening to the incomparable sound of Bach: "Gloria in excelsis Deo!"

Lance pointed out a small gypsum chandelier, perhaps two feet long, hanging in an alcove on our left. It was the first indication that we were nearing our destination. I grew more expectant with every turn, anticipating at any moment the entrance to the Chandelier Ballroom. Despite the orange tape, the maze of passages now seemed so confusing that I wondered how the first explorers had been able to find their way out. Then we were at the top of a steep decline, and Pete and Tammy were making their way cautiously down the trail below, entering what was apparently a very large chamber. I swept my head lamp back and forth through the darkness, searching for what I knew must be there. Off to my right, I could barely make out something in the distance, but it was so indistinct that I couldn't tell what it was. Yet I already knew, and my heart jumped.

The Brightest of Wonders

GYPSUM CHANDELIERS ARE among the rarest of cave formations. They grow from the ceiling or wall of a cave as long, white fingers of crystalline gypsum, frequently curving in graceful arcs and ending in bursts of selenite crystals and glistening gypsum spikes. Lance had told us that a cave would be famous if it had only one gypsum chandelier three to six feet long. As I made my way into the dark chamber and the vague thing I had seen began to divide and assume a number of definite shapes, my excitement grew until I began to feel my own heartbeat. I had heard about what was here, and I had seen photographs, but now I could see for myself. Extending from the ceiling in great clusters were dozens of gypsum chandeliers, some of them up to twenty feet long. Those on the far side of the chamber looked like pale apparitions in the semidarkness, but those in the nearest cluster glittered brilliantly in the glare of our head lamps. Above the chandeliers, ribbons of pure-white gypsum streaked the inclined ceiling in thick crusts, merging near the wall into a great field of sparkling mineral. The massive formations emerged from this and curved gently toward the wall, finally exploding into those characteristic crystal sprays, like giant sparklers on the Fourth of July.

We sat down on a large boulder in the center of the chamber to rest and eat, but as we took food out of our packs and spread extra shirts as tablecloths, it was difficult to think about anything other than the chandeliers. I wanted to see them up close. For fifteen minutes, we talked and ate sausage, cheese, and bread while the chandeliers waited patiently. After finishing we packed everything away and moved down the adjacent slope of boulders to a fork in the trail. The right fork took us to the largest and most exquisite chandelier cluster.

It was impossible not to feel a sense of profound awe and reverence as we approached those immense forms, which now looked like great bolts of lightning thundering down from a gypsum sky. I could only gaze in disbelief and feel honored to witness the splendor of that marvelous place. I even repeated to myself the words of Walt Whitman: "Prais'd be the fathomless universe, for life and joy, and for objects and knowledge curious . . ."

The trail circled the chandeliers and ended near the wall, where one formation with branching arms and legs looked almost human. Lance called it a cowboy as he sauntered to the end of the orange tape, stood next to the strangely shaped formation, and hunkered down in a bowlegged stance that duplicated its appearance almost perfectly. Our laughter broke the awesome stillness of the chamber. We then began noticing gypsum flowers growing along the trail, and I discovered a cluster of beautifully translucent petals that formed a perfect orchid. We were amazed that gypsum could have created both the small, delicate flowers and the tremendous chandeliers nearby.

After a short side trip to a large and very imposing chamber called the Prickly Ice Cube Room, we returned to the Chandelier Ballroom and began preparing for the trip back to the surface. That's when Pete suggested we have a blackout. *Of course!* We sat in a circle on the large boulder where we had eaten, then turned off our head lamps. Absolute darkness. Absolute silence. I had experienced it many times before, but this time was different. We were only a few yards away from the most spectacular formations in one of the most spectacular caves in the world. How many other caves might we have been sitting in at that moment? Yet we were in Lechuguilla.

After several minutes, Pete turned his head lamp back on, and everyone followed his lead. We had been in the cave almost nine hours, and it definitely was time to start back to the surface. As I adjusted the shoulder straps on my pack, I realized that the marvelous photographs I had seen, while giving a fair impression of the things we would see during our trip, hadn't captured the full impact of Lechuguilla Cave. I also knew that I could never adequately describe what I had seen to anyone who had never been there. How could I convey the stateliness of the gypsum passages, the glowing color of the pools, or the glory of Tinseltown and the chandeliers? Such things were beyond the power of telling. The underworld we had discovered in Lechuguilla Cave was a place of uninhibited creation and unimaginable beauty—hidden in darkness, yet filled with the brightest of wonders.

As we shouldered our packs, Pete asked if anyone else wanted to lead the way, and Tammy volunteered. I was too tired to do anything except fall in at the rear of the group. Tammy started us along the trail, and then we were moving rapidly up the steep incline and into the maze of passages we had come through earlier. I felt an unexpected surge of energy, but I knew it wouldn't last; we had several major climbs ahead of us, including the Poop Chute and Boulder Falls, and the surface was at least six hours away. Yet I was determined to make it out of the cave, if only because there was no alternative.

We refilled our water bottles at Lake Chandalar, using the sterilized plastic dipper kept at the pool for that purpose. (It prevented the pool from being contaminated with microorganisms brought in from the surface. Although mildly acidic, the water was safe to drink.) Lance had warned us that we would drink plenty of water during the trip, and he was right. I had already emptied the two liters brought from home, and both containers would be empty again by the time we reached the entrance.

At Lake Lebarge, we put on our climbing gear. As the others ascended the flowstone waterfall and continued toward the Little White Bastard, I stood beside the quiet pool and stared back into the darkness, thinking about the utterly improbable things we were leaving behind. It now seemed so lonely back there. When I heard the last muffled cry of "Off rope!" from above, I clipped onto the rope and started up, using one foot in my foot loop and the other to push myself away from the flowstone.

Lance was waiting for me at the bottom of the Little White Bastard, occasionally shouting encouragement up to Laura, who apparently was having difficulty moving up the tight squeeze. Tammy and Pete had gone up first and by now were far above us. I turned off my head lamp and stood quietly to wait my turn. Lance had once mentioned that caving requires ninety percent mental determination and only ten percent physical exertion. I hoped he was right: judging from the way I felt, determination was the only thing that could get me up the Little White Bastard.

When Laura shouted that she was off rope, Lance began his ascent, slipping up the crevice so quickly and efficiently that he made it look easy. Within moments I couldn't even detect the glow from his head lamp, much less the sound of his equipment, but I could imagine him singing more of John Prine as he went—this time about a dog named "Dingo" learning to speak German. When he finally shouted that he was clear, I turned on my head lamp, clipped onto the rope with my safety, and moved laterally into the crevice. Taking off my pack, I attached it to my seat harness with a four-foot tether; it would be easier to pull it behind me. Clipping on with my croll, I started up. Within a few feet I was sandwiched so tightly between the walls that I could barely maneuver. Yet I kept struggling upward, fitting myself awkwardly into the tight space and pushing with my legs as best I could. The climb was much longer than I remembered and seemed to take forever, but eventually I pulled myself over the lip and sprawled out on the balcony to rest before crawling up the gentle slope to the second rope.

If the Little White Bastard had been difficult, the Poop Chute was brutal agony. My frustration grew steadily as I slowly and awkwardly pulled myself up the tight passage on my back and sides, straining with my arms and fumbling to wedge my feet and knees against the rock. Small kernels of cave popcorn cut into my arms and legs like coarse sandpaper. I began cursing under my breath as I peered vainly ahead for the glow of Lance's head lamp, which would signal an end to the relentless torture. When I finally saw a faint gleam, it was the most welcome sight of the trip.

⌒ Lance said Pete and Tammy had gone on ahead and that he, Laura, and I would continue together. Dividing our group that way would cut down on our waiting time at the rope in the Colorado Room. When we finally reached the fifteen-story climb, Pete and Tammy had already ascended, and we could hear the faint echo of their voices and see their head lamps reflecting against the cave wall high overhead. I sat down to rest on the large boulder while Lance helped Laura attach herself to the rope. When she started up, he walked back to join me, and we turned off our head lamps as he took a seat on the boulder.

"She's doing just fine with the frog equipment," he observed. "I knew she would."

We watched Laura climb ever higher, alternately reaching with her arms and pushing with her legs, until she was eleven stories above us, a small figure dangling near the ceiling in a dim circle of light. She then pulled herself over the lip and scaled up the cliff, slowly disappearing as her light became a mere glimmer that moved erratically against the cave wall. It was an amazing sight, prompting Lance to whisper, "That is way cool."

A few moments later, I clipped onto the rope and started up the wall. Lance offered advice about where to place my feet against the rock. Then I was hanging freely, working my arms and legs in unison. The last I saw of Lance, he was walking back along the trail to our boulder. I concentrated on setting a steady pace, raising my legs each time I pushed my ascender up the rope, until I arrived at the bottom of the cliff and pulled myself over the lip. I looked down a final time but saw only darkness, with no sign of Lance.

Scaling the cliff was relatively easy, and moments later I crossed the upper lip, taking care to place the rope back over the pad. I was glad to see Pete waiting for me as I clipped onto the safety rope. Laura and Tammy had gone on ahead, and he left to join them as I waited for Lance. A few moments later, Lance arrived at the rope pad, straining and puffing as though he were trying to break a speed record. Disengaging from the rope, he said that he regretted not having had me time his ascent. We continued up the passage to the bottom of the flowstone slope, where Lance clipped onto the hand line.

We were now within thirty minutes of the surface. I was so eager to reach the entrance and be out of the cave that it was hard to focus on the task at hand. The trip had worn me out, and the thought of being on the surface again was about the only thing that kept me going. After Lance reached the top of the slope, I clipped onto the hand line with just my safety, as he had suggested, but about halfway up I became so exhausted that I had to attach my croll as well. Yet it was still a slippery and difficult climb to the top. As I struggled along on my knees, breathing heavily and drenched with sweat, I happened to look up at Lance. He was watching me empathetically with a pained expression on his face. When he noticed my glance he said, "I know I always give you a hard time, Doug, but you do good." That compliment meant the world to me, and it definitely gave me the energy I needed to reach the surface.

I was the last to climb the ladder up the culvert, dragging my pack behind me by its tether as it bounced over the rungs. The air was perfectly still now. Lance said it was the first time he had gone through when there was no wind. Closing and locking the heavy metal door meant saying good-bye to Lechuguilla Cave, and despite my exhaustion I felt sad to be leaving. What an experience it had been.

We reached the guano pit a few moments later and found Laura climbing the rope to the surface. I sat down on the floor near the remains of the old ladder, too tired to say or do anything. My shorts and T-shirt were torn and soaked with sweat, and I was so dirty that I seemed to be a part of the guano pile. I also felt sleepy, and I could barely keep my eyes open as I checked myself for bruises and scratches. I did notice by my watch that it was after midnight, which meant we had been in the cave more than fifteen hours.

The final climb to the surface was easier than I expected. A few moments later I was making my way up the rocky crevice and unclipping from the rope. Pushing through the bushes, I emerged into the cool desert night with an overwhelming sense of relief, drinking in the shadowy landscape as though seeing it for the first time. Everything seemed so fresh and beautiful, and there were so many stars overhead that it looked like Tinseltown had come out of the cave and spread itself across the sky to welcome us back to the surface.

The hike back to the parking area was a blur of dark shadows and twinkling stars, with the beam of my helmet lamp reflecting briefly in the eyes of a deer. At the pickups, Pete and Lance got out coolers and handed relatively cold beers to everyone (this is a required ritual at the end of every caving trip). As we sat on the tailgates, we started noticing meteors streaking across the sky, but because I couldn't get comfortable and was too tired to look anyway, I lay back across some of the packs and closed my eyes.

A short while later, we were bouncing along the dirt road, heading for home. I remember lying under the camper shell in the back of Lance's pickup, sprawled out on our equipment and too tired even to move, watching the stars through the back window. I also remember crawling over the tailgate and tumbling onto my driveway, then walking toward my front door, unable to stand up straight because my body ached so much. Beyond that I don't remember anything.

⌒ For the next few days, it seemed as though I were still in Lechuguilla Cave, crawling on my elbows and knees or pulling myself up the flowstone waterfall or the Little White Bastard. I couldn't get the cave out of my mind, and in the everyday objects and events around me I found constant reminders of the things we had seen and done on our journey into the underworld. At work I began finding opportunities to talk with visitors about Lechuguilla, speaking for the first time from my own experience. Even though I couldn't adequately describe the cave's beauty, I could relate what it felt like to make the fifteen-story drop at Boulder Falls, move in a low crouch through the aragonite forest, and stand in awe beneath the gypsum chandeliers. The visitors were very receptive, and I felt my efforts enabled at least some of them to find their own way into Lechuguilla Cave—if only in their imaginations—and experience some of the joy and wonder I had found there.

I also came to agree with Lance that we're as likely to find wilderness underground as we are on the earth's surface. The things we had seen and the solitude we had experienced in Lechuguilla were certainly as inspirational and transformative as anything I had found in the mountains or open desert, if not more so. Perhaps the idea of wilderness is yet another connection between the beauty and grandeur of the earth's surface and the beauty and grandeur of the underworld.

The same is true of beauty itself: it pervades both realms, even though it manifests itself differently in each case. I had seen the gypsum chandeliers as lightning bolts, yet they were solid objects created by the interactions between water, hydrogen sulfide gas, limestone, gypsum, air currents, and variations in temperature. True lightning bolts are bursts of pure energy that result from interactions between water vapor, air currents, variations in temperature, and electrical fields. The two couldn't be more diverse, yet both express the same beautifully sinuous form.

After several weeks of preparation, I started giving an interpretive program about Lechuguilla Cave in the visitor center theater. In my earlier program about cave formations, I had shown how the creative actions of water link the beauty of caves to the beauty of the earth's surface. Now, by comparing many of the park's Lechuguilla photographs with photographs of the Chihuahuan Desert, I wanted to show how nature's use of forms and patterns does the same thing. I also prepared a temporary exhibit for the theater's back wall, again using many of the park's photographs, with captions taken from the trip report I had submitted to Pete shortly after our return. My goal in these projects was to emphasize the unity of nature's creative spirit and help visitors realize that the unusual and seemingly unique beauty of Lechuguilla Cave is the same beauty that surrounds us every day.

Over the following months, I made two additional trips into Lechuguilla. The first was to help rescue a member of a European film crew that had been filming a documentary under a permit from the park. The man had become exhausted and dehydrated in the Chandelier Ballroom. Lance, Dave, and I were assigned to make first contact with the crew and offer whatever assistance they needed. We met them just before we reached Boulder Falls and were glad to learn that the man was all right. I made the second trip about three months later, when I went with Lance, Collin, Clarence, and a park volunteer to retrieve the film crew's equipment from the Chandelier Ballroom. Because it included several battery-operated floodlights, we used them to illuminate the chamber briefly, with spectacular results.

My journeys into Lechuguilla Cave have had a lasting influence on the way I see things. Any encounter with a cave of this scope forces us to measure ourselves against the scale of its awesome size and features, and then against the power and subtlety of the natural world itself. As a result, we gain perspective and balance. That's why my journeys into Lechuguilla Cave will always remind me of an Ojibwa saying I discovered years ago in my reading: "Sometimes I go about in pity for myself, and all the while a great wind is bearing me across the sky."

CHAPTER TWENTY-ONE

Time Passing

THE NIGHT WAS absolutely still, except for the faraway hooting of an owl. We were camped on the open desert below the escarpment near the mouth of Big Canyon—Lance, Dave, Pete, Tammy (the seasonal), Beth (the volunteer from England), and me—and we were planning to spend the next day hiking up the canyon's left fork. I assumed my friends were asleep, but I lay awake in my sleeping bag enjoying the cool night air. The incredibly lovely three-quarter moon had transformed the escarpment into a massive wall of silvery-gray light, interrupted only by a few dark shadows and the gaping void that was Big Canyon.

I was trying to visualize the Permian reef and the ocean waves that had broken against it millions of years earlier. The escarpment had been alive then, a teeming mass of sponges, algae, brachiopods, nautiloids, and other small creatures clinging tenaciously to the edge of the ancient Permian sea. Because this was long before the evolution of our present corals, the reef was quite different from the reefs we know today. How things had changed. The sea was gone, and the reef had been pushed above the surrounding terrain like a mushroom popping up through the detritus on a forest floor. The transformation was so extraordinary and far-reaching that the reef now dominated all of southeastern New Mexico.

I thought back to that afternoon almost six years earlier, when I had driven across the plains of West Texas toward my job interview at Carlsbad Caverns. I hadn't known anything about the reef then, and I certainly hadn't realized that the cliffs I saw gleaming in the distance were a part of it. Again, things had changed. The reef was now as familiar as my own name, and it was never far from my thoughts. I worked inside it, hiked across it, bicycled through it, climbed up and down on it, even slept above it. It was the pervasive backdrop to everything I said or did, and it was a final link between the Chihuahuan Desert and the caves of the Guadalupe Mountains.

Over the preceding years, I had seen how the desert and its caves are connected through myths about the underworld, the creative actions of water, my four interpretive themes—especially the idea of exploration and discovery—bats and other animals, the concept of wilderness, nature's use of forms and patterns, and the pervasiveness of natural beauty. Now I could see that desert and caves come together in the reef and that neither can be separated from the other because of the reef's unifying presence.

Think about it: The desert covers the reef's surface, while the caves honeycomb its interior. Desert thunderstorms flood the reef's dry washes, while small amounts of rainwater seep through the reef into the caves. The desert's extreme heat cracks the reef's surface and sends heat waves dancing across its barren slopes, while the caves remain cool in the reef's dark interior. Desert plants force their roots into the reef's joints and crevices to help replenish its thin, barren soil, while the caves have transformed much of the reef's limestone into calcite, gypsum, iron oxide, and other minerals. The Chihuahuan Desert and Guadalupe caves are as much a part of the reef as the tiny fossils I often discovered while hiking through its canyons.

Because it's difficult to imagine the reef's extreme age, I used an analogy when talking with park visitors: if we let one inch represent one year, it would take a line 4,182 miles long to represent the 265 million years that have passed since the reef stopped growing. The line would stretch from Los Angeles to Chicago and back to Los Angeles, with more than one hundred miles left over. The caves are much younger, of course, with ages between four and twelve million years, while the desert is younger still, with an age of only seven to ten thousand years. At the end of the last Ice Age, when glaciers retreated and the climate became warmer and drier, the Chihuahuan Desert had moved slowly northward from Mexico to envelop the reef. Now all three—reef, caves, and desert—are linked in an ever-changing panorama of creation and destruction that began in the Permian Age and will continue inexorably into the distant future.

⌐ One morning as I was returning to the elevators after patrolling the Big Room Trail, a visitor approached me near the underground lunchroom and asked, "How do we know this limestone was once a reef?" I always welcomed questions about the reef, because it's just as important to the story of Carlsbad Cavern as the Big Room or the squiggly little helictites that grow out of the cave wall near the Hall of Giants. We have to understand the reef to fully appreciate the cave.

"Well, sir," I began, "there are a number of reasons. First, there are—"

The man interrupted me with another question: "Do you believe in evolution?"

Oops. That was something I hadn't expected, and because I was fairly certain the man had changed the subject for a reason, I tried to answer carefully.

"Well, I wouldn't say that I 'believe' in evolution, the way a child believes in Santa Claus or the Easter Bunny, but I do think the evidence in support of evolution is overwhelming. I suppose the best way to put it is that I accept evolution as an established fact."

The man looked at me with what appeared to be an expression of sympathy and said, "There is an alternative, you know. You should read the book of Genesis." Then he walked away toward the elevators, turning to give me a final glance as he added, "Try it!"

That was a frustrating contact because the man hadn't given me a chance to answer his initial question, something I could have done without any reference to evolution. As a start, I could have taken him over to the revolving door at the elevator lobby and shown him the impressions of small sponges preserved in the cave wall as well as the fossil of a trilobite, a tiny creature that lived along the reef and whose appearance always reminded me of today's horseshoe crabs. Then I could have explained that the structure of the reef is preserved in the Guadalupe Escarpment. It's clearly visible in Carlsbad Cavern as we walk down the Natural Entrance Trail and continue around the Big Room Trail, and it's also visible when we hike into any of the escarpment's canyons. In Guadalupe Mountains National Park, the Permian Reef Trail even climbs the side of McKittrick Canyon, where a cross section of the reef is fully exposed. Moreover, because the reef was hundreds of miles long, additional sections are visible today in the Apache Mountains and Glass Mountains of West Texas. So we have plenty of evidence that today's limestone was once a reef.

What does a cross section of the reef look like? Imagine yourself descending into the twilight zone of Carlsbad Cavern along the Natural Entrance Trail. In Permian times, the limestone around you was muddy sediment at the bottom of a shallow lagoon that extended along the back side of the reef. If you stop along the trail where the ceiling is lowest and look overhead, you can see perfectly preserved mud cracks, which formed during a temporary dry spell. The sedimentary limestone that formed beneath the lagoon is now part of what geologists call the "backreef" because of its location behind the reef. This uppermost layer is called the Tansill Formation.

As you continue along the trail into the cave's dark zone, you'll find yourself descending into a second layer of backreef sediment directly below the Tansill, called the Yates Formation. Unbelievably, it's about twenty stories thick, which tells us the reef and its lagoon were around for a very long time. If you stop at the Whale's Mouth and look up at the north wall of the Main Corridor, you can see the dividing line between the two layers, marked by a horizontal row of stalactites where water seeps out of the wall.

By the time you reach the Big Room at the bottom of the Natural Entrance Trail, you've entered the reef itself. Now the limestone is solid, without horizontal layers, and if you look closely you'll begin to find the impressions of sponges and other small creatures that comprised the reef. You'll also realize that the reef was very wide, because it extends all the way to the far end of the Big Room.

When you finally reach the front of the reef at the Bottomless Pit, you'll find something altogether different. If you look up at the walls and ceiling, you'll see more limestone layers, but this time the layers are diagonal rather than horizontal, and they slope away from the reef. That's because they're made of talus, small chunks of the reef that broke away and tumbled into the sea to form a slope, like the one at the base of El Capitán

238

in Guadalupe Mountains National Park. Because the sloping layers are located in front of the reef, geologists call them the "forereef."

That's what a cross section of the reef looks like. Whether we walk the trails through Carlsbad Cavern or hike into one of the escarpment's canyons, we'll always find the horizontal layers of the backreef behind the solid limestone of the reef, and the sloping layers of the forereef directly in front of it.

While it's impossible to say exactly how long the reef was alive and growing, the evidence shows that its vertical growth kept pace with the rising sea level—an increase of many hundreds of feet—and that it slowly migrated in the direction of the sea by growing on top of its own talus slope. It's unfortunate that most people have never heard of it, because geologists consider it to be one of the world's premier fossil reefs, and its preservation for 265 million years is truly astonishing.

~~ One morning as I was working at the visitor center information desk, Chandra said something that caught my interest (you may remember her as the seasonal interpreter who owned a cattle ranch with her husband about fifteen miles south of the park). She had just trailed one of the King's Palace tours, and after recording the number of visitors in the tour log she said to one of the cashiers, "By the way, Big Canyon came down last night." Big Canyon came down? What was she talking about? She then added, "McKittrick came down, too, but I don't know about Black or Gunsight."

I was stumped. How does a canyon "come down"? I tried to imagine Big Canyon pulling itself out of the escarpment and lumbering off into the desert toward Chandra's ranch, but I couldn't do it. It wasn't until later that I put two and two together. There had been heavy thunderstorms along the escarpment during the night, and they had caused flash floods in Big Canyon and McKittrick Canyon. "Coming down" meant the floods had swept debris out of the canyons into the open desert. It seems I had learned another southwestern way of saying things.

Chandra had referred to an ongoing process that was slowly but inexorably changing the reef. It may have been a geologic marvel, but it was gradually beginning to disappear, the way snow and ice melt and disappear in warm sunshine. Every time a thunderstorm hurled its rain against a slope, every time a chunk of limestone crumbled from a cliff, every time a flash flood surged down one of the canyons, pushing the rocks and boulders in its dry wash that much closer to the open desert, a little more of the reef was carried away. It had been happening for millions of years, and the slow accumulation of changes was adding up: the massive canyons had eaten through the forereef, into the reef itself, and even into the horizontal layers of the backreef.

The story was evident during our hike up the left fork of Big Canyon. Shortly after sunrise, the wind became so strong and cold that it felt like winter rather than early April, and we shivered as we stood around eating breakfast. After packing away our camping gear, we drove the remaining distance to the canyon's mouth, where a few stray cows lumbered across the road just ahead of us. Looking up the canyon, we could see the horizontal layers of the backreef lying on top of the most distant cliffs, directly above the solid limestone of the reef. (As the reef migrated toward the sea, the backreef had followed it by growing above the older parts of the reef, just as the reef had grown above the diagonal layers of its talus slope.)

We parked next to a broken-down corral near the remains of a windmill and a dilapidated bunkhouse, then followed the desert vegetation into the canyon's broad mouth. Laughing and talking, we hiked below typically sheer cliffs and their jumbled talus slopes—we were passing through the forereef—to the first fork in the dry wash. Lance chased a few cows along the way, shouting belligerently until he met a bull and beat a hasty retreat back to the rest of us. We took the left fork and hiked up the wash through sotols, desert willows, prickly pears, and other desert plants until we began to see a few ponderosa pines. Even in this early stage of the hike, we could see that we were in one of the most awe-inspiring canyons in the Guadalupe Mountains.

I paid close attention to the dry wash, trying to decipher what it had to say about the most recent flash flood. The largest boulders told me where rapids had formed, while patterns in the smaller rocks, gravel, and sand showed where the swiftest currents had run and backwater eddies had circled. It was like reading the twists and turns of a melody on a page of sheet music: it goes up here, down there, makes a turn here, repeats itself there. Many of the rocks were smooth and flawless, indicating that they had come from the solid limestone of the reef, while others displayed small, concentric circles known as "pisoliths," showing that they had once been part of the backreef (the formation of pisoliths isn't fully understood). A few even retained the impressions of small nautiloids or other marine creatures.

Within two miles, the wash became so choked with huge boulders and rock outcrops that we had to start boulder-hopping. The limestone was solid now, meaning we had hiked through the forereef and were in the reef itself. The canyon's sheer walls gradually closed around us to form a narrow, twisting corridor of beautifully sculpted rock. In a few places, water dripped below moss-covered ledges, and we began to find perfectly clear pools of emerald-green water, some with cascading waterfalls, lying in shallow depressions along the canyon bottom. At one pool, we heard the faint murmur of a waterfall that was hidden within a jumble of massive boulders and smaller rocks. Billowing clouds of green algae choked pools on the sunny side of the canyon, prompting me to imagine myself flying in an airplane over bright-green thunderstorms. A few pools covered most of the canyon bottom, making it difficult to get around. We had to climb the steep slopes on either side until we were hanging precariously five or six stories above the canyon floor, inching from handhold to handhold. It was a relief when we finally descended on the far side of the largest pool.

As the hike became more difficult, Pete and Beth decided to fall back and go at a slower pace, while the rest of us pushed ahead. In an exceptionally rugged area, we came to a dark-green pool that blocked the canyon completely, with no way of climbing the sheer cliffs on either side. We estimated it was about fifty feet across, but we had no way of knowing how deep it might be. Determined to keep going, Lance took off his boots and waded in, only to come hopping back when he discovered the water was ice-cold.

Taking off my own boots and rolling up my pants legs, I went in next and tried to reach the cliff on the right side of the pool, where there appeared to be a submerged ledge. Perhaps I could walk across on it. Instead, I slipped on the bottom and went into the water up to my waist. Lance didn't miss his chance, calling, "Way to go, Doug. How does it feel to be the clumsiest person on the planet?"

The cold water was a problem because if we did get across, our clothes would be wet for the rest of the hike. Dave suggested we take off our packs and clothing as well as our boots—everything but our underwear—and hold them over our heads as we tried to wade across, and that's what we finally decided to do. After stripping down to his briefs, Lance headed in first, swearing he would make it across. Slowly wading into the middle of the pool, he found that the water came up to his chest. When he finally emerged on the far side, he began jumping vigorously up and down in an effort to keep warm.

I waited for Dave to reach the other side before going in myself, with my boots, pack, and clothing held over my head. At the halfway point, the water reached my armpits and was so cold I could hardly catch my breath. Then I slipped on the bottom again and plunged forward into the icy water, taking my boots and clothing with me. Dave and Lance thought that was hilarious.

"Hey, Doug, why don't you fall into the water and get wet?"

"Have you found that rope in the Rift yet, Doug?"

"I think he's too busy showing off."

I tried to ignore the ribbing but couldn't get past realizing that I had no other clothes to wear. Although I made it to the other side, I wasn't happy.

We went a short distance ahead to give Tammy some privacy as she crossed the pool. Putting our boots and clothing back on, we draped our underwear over bushes and tree branches to dry in the sun. I had no choice but to wear my wet pants, although Dave mercifully loaned me a dry shirt from his pack. When Tammy joined us, we continued up the canyon and discovered more emerald-green pools, disturbed only by the circular ripples of tiny water striders skimming over their surfaces. The cliffs were fantastic, often overhanging the narrow canyon bottom and always streaked with long ribbons of desert varnish.

Lance and Dave noticed two small caves at the top of a nearly vertical slope and climbed up to have a look, while Tammy sat on a nearby rock to watch. Not wanting to stop, I continued up the canyon on my own, expecting at any moment to find a sheer cliff that would finally block our way. When the others eventually joined me, we had indeed gone as far as we could. The hike was over, except for the long and difficult trek back to the mouth of the canyon. It was almost dark and my pants were dry when we finally climbed into our vehicles for the drive back to the highway. The cows were nowhere to be seen.

⌐ The most intriguing thing about our hike into Big Canyon was that it had taken us through the entire history of the reef. We had seen for ourselves that it had grown higher, that it had migrated toward the sea, and that it had grown over its own talus slope. We had also seen that erosion was enlarging the canyons and that the reef was slowly beginning to disappear. That was the reef's great lesson: while change may come at an agonizingly slow pace, all things do change and eventually pass away. It's as true of landscapes as it is of our own lives, as Tennyson noted in one of his poems: "The hills are shadows, and they flow from form to form, and nothing stands."

Yet the hike had shown something more: The canyons had allowed the desert to penetrate the reef's interior, so that yuccas and prickly pears now grew where sponges, brachiopods, and trilobites once flourished. Further, the two small caves Lance and Dave had visited were a reminder that the Guadalupe caves are an integral part of the reef's story and that we're indebted to the canyons for bringing them to light. If Big Canyon hadn't eroded its way into the reef, those two caves would have remained forever hidden, and we wouldn't even have known they were there. That was another amazing aspect of the reef's story: the erosion of the canyons had created every one of the openings that give us access to the caves, from the tiny entrance into Chimney Cave to the massive entrances of Frank's Cave and Gunsight Cave. Without Bat Cave Draw, there would be no Carlsbad Cavern.

The erosion continues today, of course, although it's so gradual we seldom notice it. A few years before I started working at Carlsbad Caverns, a large chunk of the Natural Entrance's rock overhang had collapsed, and the Natural Entrance Trail had to be closed while the rubble was being cleared away. According to Lance, when the maintenance workers arrived at the scene they found a baseball cap sticking out from under one side of a huge boulder and tennis shoes from under the opposite side, apparently placed there by a practical joker on the park staff. A humorous story, but one with a clear implication: the Natural Entrance to Carlsbad Cavern is getting bigger.

Also, the first time I hiked from the park's scenic drive down to the bottom of Rattlesnake Canyon, I noticed an odd-looking piece of limestone jutting up from the trail. Stopping for a closer look, I couldn't understand

243

why it seemed out of place. Then it dawned on me: it was flowstone, the bottom of a beautifully crenelated drapery formation, like the draperies along the thirty-story climb into Chocolate High or near the Rock of Ages in Carlsbad Cavern. Sometime in the past, a cave had existed where I was standing. What a revelation. It hadn't occurred to me that some of the escarpment's caves might have been completely devoured by the erosion that had created the canyons, but that obviously was the case.

Later, in conversations with other interpreters and members of the cave-resources staff, I learned that geologists suspect a truly amazing possibility: the disappearance of a massive cave that may have existed in the middle of Slaughter Canyon. Anyone familiar with Slaughter Canyon Cave and Ogle Cave knows they're at the same elevation, even though they're more than a mile apart and on different sides of the canyon. Clearly, they could have been opposite ends of the same huge cave, which gradually disappeared as the canyon grew larger. And that brings up some fascinating questions: If there was a missing cave, what was it like? Did it have a chamber even larger than the Big Room? Did it have features even more spectacular than the gypsum chandeliers in Lechuguilla Cave? Did it house a colony of Mexican free-tailed bats even larger than the one in Carlsbad Cavern? We'll never know.

Finally, what about the caves that haven't yet been exposed by erosion and are completely unknown to us because they have no entrances? They're still waiting in the reef, locked in absolute darkness and silence until the continuing erosion of the canyons eventually exposes them. Limited as we are by the slow pace of geologic time and the brevity of our own lives, we may never see the mountains' greatest underground wonders.

CHAPTER TWENTY-TWO

Saying Good-Bye

OUR HIKE INTO Big Canyon confirmed what I had long since come to accept: that change is both universal and inevitable. Despite the illusion of permanence, everything that flourishes will come to an end—just like the Permian reef and Guadalupe caves. The proof of this in my own life was the end of my assignment at Carlsbad Caverns. After almost six years of working in and around caves, learning to climb rope, becoming an experienced caver, and enjoying the beauty and challenges of the Chihuahuan Desert and Guadalupe Mountains, it was time to move on to another park. My retirement was just a few years away, but I still had enough time for one more assignment as a frontline interpreter, and working aboveground in another southwestern area seemed appealing. The park's decision to close "On the Hill," the employee-housing area, coupled with my reluctance to move into the town of Carlsbad, finally made me start searching for another position.

I didn't look forward to leaving Carlsbad Caverns: my assignment there had been the most challenging and enjoyable of my career, and it had brought the most rewarding friendships of my life. Yet I could take heart from the Permian reef. Even though it was slowly disappearing, it proved that nature was just as reluctant to give up the past as I was. Every one of its fossils, from the smallest sponge to the largest ammonoid, as well as every preserved mud crack and even the limestone itself, was a memory of something that had happened 265 million years earlier—something nature was unwilling to forget. And just as nature could appreciate its own past through the memories it had stored in the reef, I would be able to relive my years at Carlsbad Caverns through the memories I took with me into retirement, memories that would eventually allow me to write about my experiences.

Even as I began to prepare for my next assignment, my friends' lives were also changing. Lance had decided to become a protection ranger and had already completed the required training. He liked his new law-enforcement duties at the park and had become adept at making traffic stops and patrolling the backcountry on foot. He was the ranger who discovered the murder scene in Rattlesnake Canyon, after finding the young men's car parked along the scenic drive and hiking down the trail to the canyon's dry wash. It took some effort to get used to the fact that my friend was no longer an interpreter, but he had his own career plans, and I certainly wished him well.

While visiting Colorado, Lance had met Leah, a wonderful woman who became his significant other and eventually his wife. A high school English teacher and homeowner, she was Lance's opposite in most ways, but they hit it off immediately and proved to be the perfect match. Because Lance was eager to develop his career, he began applying for law-enforcement positions at other parks and eventually accepted a job at Big Bend National Park in Texas. He and Leah were married at Rattlesnake Springs just before they left Carlsbad Caverns.

Iffy departed shortly after Lance for a string of seasonal positions that began at Badlands National Park in South Dakota. While at Black Canyon of the Gunnison National Park in Colorado, he happened to meet Joanne, a park volunteer and talented artist who later became his wife. Joanne had a more settled outlook than Iffy, and her influence was strong enough to make him give up his wandering ways. Following Lance's example, he opted for a career in law enforcement and completed the required training shortly after accepting his first permanent job at Guadalupe Mountains National Park, where he and Joanne were married.

Dave was the last of my three friends to leave Carlsbad Caverns. He had been trying to get a permanent job with the National Park Service for as long as I had known him, but he finally gave up and became an environmental inspector for the State of Kentucky. Within a few years, he was offered a permanent position at Carlsbad Caverns, but by the time he returned to New Mexico I had already left for my new assignment. Dave's second stint at Carlsbad introduced him to Marjorie, a career-oriented interpreter who served as the park's education specialist and who later became his second wife. Dave confides that it was the charm of Marjorie's Southern accent and her level-headedness that won his heart.

Today my friends have rewarding careers and beautiful families, and we visit one another often. Lance is the emergency-services manager at a large park in the Southwest and is heavily involved in its protection programs. It's hard to imagine him as the lanky young interpreter I knew at Carlsbad Caverns, eagerly searching for undiscovered caves in the Guadalupe Mountains, yet he's as sarcastic as ever and still enjoys giving me a hard time. Dave serves as the volunteer coordinator at a large southeastern park, managing hundreds of volunteers who construct trails or assist with park cleanups and other projects. He juggles so many activities at work and home that I don't know how he keeps up with himself, but somehow he succeeds. Iffy is a protection ranger at a small park in the Southwest, patrolling its roads and trails and enforcing regulations. His jet-black hair is just beginning to show a little gray. All three of my friends are doting fathers, and it should be no surprise that they're still active in the outdoors and are teaching their children to climb rope.

My friends' departure from Carlsbad Caverns left me rudderless and lonely on my days off, and I had to keep reminding myself that we were going to see one another frequently over the coming years. In time I accepted a position as a frontline interpreter at Big Bend National Park, where I joined Lance and Leah about a year after they moved there. Big Bend's rugged scenery and exceptional hiking opportunities in the Chihuahuan Desert and Chisos Mountains made it the ideal park, and I spent four happy and productive years there before I finally retired, thirty-three years after becoming a ranger trainee at the Albright Training Academy. Given my love for the Southwest, I retired to the juniper-piñon foothills of central New Mexico, where I'm close to the hiking trails of the White Mountain Wilderness and Lincoln National Forest.

While at Big Bend, I learned that one of my projects at Carlsbad Caverns—a training handbook Pete had asked me to write for the Hall of the White Giant caving tour—was still influencing the park's interpretive operation. One afternoon as I was working at the information desk in the Panther Junction Visitor Center, three young men came in to look at the museum exhibits. I greeted them and asked where they were from, and one of them said they were working for the summer as seasonal interpreters at Carlsbad Caverns. When I replied that I also had worked as an interpreter at Carlsbad, they looked at my name tag, and the one who had just spoken asked, "Are you the same Doug Thompson who wrote the Hall of the White Giant handbook?" When I said yes, his eyes opened wide and he whispered, "Oh, wow!"—with a tone of reverence in his voice that would have flattered a movie star.

⌒ By the time I left Carlsbad Caverns, I had achieved all three of my goals. Learning about the caves of the Guadalupe Mountains taught me that nature's creative genius can be found in unexpected places and that it often produces its most extravagant wonders when using the most unassuming materials. Regardless of where it is or what it has to work with, nature always finds a way to do extraordinary things, which gives rise to a world of astounding beauty. Caves also increased my respect for the creative power of water, especially when it interacts with limestone and gypsum—both of which were entirely new to me. I had learned in my high school chemistry class that water is "the universal solvent" because it can dissolve almost anything if given enough time. I confirmed that truth for myself in the caves of the Guadalupe Mountains, and I'm now reminded that caves are places of creation every time I use a drinking fountain or take a shower.

Exploring the Chihuahuan Desert through my hikes and other activities along the escarpment only strengthened my love for the Southwest. I almost envied the jackrabbits, coyotes, mountain lions, and other desert creatures for living in such grand and rugged surroundings, and I relished every minute of my aboveground adventures. The desert taught me that life and beauty can flourish under the most extreme conditions and that austerity and hardship have their place in the natural scheme of things.

A park visitor once told me she didn't like desert parks because there was "nothing in them," at which I immediately thought of a passage from the Gnostic Gospel of Thomas: "The Kingdom of the Father is spread upon the earth and men do not see it." Deserts have important things to tell us, and we need to listen.

Achieving these two goals also taught me that caves and the world of the surface are intimately connected. I had always known that rainwater seeps into caves, but I hadn't considered other important links between nature's opposing realms, such as myths about the underworld, the nightly foraging of bats, or nature's pervasive beauty. Despite their profound differences, caves and the surface are opposite sides of the same creative coin: each has something to tell us about the other. I learned more about the natural world and its interconnections during my years at Carlsbad Caverns than at any other time in my life, and I'm forever indebted to the extraordinary caves and desert landscapes of West Texas and southeastern New Mexico.

Finally, becoming an experienced caver changed my life dramatically, gave me skills I continue to use, and taught me important things about myself. My first trip into Spider Cave proved I could overcome my own fear by simply asking, "Where is it written?" That lesson has stayed with me and been reinforced many times over on trips into ever more challenging caves. My first long drop into Ogle Cave showed that I could master the challenges of vertical caving. Climbing didn't come as easily to me as it did to Lance and some of the other talented climbers on the park staff, especially in the beginning. Yet I gained confidence and experience with every rappel, and I'm extremely proud of my accomplishments on rope during those years. Caving and climbing have taught me that if I look deeply into myself, I can find the ability to achieve remarkable things.

Which brings me to the Ojibwa saying I quoted earlier: "Sometimes I go about in pity for myself, and all the while a great wind is bearing me across the sky." I first took this to mean that appreciating the beauty and grandeur of the natural world gives us perspective and balance. Yet it also suggests that letting go of our innermost fears while trusting in life and our own abilities can bring unexpected rewards and deep satisfaction. This applies not only to caving but also to my entire experience at Carlsbad Caverns, beginning with my decision to seek a frontline interpretive position and carrying through my encounters with the natural world. Of all the things I learned during those six years, this was the most important.

To illustrate the scope of this truth, I want to tell you about a young man whose love for the Southwest remains unsurpassed, and whose passion for exploration and discovery places him on a level with Jim White—a young man whose name you may not recognize.

⌐ I first read about Everett Ruess more than ten years after leaving Carlsbad Caverns, when Iffy gave me a book that featured many of his letters and journal entries (I'm sure you can guess that Iffy hadn't read it). Ruess's strange saga began in 1930, when, at the age of sixteen, he began a five-year odyssey that would take him from his parents' home in Los Angeles to the rugged California coast around Carmel, the Sierra Nevada Mountains, and the most remote wilderness areas of Arizona, northwestern New Mexico, and southern Utah. Traveling mostly on foot and with only one or two pack animals—he preferred burros but also used horses—he ventured into the deserts and canyons of the Southwest at a time when there were few reliable roads, for the sole purpose of witnessing and recording what he called the "unendurable beauty" of the American Southwest. The result was a collection of writings, block prints, and paintings that captured his unique vision of the natural world.

Ruess's wanderings were a difficult and dangerous undertaking, yet he wrote in a letter to one of his friends, "I like adventure and enjoy taking chances when skill and fortitude play a part. If we never had any adventures, we would never know what 'stuff' was in us." His letters and journals tell a remarkable story: how he shared his coffee with a Navajo family one night—he could speak some Navajo—after following the gleam of their campfire across the desert; how he watched his packhorse, Nuflo, stagger sideways, fall to the ground, and die in a remote desert canyon; how he worked for a short time on a ranch in Arizona, then took part in the Fourth of July parade in nearby Holbrook, wearing his black Stetson and green bandanna; how he spread out his belongings to dry in the sun after another packhorse foundered in a river during the long trek to Mesa Verde; and how he paused one night to wait out a thunderstorm in Arizona's Lukachukai Mountains: "We halted under a tall pine, and my sombrero sheltered the glow of a cigarette. The burros stood motionless with heads down and water dripping off their ears."

Far more than most people, Ruess grappled with life on its own terms, stoically enduring hardships, loneliness, and recurring illness as he doggedly pursued his goal. In November 1934, while venturing into the treacherous slickrock canyons along the Escalante River in southern Utah, he disappeared at the age of twenty and was never seen or heard from again. His story is enshrined today among the Southwest's most enduring legends, and he has a small but steadily growing number of devoted admirers.

Ruess also has his critics, who see him as a self-absorbed individual-ist who imposed on his parents for financial support, and who see his writings—in the words of biographer David Roberts—as little more than "the fevered strivings of a precocious but self-conscious idealist." Perhaps. Yet he captured the beauty and spirit of the Southwest more eloquently than many older and more experienced writers, and even his critics agree that he accomplished the task he had set for himself. Witness his poem *Wilderness Song*: "Say that I starved; that I was lost and weary . . . lonely and wet and cold, but that I kept my dream."

I mention Ruess primarily because of two brief passages in his letters. While most of his writing is descriptive, in these few sentences he reaches into the depths of his feelings to reveal the transformative power of both the natural world and the inescapable challenge of life.

> I have been feeling so happy and filled to overflowing with the beauty of life. . . . It is all a golden dream, with mysterious, high, rushing winds leaning down to caress me, and warm and perfect colors flow-ing before my eyes. Time and the need of time have ceased entirely. A gentle, dreamy haze fills my soul, the rustling of the aspens lulls my senses, and the surpassing beauty and perfection of everything fills me with quiet joy and a deep pervading love for my world.

And again:

> To live is to be happy; to be carefree, to be overwhelmed by the glory of it all. Not to be happy is a living death. Alone I shoulder the sky

251

and hurl my defiance and shout the song of the conqueror to the four winds, earth, sea, sun, moon, and stars. I live!

Everett Ruess had discovered that if we draw on our inner strengths and remain open to the limitless possibilities of life, we may find ourselves borne aloft and carried to unforeseen and perhaps unimaginable destinations. It happened to him when he left his parents' home in Los Angeles at the age of sixteen. It happened to me when I drove across the plains of West Texas and saw the Guadalupe Mountains for the first time, floating like clouds above the distant horizon.

BIBLIOGRAPHY

Cave Exploration

Doucette, Don. "Chocolate High, Carlsbad Cavern: A Preliminary Report." *NSS [National Speleological Society] News* 51, no. 7 (July 1993): 184–86.

Nymeyer, Robert. *Carlsbad, Caves and a Camera*. St. Louis, MO: Cave Books, 1993.

Reames, Stephen, Lawrence Fish, Paul Burger, and Patricia Kambesis. *Deep Secrets: The Discovery and Exploration of Lechuguilla Cave*. St. Louis, MO: Cave Books, 1999.

Taylor, Michael Ray. *Caves: Exploring Hidden Realms*. Washington, DC: National Geographic Society, 2001.

White, James Larkin. *Jim White's Own Story: The Discovery and History of Carlsbad Caverns*. 1938. Reprint, Carlsbad, NM: Carlsbad Caverns–Guadalupe Mountains Association, 1998.

Widmer, Urs, ed. *Lechuguilla: Jewel of the Underground*. Basel, Switzerland: Caving Publications International, 1991.

Caving

Jones, Cheryl. *A Guide to Responsible Caving*, 4th ed. Huntsville, AL: National Speleological Society, 2009.

Owen, Peter. *The Book of Outdoor Knots*. New York: The Lyons Press, 1993.

Rea, G. Thomas, ed. *Caving Basics: A Comprehensive Guide for Beginners*. Huntsville, AL: National Speleological Society, 1992.

Deserts

Alden, Peter, Brian Cassie, Peter Friederici, Jonathan Kahl, Patrick Leary, Amy Leventer, and Wendy Zomlefer. *Field Guide to the Southwestern States.* National Audubon Society Nature Guides. New York: Alfred A. Knopf, 1999.

Childs, Craig. *The Secret Knowledge of Water.* Boston, MA: Little, Brown and Company, 2000.

Cunningham, Richard L. *50 Common Birds of the Southwest.* Tucson, AZ: Southwest Parks and Monuments Association, 1990.

Fischer, Pierre C. *70 Common Cacti of the Southwest.* Tucson, AZ: Southwest Parks and Monuments Association, 1989.

Hanson, Jonathan, and Roseann Hanson. *50 Common Reptiles and Amphibians of the Southwest.* Tucson, AZ: Southwest Parks and Monuments Association, 1997.

MacMahon, James A. *Deserts.* National Audubon Society Nature Guides. New York: Alfred A. Knopf, 1985.

Mielke, Judy. *Native Plants for Southwestern Landscapes.* Austin: University of Texas Press, 1993.

Olin, George. *50 Common Mammals of the Southwest.* Tucson, AZ: Southwest Parks and Monuments Association, 2000.

Pate, Dale, and Ronal Kerbo. *On the Desert's Edge: A Journey of 36 Years in and around the Guadalupe Mountains, New Mexico and Texas.* Littleton, CO: Flat Rock, 2013.

West, Steve. *Northern Chihuahuan Desert Wildflowers.* Helena, MT: Falcon, 2000.

Geology

DuChene, Harvey R., and Carol A. Hill. *The Caves of the Guadalupe Mountains.* Huntsville, AL: National Speleological Society, 2000.

Hill, Carol A. *Cave Minerals of the World.* 2nd ed. Huntsville, AL: National Speleological Society, 1997.

———. *Geology of Carlsbad Cavern and Other Caves in the Guadalupe Mountains, New Mexico and Texas.* Bulletin 117. Socorro: New Mexico Bureau of Mines and Mineral Resources, 1987.

Jagnow, David H., and Rebecca R. Jagnow. *Stories from Stone: The Geology of the Guadalupe Mountains*. Carlsbad, NM: Carlsbad Caverns–Guadalupe Mountains Association, 1992.

History

Bartlett, John R. "Horse-Head Crossing to Delaware Creek." 1850. Reprinted in *God's Country or Devil's Playground: The Best Nature Writing from the Big Bend of Texas*, edited by Barney Nelson, 175–97. Austin: University of Texas Press, 2002.

Fradkin, Philip L. *Everett Ruess: His Short Life, Mysterious Death, and Astonishing Afterlife*. Berkeley: University of California Press, 2011.

Geronimo. *Geronimo: His Own Story*. Translated by S. M. Barrett. 1906. Reprint, New York: Penguin, 1996.

Jameson, W. C. *Legend and Lore of the Guadalupe Mountains*. Albuquerque: University of New Mexico Press, 2007.

Kersten, Jason. *Journal of the Dead: A Story of Friendship and Murder in the New Mexico Desert*. New York: HarperCollins, 2003.

Nymeyer, Robert, and William R. Halliday, MD. *Carlsbad Cavern, the Early Years: A Photographic History of the Cave and Its People*. Carlsbad, NM: Carlsbad Caverns–Guadalupe Mountains Association, 1991.

Roberts, David. *Finding Everett Ruess: The Life and Unsolved Disappearance of a Legendary Wilderness Explorer*. New York: Broadway Books, 2011.

Ruess, Everett. *Wilderness Journals of Everett Ruess*. Edited by W. L. Rusho. Salt Lake City, UT: Gibbs Smith, 1998.

Rusho, W. L. *The Mystery of Everett Ruess*, 1st revised ed. Layton, UT: Gibbs Smith, 1982.

Mythology

Bright, William. *A Coyote Reader*. Berkeley: University of California Press, 1993.

Campbell, Joseph. *A Joseph Campbell Companion: Reflections on the Art of Living*. Edited by Diane K. Osbon. New York: HarperCollins, 1991.

———. *Myths to Live By*. New York: Bantam, 1972.

———. *Primitive Mythology*. Vol. 1: *The Masks of God*. New York: Penguin, 1976.

Cheek, Lawrence W. *Kokopelli*. Tucson, AZ: Rio Nuevo Publishers, 2004.

Erdoes, Richard, and Alfonso Ortiz, eds. *American Indian Myths and Legends*. New York: Pantheon Books, 1984.

———, eds. *American Indian Trickster Tales*. New York: Penguin, 1999.

Mourning Dove (Humishuma). *Coyote Stories*. Edited by Heister Dean Guie. Lincoln: University of Nebraska Press, 1990.

Nickelsburg, George W. E., and James C. VanderKam, trans. *1 Enoch: A New Translation*. Minneapolis, MN: Fortress Press, 2004.

Pagels, Elaine. *The Origin of Satan*. New York: Vintage Books, 1995.

Tyler, Hamilton. *Pueblo Gods and Myths*. Norman: University of Oklahoma Press, 1964.

Waters, Frank. *Book of the Hopi*. New York: Penguin, 1977.

Nature

Crane, Candace. *Carlsbad Caverns National Park: Worlds of Wonder*. Carlsbad, NM: Carlsbad Caverns–Guadalupe Mountains Association, 2000.

Dillard, Annie. *Pilgrim at Tinker Creek*. New York: Harper's Magazine Press, 1974.

Muir, John. *The Mountains of California*. 1894. Reprint, Hamburg, Germany: Tredition Classics, 2012.

Thoreau, Henry David. *Walden*. 1854. Reprinted in *Walden and Civil Disobedience*, edited by Sherman Paul. Boston, MA: Houghton Mifflin, 1960.

Poetry

Dickinson, Emily. *The Poems of Emily Dickinson*. Edited by Thomas H. Johnson. Cambridge, MA: The Belknap Press of Harvard University Press, 1983.

Frost, Robert. *Robert Frost's Poems*. Edited by Louis Untermeyer. New York: Washington Square Press, 1971.

———. *Selected Poems of Robert Frost*. New York: Barnes and Noble Books, 1993.

Milton, John. *Paradise Lost*. 1667. Reprint, edited by David Scott Kastan. Indianapolis, IN: Hackett Publishing Company, 2005.

Tennyson, Alfred, Lord. *Alfred, Lord Tennyson: Complete Works*. Delphi Poets Series. Hastings, UK: Delphi Classics, 2013.

Whitman, Walt. *Walt Whitman: Complete Poetry and Collected Prose*. New York: Literary Classics of the United States, n.d.

Prehistory

Brody, J. J. *Mimbres Painted Pottery*. Santa Fe, NM: School of American Research Press, 2004.

Childs, Craig. *House of Rain: Tracking a Vanished Civilization across the American Southwest*. Boston, MA: Little, Brown and Company, 2007.

Cordell, Linda S., and Maxine E. McBrinn. *Archaeology of the Southwest*. Walnut Creek, CA: Left Coast Press, 2012.

Frazier, Kendrick. *People of Chaco: A Canyon and Its Culture*. London: W.W. Norton & Company, 2005.

Noble, David Grant, ed. *In Search of Chaco: New Approaches to an Archaeological Enigma*. Santa Fe, NM: School of American Research Press, 2004.

———, ed. *The Mesa Verde World: Explorations in Ancestral Pueblo Archaeology*. Santa Fe, NM: School of American Research Press, 2006.

Roberts, David. *In Search of the Old Ones: Exploring the Anasazi World of the Southwest*. New York: Simon and Schuster, 1996.

Technical Rescue

Laidlaw, Kenneth N. *Considerations for Technical Rope Rescue and Introduction of TAC Rope Kit*. Berkeley, CA: Privately printed, n.d.

Phillips, Ken. *Basic Technical Rescue*, 9th ed. Grand Canyon National Park, AZ: National Park Service, 2004.